Prison Diaries

Prison Diaries

Edward Kuznetsov

Translated by
HOWARD SPIER

Introduction by
LEONARD SCHAPIRO

STEIN AND DAY/*Publishers*/New York

First published in the United States of America, 1975
Copyright © 1973 Original Russian, Les Editeurs Réunis, Paris
Copyright © English translation by Vallentine, Mitchell & Co. Ltd.
Printed in the United States of America
Stein and Day/*Publishers*/Scarborough House,
Briarcliff Manor, N.Y. 10510

Library of Congress Cataloging in Publication Data

Kuznetsov, Eduard.
  Prison diaries.
  Translation of Dnevniki.
  1. Political prisoners—Russia—Personal narratives.
  I. Title.
H.V 8959.R9K9813   365'.45'0947   74-29320
ISBN 0-8128-1810-5

Introduction

Between 15th and 24th December 1970 in Leningrad the trial took place of eleven persons on charges of treason. Among them was Edward (Edik) Kuznetsov, the author of this diary. Apart from two persons, all the defendants were Jews, except that Kuznetsov is only half Jewish, and in fact legally classified as Russian. He has, however, persistently claimed that he wishes to be officially classified as Jewish by nationality.

What happened was that this group of friends, inspired, like so many Soviet Jews, by the lodestar of Israel, frustrated in their attempts to emigrate legally and goaded to a state of despair by the now familiar manifestations of Soviet antisemitism, conceived a desperate plot. This was to seize an aircraft at Smolny airport, bound for Murmansk. The intention was that some of the group should board the plane as passengers at Smolny, while the rest would join at the intermediate stop of Priozersk, take possession of the plane, and one of their number Mark Dymshitz, would then pilot the machine to Sweden. The hijacking fixed for 15th June 1970 never took place: indeed as the day approached the probability of failure became increasingly apparent, and it was only despair and fatalism that made these young people persist in the attempt which in fact at some stage plainly became known to the Soviet authorities. The scheduled flight was cancelled, and members of both groups arrested before they had even made any bid to seize the plane. The only weapon available to the group was a home-made pistol, unusable as a firearm.

There was no doubt that the defendants had committed offences under Soviet law, namely preparation for an attempt to cross the Soviet border illegally; and an attempt, or preparation for, the illegal taking possession of state property. Neither of these offences involves, in Soviet terms, very heavy sentences of imprisonment. The Soviet authorities, however, were determined to use this trial as a propaganda exercise, and their conduct of it was, as is usual in such circumstances in the Soviet Union, not very much inhibited by legal formalities or by the nature of the evidence. And so all the accused, except one, were charged not with the attempted illegal crossing, which was not disputed, but with an attempt to commit treason, the gravest offence in Soviet law; and with the attempt to *steal* state property on a large scale, in spite of the fact that theft is defined in Soviet law as the "appropriation" of property, as distinct from the mere taking possession of property: yet it was plain that the defendants had had no intention of appropriating the aircraft.[1]

In the result two of the defendants, the author of this book and Mark Dymshitz, were on 24th December sentenced to death, and all but one of the remaining defendants, who included Kuznetsov's wife, Sylva Zalmanson, to terms of imprisonment varying from eight to fifteen years of penal camps "with strict regime", or "with special regime". One defendant, who it was stated had been "co-operative", was let off with a sentence of four years on the lesser charge of attempting to cross the Soviet border illegally. On 30th December the two death sentences were commuted to sentences of fifteen years of camp "with strict regime" (Dymshitz), and the more severe "special regime" (Kuznetsov). This act of "clemency" could have been the result of the very considerable public agitation which the sentences evoked both outside the USSR, and by many brave people, including many non-Jews inside the USSR. But it could also have been a premeditated exercise *in terrorem*, which is not without famous parallels in the centuries of Russian oppressive rule.

The author of this diary had already served seven years in "strict" and "special" regime camps and in Vladimir prison for

[1] For an excellent discussion of the legal aspects of this trial see René Beermann in *Soviet Jewish Affairs* No. 2, Nov. 1971, pp. 3–8.

Samizdat[1] and for taking part in unauthorized public poetry readings in Moscow. After his release in the autumn of 1968 he moved to Riga, where he married. Less than two years later he was under arrest again. His indomitable spirit, courage and will power determined him to produce this diary. It is intended to show those of us who are fortunate enough not to live in a lawless police state, where a political prisoner is *caput lupinum*, what thousands of brave but desperate young men and women, who are in no conceivable sense "criminals", are at this very moment, as I write these lines or as you read them, going through. Kuznetsov succeeded with great ingenuity in writing his diary both in prison in Leningrad and in camp thereafter, in concealing all but a portion of it from the authorities, and above all in getting it smuggled out of the camp to Moscow. From there it reached the West and achieved publication in Russian, in Paris in 1973. The present translation has been prepared from this Russian edition. How the diary got out is not known, but the Soviet authorities have done their best to implicate a number of people—with what justification cannot, of course, be surmised. Towards the end of 1973 the wife of Academician Sakharov, Elena Bonner, was interrogated in connection with this diary, and threatened with prosecution. At least two prominent dissenters, Gavriel Superfin and Viktor Khaustov, have been sentenced to five and four years of "strict regime" camp, followed in Superfin's case by two years of exile, for their alleged part in smuggling the Diaries out to the West. That is all that is known at present.

Pavel Litvinov, one of the foremost Soviet fighters for human rights, has described the Diaries as a "human document of striking sincerity and depth". Certainly they are that. One finishes reading them with a sense of humility and admiration, indignation and pity. I am as hardened, I suppose, as any historian of the Soviet Union, to the brutality, inhumanity and deliberate degradation with which the Soviet authorities, from the first days of Lenin's regime until the present day have

[1] Circulating uncensored writings.

9

treated those who have refused to conform to the regime. Even so, like Solzhenitsyn's "Gulag Archipelago", with which this book stands comparison, Kuznetsov's sober and factual account, always in a low, somewhat ironical, at times cynical key, opens up a new casement on the world of human depravity. One cannot but admire both this young man's courage and his strength of character in preserving his personality and dignity in the face of the years of desperate suffering which have been his quite unmerited fate. But those of us who are fortunate enough to live in a civilized society should also have the humility to recognize the spiritual power which lies behind this young man's effort to escape from oppression and indignity. He has suffered both as a Jew and as a Russian for his persistent refusal to show the kind of conformity to which many honest men in the Soviet Union now find it impossible to submit.

I hope Jewish readers of this book will not regard this story as merely one more example of Soviet antisemitism. It is much worse than that. It is a part of the fate of all Soviet citizens, whether Jewish or not, who are unwilling to conform and to suffer in silence the persecution and repression meted out to their fellows for their religious beliefs or for their action in defending human rights. The fate of the Soviet Jew differs only from his fellow dissenters who are not Jews in that he has a greater possibility of escape. There are many Baptists, Orthodox, Crimean Tartars, Ukrainians and others who have suffered as harshly, or even worse, in their conflict with the Soviet authorities as the defendants in the Leningrad trial. The persistence of the Soviet police state which tramples on human rights and dignity in *all* cases where conformity is refused is the real point of importance. It is a regrettable fact that so many Jews were until recently ardent apologists of the Soviet regime—no doubt for ideological reasons, which to me always seem to be the worst of all reasons; and only became critical of the Soviet regime when they discovered in the Soviet Union what they believe is antisemitism. Actually, it is much more than that: it is the normal reaction of a police state against a section of the community which has discovered a way of escape. The worst aspects of the Soviet regime have over the years been strengthened, perpetuated even, by the support for official Soviet lies and deception which they have received for years from fellow-travellers all over the world, many of them Jews. If Kuznetsov's *Diaries* help to put an end to this betrayal of the human spirit of which so many of us have been guilty, he will not have suffered in vain. For the day is probably gone when any regime, however powerful, can flout foreign opinion indefinitely. Sooner or later economic or political considerations will force it to modify the worst features of its conduct—provided, of course, that it cannot successfully befuddle foreign public opinion with glib lies and denials. To ensure that the deception of the dictators and the tyrants should never succeed is the duty of all of us. Edward Kuznetsov, and the many brave men and women like him who have suffered and continue to suffer under repressive regimes in many parts of the world for their courage in protesting, have pointed out to us what should be our constant duty.

A few words in conclusion about the author and his wife. Edward, so far as is known, remains in Camp No. 10, in Mordovia, the only "special regime" camp of that complex. The reader will get a good picture of what the "special regime" is like from this book. Latest reports suggest that Kuznetsov's health has already been impaired, and there are fears for his condition. His wife, Sylva, was imprisoned in another camp. Let me quote a few words from the statement of this remarkable young woman at her trial.

"I am stunned by the penalties the procurator has demanded . . . for something that has not been done . . . I don't think that Soviet law can consider anyone's intention to live in another country as treason . . . Israel is the country with which we Jews are bound spiritually and historically. . . Even now I do not doubt for a minute that sometime . . . I *will* live in Israel . . . Next year in Jerusalem! . . . 'If I forget thee, Oh Jerusalem, let my right hand lose its cunning'." (As she repeated these words in Hebrew she was silenced by the Court.) Accounts reaching her friends bore witness to the persistent toughness of spirit which she showed at her trial. In spite of deteriorating health she took part with Ukrainians and others in hunger strikes and wrote innumerable petitions and complaints. Very recently, in one of those spasmodic acts of clemency with which the Soviet authorities occasionally temper injustice, Sylva Zalmanson was released and is now in Israel. There are few of us, in the Jewish Community and outside it who will not feel intense relief at the thought that she at least is free and whose good wishes for her future will not accompany her. One of those wishes and hopes must surely be that Edward Kuznetsov may soon be allowed to join her in Israel. They have both suffered enough. Perhaps some day they will read the few words I have written about them. I hope they will realize that the thoughts of many of us were with them during the time of their suffering, even if we were powerless to bring it to an end.

London   Leonard Schapiro

Contents

Illustrations

The Diaries of Edward Kuznetsov

Part 1—1970

27th October

The investigation is over. At last they have given me a pencil and paper.

Not that I didn't have them before, but what can you do when your guards sniff every single bit of paper you've got, every little pencil mark?

Nor is my head so full of brilliant ideas. I just like sitting here with my jotter in front of me and thinking profound thoughts, or puffing a cigarette now and again, or setting down on paper the very least passing thought that takes my fancy.

Curious, even in the few lines I've written I had to cross out two words already (I didn't want the guards to see them) and write one in.

Can it be I'm vain enough to believe anyone will ever read this? Surely anyone's behaviour tends to be somewhat un-natural, if they even *suspect* someone is looking over their shoulder.

The cells are in two sections here; they're called "doubles". Two days after my arrest I was joined by an oldish man named Liapchenko who was afflicted with every disease one could possibly have. He had collaborated with the Germans during the War, served ten years, and had been freed in 1955. After this he had appealed against his sentence and been arrested again—14 years later. He's certain they're going to shoot him.

We were together for a fairly peaceful six weeks or so, and then were flung into different cells. Then I found myself with Yuri Kozlov, who was no more than a couple of years older than I. He'd been in a camp in the Komi ASSR, but I've no idea whether they transferred him here to serve another term, or for some other reason. He never discussed it and I never thought it a good idea to be too inquisitive—people just don't bare their souls to you in a place like this. I got on with him reasonably well, though on occasions our cell was anything but quiet and orderly. But after a month I began to grow tired of him, and my only desire from then on was to change his extrovert cordiality for a misanthropist's stone-cold silence.

Since 2nd September, I have been sharing with Vladimir Pavlovich Saltykov, an artist, sentenced to four years for "hooliganism". He'd been transferred from the "Crosses"[1] to the "Mansion"[2] as a witness in a gold-trafficking case. But he's no "artist", as I was to find out soon enough: he used to paint posters, that's all. He's about 50, extremely light-hearted, inexhaustibly vulgar and full of all the jokes you associate with the provincial. His trouble is the authorities don't care for him or his bald head, or his stuttering or the way he gesticulates whenever he speaks. It didn't take me long to impress upon *him* that silence is the best means of contact in situations where people are forced to live together. If I forget the rhythmic scrape of his heels on the floor as he stalks up and down the cell, or his habit of whistling his thoughts to an accompaniment of operatic arias, or his diabolical snoring night after night, then I suppose I really have quite a tolerable cell-mate! What can you do?

28th October

A couple of weeks before the implementation of Art. 201 (Criminal Code of the RSFSR), I wrote rejecting the services of a lawyer. For do I not know (and not through personal experience alone) how helpless, how lumbering, how timid, lawyers often are in these political trials! And not only that: once I'm not allowed to say everything I want to say—which I'm quite prepared for—it's better to say nothing at all. During the investigation I was given the opportunity to apply a little logical analysis, and what happened? I had both the investigator

[1] Nickname of Leningrad Prison.
[2] i.e. Leningrad KGB (Secret Police) HQ.

and the procurator, time and time again, cornered in their own logical blind alleys—yet they felt quite at ease and hardly seemed to notice.

These people have usurped power over human destiny and dare pass themselves off as the repositories of absolute truth! The only trouble is this truth isn't in their heads—it's in the lower parts of their bodies. If you so much as suggest that they indulge in the bare minimum of theoretical reasoning, then all your entreaties will inevitably fall upon deaf ears. All I can expect is the usual diet of quasi-legal "Socialist Justice".

I do *not* consider myself guilty before the Soviet Union—rather the contrary!—and I have no desire whatever to take part in any legalistic game they may care to play with me, if it is to be played strictly according to their rules.

I am no longer 20 years old, and I am no longer "burning with the desire" to change the world. God, how I despise all this Byzantinism! If only there were a St. George's Day for those whose hearts yearn for another country!

Although I made it quite clear that I refused to have a lawyer, I might as well not have bothered; here he is, just the same—a Jew, stockily-built, 40 or thereabouts, with a stoop in his back, and a twinkle in his eye, one Yuri Iosifovich Lury. I didn't want anything at all to do with him, but it transpired that he hadn't been appointed by the court, as is normally the case, but hired by my friends (who, he says, might be offended if I were to refuse his services). He is my first glimpse of the world outside, and I gave in. It's no laughing matter to alarm any friend the KGB has got hold of, though, generally speaking, only a friendship you've kept in the camp is a genuine one . . . But I'll say more about this later, it's leading me too far astray from my subject.

Lury is nobody's fool. We had a good chat, preening ourselves on our wit and literary likes and dislikes. But there was no getting away from it: my case is very weak indeed. What was the point of denying it? I have to expect 15 years, so it would make no difference if I don't plead guilty to each charge and insist they charge me under different articles; Lury would admit the charges and do his very best to get my punishment reduced— miracle of miracles!—to 14 years. I'm beyond caring, one way or the other. Lury is living news from the outside, a creature of warmth amidst a mass of bureaucratic inquisitors. This isn't the place for "inquisitors" anyway: here is none of that spiritual delicacy, none of that atmosphere in which they most willingly pursue their operations.

Lury is typical: the winds of the Diaspora blow too cold for the Jew to remain upright. Few succeed. He who seeks advancement, he who craves the Pharaoh's way of life, is always distinguished by a forced heartiness and a jovial hypocrisy masked by zealousness; even as he begins to feel the slightest sense of involvement, up sprouts the tiny mustard-seed of alienation, of irony and scepticism, as he learns he can never be more than an outsider, never more than one who can observe with his intellect only—for he knows, deep in his heart, he is only doing *their* work.

29th October

Apparently the trial is to take place in about six weeks time. Before the New Year, at any rate. There is no doubt whatsoever that I'll get 15 years. I have known of so many cases where men got 15 years for "betraying their homeland" in circumstances nowhere near as serious as ours. God help you, if you even steal a few roubles!

I remember the case of Kostia Tsarev, a good-looking young fellow, only 20 years old. I was sharing a cell with him in Vladimir prison; I had about three months to go before being freed, when they brought him and four others over from Mordovia to serve fresh terms for rowdyism in the punishment block; some had had two years, others three years, added on to their sentences, and they were extremely pleased to have got off so cheaply! Kostia had been a soldier in the German Democratic Republic, and one day he thought he'd throw all caution to the winds; so he drank himself paralytic and slept the whole night in a ditch! When he woke up in the morning, he was petrified when he realized they might take him for a deserter. Being a lad from the country—the type usually recruited for occupying forces—he had a very vague conception of the law. Indeed, all he'd ever done before was to get away with minor disciplinary infringements and he'd even been commended as an "excellent military and political student". But Kostia was infinitely more afraid of the public disgrace of being punished for infringements of discipline than he was of death itself. So, it flashed through his mind; why not run away, why not cross the frontier? He'd never before, on his own admission, given any thought to the West, and if he had ever compared East and West, then it was only in the newspaper editorials he'd read or in the "eloquence" of his political lecturers. From time to time, though, he'd heard of "deserters" or "traitors" being sentenced in their absence. (It's a well-known fact that every successful "deserter" is sentenced to death in his absence.) It was this that had made him think—in principle—that he too might flee to the West. Now this very thought was playing on his mind. As far as I know, he was arrested the very next day, when the GDR police stopped him in a railway station and handed him over to the Soviet authorities.

The investigator was like a father to him, sympathetic, sitting patiently as he explained the naive, mixed-up fears that had driven him to such an awe-inspiring crime:

"Come on now, if you'd have got to the German Federal Republic, they'd have stuck you straight into their counter-intelligence, wouldn't they?"

Well, of course, Kostia agreed with him.

"And then, you never even destroyed your soldier's booklet, you didn't burn it, or tear it up, did you? That means they would have found out the number of your unit."

"Yes, you're right," Kostia had to agree with him, sadly.

"Come on, tell me honestly, like a good Russian, would you

really not have told them the names of your officers, and what sort of ammunition you have, or whether you use submachine guns or whatever, and wouldn't you have told them all about your garrison? They'd know how to make you talk, you know!"

Kostia had to agree with him that he probably would have told them all they wanted to know. But, when all of a sudden, the investigator became incensed at this apparent lack of principle and apathy, Tsarev asked him nervously what was the worst that could happen to him. Your case might not reach the disciplinary commission, he was told, but you certainly won't get off lighter than two weeks in the guardhouse, a reprimand, and transfer to another unit—though in Russia this time.

Kostia was very pleased at the idea of being sent to another unit. The commander, he thought, was bound to put him to shame, it would be a blemish on the whole unit, they might lose their Red Banner, and so on and so forth.

The Military Tribunal sentenced him to 10 years for attempting to betray his country by fleeing to West Germany, where "his intention had been to hand over military secrets to counter intelligence."

30th October

We've been moved from cell 247 to 242. Lenin's old cell, 193, is just below us. It's kept unoccupied, a relic not to be profaned. If you look at our block from the yard down below, it's the fifth window from the right on the fifth floor that immediately catches your eye. In contrast to the gloomy regularity of the rusty shields on all the other windows, its freshly-scrubbed panes flash in the light of day. It's covered by a grill, has panels of glass instead of plastic and lacks the shield, which, even on a sunny day, darkens the ordinary cell. On the dawn of the Revolution—or, as a friend of mine put it, of the "Dissolution" —they were going to destroy all the churches and prisons, they said. As far as the churches are concerned, they seem to have done the job fairly thoroughly, but something must have gone terribly wrong when they started demolishing the prisons. Perhaps it was only to be expected. For they intended not only to preserve all that was best in the old feudal-bourgeois culture, but to intensify the class struggle by displaying the even greater achievements that Socialism was capable of, and however convenient a system of concentration camps may have been (in the economic sphere, particularly), they would have had to build a whole new chain of prisons. As it is, they seem to make do well enough with the old ones, and it's very rare indeed that they spend anything on new buildings. No, I must be fair; sometimes they do announce that there has been a significant decrease in crime, and when this happens, the powers-that-be must take swift action—like for example, demolishing the Leningrad women's prison. They decided the "Crosses" was good enough for criminals of both sexes. And, of course, it *was* good enough. The only trouble is you now have seven or eight prisoners sharing a cell like ours. That's why each of us treats his 12 square yards like his own private villa.

It's the exterior of the prisons that has changed most, from what I can see: each window has a shield fixed on now. In some prisons (Vladimir, for example), if you look closely enough at the fresh-brick masonry, you can see the "old-regime" windows were four times wider than they are now. Four blocks of the "Mansion" are empty; maybe they're being held in reserve. We occupy only the fifth and sixth floors of one of the blocks: 50 of us, about half perhaps being dealers in illegal currency, or bribe-takers or embezzlers. It was in 1960, if I'm not mistaken, that the KGB took this added burden upon itself, and although all these "economic saboteurs" have to sit out their terms in normal camps, it is the KGB which investigates their cases—something which pleases the prisoners no end!

The atmosphere in the "Mansion" differs very little from that in the Lubianka[1] or Lefortovo. Now that I'm used to

[1] Moscow KGB HQ.

prison life again, I find I am confusing 1970 with 1961—I'm living in the past as well as the present.

As if illustrating how superficial is the traditional comparison between Muscovites and Leningradites (conviviality v. dryness, disorderliness v. fastidiousness, etc.), the prison rituals are not adhered to so strictly here as in the Lubianka or Lefortovo. Here they don't give you that sinister order, "K, get yourself ready!" They just bang your food hatch and call your name out, and tell you where they're taking you. As they escort you along, the guards avoid any unscheduled meeting with other prisoners, crack their fingers (like they do in Moscow), jingle their keys, whistle through their teeth, and shout at regular intervals, "Out of the way of the convoy!" Perhaps the Leningradites themselves do not know in what contempt the regulations are held.

As far as I can see the number of guards has doubled twice already. So many prisoners are here from so many different cities! I have heard guards say they've been sent here on an official mission or as probationers.

I wonder if this has any bearing on our case. Over 40 investigators have been preparing us for the forthcoming trial: from investigators "with responsibility for highly important Government affairs" to KGB area, regional and town departmental heads, from 1st lieutenants to colonels. Every two or three weeks I've been getting a new order to sign, for, "due to the particular complexities of our case," more and more "investigators" have had to be drafted in.

31st October

I'm convinced my cell-mate's a "plant". He's been taking much too great an interest (according to prison "Etiquette" that is) in certain details of the case and for much too long a period of time. I never jumped to any conclusions, I was always prepared to restrain any suspiciousness I might have felt though, I dare say, it was natural enough in the circumstances. There are so many informers and spies, the place is swarming with them. Or maybe I'm just trying to make myself more important than I am!

I don't know. The KGB are so good at hypnotizing people and poisoning their minds. The prisoners here are generally the stupidest of people. Even if you were to turn them upside down, nothing worthwhile would fall out, only inflated vanity or a few drops of venom.

In such close proximity to people like this, lack of ceremony is inevitable and, let things slide just a little, and you're hob-nobbing with the swine.

I always try to keep my distance from a cell-mate, not because I'm unsociable, but some times I just cannot bear the silence to be broken; I must preserve such rare and beautiful moments. I resort to any tricks I can, solely to get the message over to my cell-mate, that when this bilious, irascible and insolent man is reading, when he's pacing up and down his cell in deep concentration, or when he's sitting on his bed with his hands over his eyes—these are the times when it's better to leave him alone, not to start a conversation with him, or whistle, or do anything that might possibly disturb him! If you do, you are likely to be met by a very unpleasant remark indeed or, worse still, there's likely to be a "scene".

Why should this be? Is it my paucity of thought, or my hypersensitivity to any obstacles standing in my path, or even a subconscious need I have to justify my inability to concentrate? I'm so easily distracted and annoyed if I think someone's going to ask me a question at any moment, or start a conversation, or cough, or even look at me. I'm practically a bundle of nerves. Is this neurosis I have about noise *really* bringing me round, full circle, back to my old subject: how one should live, not just for today or tomorrow, but in general? Ethics are the focal point of my thoughts. Ideas are like gems to me. What would a bunch of psychiatrists, with all their boring standards of normality and abnormality, think of me?

Even when I was 18, I would dream of spending the rest of

my life in a little wooden hut at the edge of the world; snow would be on the ground as far as the eye could see; everywhere the bleak silence of pre-creation. How I wished everything were pervaded with the certainty that nobody would ever alarm me, that I had all the time in the world in front of me, no need to hurry anywhere . . . Then I could solve all those questions that deeply troubled me . . .

My time allowed for exercise will soon be up; think I'll turn back now. I don't go out for a walk any more like I used to; all I want is just to be left alone for one hour.

Here's how I found him out. I was just about to doze off when he called out quietly. There was a strange note to his voice that set me on my guard. I didn't say a word, I carried on breathing as evenly as I could. I heard him get up from his bed and quietly start pulling my volume of Karamazov from under my pillow, where I also keep this jotter. So far, I've been pretending I'm working on the Karamazov and, my diary still being in embryonic form, I hadn't much bothered about hiding the jotter. When I turned over as if about to awaken, he jumped back nervously and, pretending to hum some tune or other, began striding up and down the cell.

I must think about hiding it somewhere; the problem is, where? The cell is almost bare, and we're searched once a week. I wonder if I could get rid of him somehow. They'd only put someone else in, what's the difference.

2nd November

In general terms, there are three different attitudes you can adopt towards keeping a diary, as long as you have to keep writing under the permanent threat that it may fall into the hands of those whose power over you is absolute. The first is to confess and repent totally, admit your mistakes, and, counting on the Chekists[1] gullibility, declare yourself ready to be born anew, albeit step by step, until you're grown into an ecstatic supporter of "Big Brother". (I know of such cases.)

[1] The Cheka was the original name of the KGB.

The second is not to write at all so you can't give your enemies any material they may be able to use later.

The third is this: if you *do* write, and there are many reasons why people do (reasons which may appear banal, or naive, and perhaps only seldom of any real importance—like satisfying an inner need, for example), then you must not write anything that might possibly harm anyone else. You can put *yourself* at risk as much as you like, of course—that goes without saying!

3rd November

"Freedom is a conscious necessity". Freedom is a *state* of being and it is incorrect to regard it only as an act of consciousness. This state is characterized by its relationship to necessity, i.e. has the individual overcome it, is he overcoming it, has he subordinated himself to it? These three states manifest themselves as momentary or protracted processes, and have differing links with knowledge. Indeed, one can apprehend necessity and yet be subordinated to it. What, then, is freedom? (The yearning to apprehend freedom and to submit to it "freely" has no direct bearing on the ethical principles of free will.)

Ergo, freedom is necessity overcome, or the capability and possibility of overcoming it. Or sadder still: freedom is the possibility to consciously choose a master for oneself, while at the same time retaining one's right to leave him for another at any time.

Of course, such dabblings in rationalism must inevitably be based on a series of axioms, which alone can make them acceptable. We might add to these, for example, the tacit assumption that a concrete necessity can be fully apprehended—without any mention of its affinity to the whole network of necessities in which a man is immersed, and which is properly called life itself . . .

They haven't put the second window-frame in yet and the radiator's no warmer than a corpse's arse!

At about 10 o'clock this morning I heard the sound of an

orchestra playing from the direction of Liteiny Prospect followed by the stamping of feet. All of a sudden, through the window of my cell came the most dreadful wailing: "You fellows from China, here we are—get us out of here!" Then I heard a burst of hysterical laughter, guards rushing down the corridor, and a nervous, high-pitched whispering; finally, all hell was let loose! I think they must have dragged the trouble-maker off to the punishment block.

4th November

I must find some way of getting rid of my cell-mate. I could, I suppose, just tell them to come and "tear" their "plant" out. Though if I said this I would have to make it plain that I would smash his skull in if they didn't. But they usually do act and fairly quickly. That's my last resort—if all other means fail me. In the meantime I'll use a well-tried method: I'll find some way of provoking an argument with him and then use it to put a stop to any further conversation between us. Then my "plant" won't be able to dig anything up, and he'll have to be taken out. I know they'll put someone else in his place, but that I can't do anything about. I'll probably be by myself for a short time but, under the new law, no prisoner is allowed to be without a cell-mate.

5th November

No sooner said than done—we're no longer on speaking terms! I don't go out for exercise as I did before.

I tried to get hold of some legal literature—not a hope! They won't even give me the USSR Constitution. It's no easy matter to get hold of any books you want here. The library's not too bad, but there's no catalogue or librarian. The librarian's job is done by prison personnel in rotation. This is why you quite often get ridiculous things like this happening: I asked for something by Kony[1] and they gave me "Riders and Horses" by someone called Fedorov. When I complained the "librarian" showed me his form: "There you are, you *did* ask for something about horses . . ."

You are allowed two books a week, but that's hardly enough for three days' reading. You can protest as much as you like, it doesn't make any difference. I had hardly got over the shock of being arrested when I thought I'd see what could be done about the book situation. It didn't take me very long to find out that this state of affairs was no accident and not due to any neglect on the part of the authorities.

Major Kruglov, the prison governor, a dark, long-nosed 45 year-old, bumptious as the maître d'hôtel in a second-rate restaurant, summoned me to his office (on account of my refusal to say anything during interrogation). There he was kind enough to enlighten me on the prisoner-book situation. His summing up was perfection itself and contained a reference to the well-known prison adage, "We're not the Academy of Sciences here, you know!" I was later to hear this gem again, from the Procurator, Ponomarev, from the investigators, and even from the guards. The prison *isn't* an academy—there's no doubt about that!

During the seven years of my previous sentence I was constantly getting into trouble, so desperate was I to lay my hands on some books—any books!—and I frequently felt the weight of the authorities' displeasure on my back. In Vladimir prison I tried over six months to get permission for an English language text-book. At last I got it—and the very next time I was searched, it was confiscated, because I "wasn't allowed to have such things!" Yes, of course, I complained—bitterly— only to be rewarded with 10 days in the punishment block.

In 1963 nearly all the foreign authors were withdrawn from the shelves, but how they separated the sheep from the lambs, I could never quite understand. In camp 7 there was a time

[1] Anatoly Kony. (1844–1927) St. Petersburg University Professor of Law. In Russian "kony" also means "horses".

when even "Krokodil"[1] was forbidden, in case the cartoons aroused any "anti-Soviet laughter". Pre-revolutionary books are the very stuff of sedition. That's how I lost my *Zarathustra*, a half-dozen volumes of Hegel, and—I haven't got over it yet— a two-volume edition of the works of Uberweg-Heinze. Until 1969, at least, you could receive printed matter by post, but not now. Thus do our intellectual wardens expound the philosophical content of their objections: "What's this? You want foreign literature! We shouldn't even give you Soviet books—all you ever do is read what you like into them!"

6th November

When politics is the politics of decadence, Rousseau's assertion that "every useless citizen is a dangerous citizen" becomes an incentive to sweep clean, to purge, not only the Party rank and file, but others beyond it. Yet this is only before the State has grown to maturity and when the number of its clandestine officials is as yet imprecise. Later, when he sees all the red banners urging him to participate in social-political activity, the Soviet proletarian learns his lesson for the day, the favourite saying of the Mafia: "He that is deaf, dumb and blind, will live a long and happy life."

There were many warriors among the saints of Russian orthodoxy: was it the cult of violence, perhaps? . . .

"If there is no God, then all is permissible," proclaimed Dostoyevsky. Here he was in total agreement with Voltaire's, "If God did not exist it would be necessary to invent him." But apparently Dostoyevsky was not so concerned with whether God existed or not, but rather with the social and moral consequences of his discovery (or illusion) that He was "dead".

In practical terms, (if we may forget for a moment the complexity of almost every thought Dostoyevsky ever had) he was really underlining the need for *any* doctrine that keeps the subconscious in check.

[1] Soviet satirical periodical.

28

7th November

I'm fed up to the teeth with strong personalities and super-powers claiming to be messiahs! In this century the problem has not been one of reducing the evils that already exist, but rather of resisting their growth. The optimists, and particularly the Chekists among them, are so much more to be feared than the sceptics or those who see life as nothing but one great tragedy. The optimist is so secure in the knowledge that his, and only his, convictions are the truth, that he must rush and build Utopia in his own lifetime. But will he hesitate to destroy all who stand in his way: after all, they are only a hindrance, merely blocking the path to heaven! The more convinced and morally justified the monomaniac the more he reeks of the blood of the innocent.

8th November

One day you realize how long it is since you last picked up a book, even the most famous one, with any trepidation or excitement at all. How different when I was a youngster and I believed there were books which gave you all the truths immediately. Now everything you read is allusions or undercurrents. It's boring to be an adult.

9th November

How wonderful—we're still not speaking to one another!
***[1] The merchant is the typical Russian. The talented Russian is usually a petty tyrant, a despot, fickle and unpredictable, a braggart, yet a slave . . .
*** Life is ironic: only the oppressed and down-trodden ever talk about justice and this alone should give us sufficient grounds for distrust. Uninspired rationalism and the spreading of enlightenment weave doctrinal nets out of the chaos and

[1] Three asterisks as used by Kuznetsov here and elsewhere in the diaries denote breaks in his thoughts.

absurdity of life, and if they manage to make any flexible cells at all, they call them dialectics. But any cell is far too large for the true meaning of life. Banal wisdom, whether of subjective or Party hopes and desires, the conceptionalized (read: profaned) reading of history, the construction of edifices—all you have to do is stuff them (for appearances' sake) with specially selected "concrete" material for all times and for all nations (no need to paper over the cracks, they can always be filled in with whatever nation-time specification is the order of the day), rationalizations of historical progress from the point of view of the petty-bourgeois wisdom of the government machine . . .

*** Two guards suddenly burst in on me, searched me all over and nearly turned the cell upside-down. They would have taken my papers too (evidence is evidence!) if I hadn't managed to talk them out of it. I gave them an assurance that these were only drafts of my trial speech. I've lost my thread for the moment . . .

I lack passion, I lack that profound confidence in the value and originality of my experience and thoughts which alone could give me the strength to set them down on paper.

It's much more pleasant and infinitely more convenient (nor does it pose any threat to your vanity) to be a consumer of spiritual goods.

In Zen Buddhism creativity and appreciation of art are of equal merit: it is the ability to create which is all important: the incarnation of that which is created is considered only of secondary significance. This evidently explains the incompleteness of their works or art: it is the natural result of the awesome attachment they have to something intimate, secret, fragile. "He who has eyes to see (let him see!)"—i.e. respect and trust for him and scorn and indifference for the blind man . . .

11th November

Were the mad genius not so naive he would never think of

tackling the fundamental problems of life. For talent shrinks in the face of ontological problems, or rather, stands in reverence before them. This is why the "holy Tsars" always increased Russia's military potential. The Russian does not know freedom—only free will.

The first pogrom took place in 1113, in Kiev. The following is from Tatishchev's[1] *History.*

". . . Seeing their plight, the Jews gathered together in a synagogue and long defended themselves; Vladimir, full of hate for them, sent them all into exile. From that time there have been no Jews in our Homeland, and the people generally killed those who dared to come to Russia."

This last statement is not, of course, totally accurate, but it is very significant nonetheless.

*** The whole of my life have I spent in communal apartments, in army barracks, and in camps . . . How long can you live on stinking herrings and dream of one day possessing your own room, where just to put a lock on your door would be Utopia itself? How willingly would I exchange 15 years of camp barracks for 20 years of solitary in a cell! Sinyavsky's definition is brilliant: a camp is something between a communal apartment, a lunatic asylum and a children's nursery. For the convict, that is. But what about the authorities? For them the camp is the backyard of the Soviet empire, where the state wears its night-clothes during the day and neglects its demagogic make-up.

12th November

Major Kruglov summoned me to his office because they discovered a one-inch nail when they searched my cell. He threatened to put me in the punishment block. Thank God I haven't been convicted yet or he would have done more than just threaten me. When I was in Vladimir prison they once found a sharp piece of steel on me, and I got two weeks in the

[1] V. N. Tatishchev. (1686–1750), early Russian historian.

punishment block plus three months' deprivation of the right to use the prison shop. The only thing is, I'd been working in the joiners' shop, and I was surrounded by metal . . .

I learned from my conversation with Kruglov that if he had his way, he would drive all the Jews out of the Soviet Union, because "they're cunning and don't serve the Soviet state faithfully". This is a very common view among Government and Party officials. In the camps the remarks you hear are somewhat different (different in form, that is), e.g. everything's owned by the Jews, Brezhnev is a Jew, Kosygin is a Jew, etc. Prisoners are not greater antisemites than the rest of the population. It's simply that the barracks-cell type of existence they lead gives rise to the more traditional forms of prejudice; whichever guise it wears depends on which way the current political wind is blowing. This antisemitism is incredibly idiotic, faceless though many-sided, ridiculously argued, pathetic in its stupidity and its nightmarish lack of concern for any sort of rationalism.

I remember once, I had been careless enough to praise Antonioni's "Red Desert" (published in *Inostranok*). One of my cell-mates, who happened to be a monarchist and an admirer of Konstantin Leontyev, read a few pages and looked at me suspiciously:

"It's rubbish," he said, "This woman eats a bread-roll in the middle of the street! How can she be starving—she's rich, isn't she?"

I was just about to doze off when I heard someone else ask him:

"Is it worth reading?"

"It's a lot of nonsense," he replied, "it's the Jews up to their old tricks again."

A couple of months later, in another cell, someone said:

"I hear you wrote some Jew play."

"Why should I write a Jewish play?"

"Well, I don't know . . . it was about a deserter or something."

32

I tried as hard as I could to convince him that I'd never written anything in my life and that it was Antonioni who had written the play. A waste of time. Not long afterwards, every paper I had was taken in one of the usual searches. Most were confiscated and I was returned just a few of my papers and warned I'd better not write any "Zionist novels (!)"

For a multitude of reasons, it's much harder to be a Jew in a camp than anything else, mainly because Russophiles of all classes—and they are a fairly large percentage—consider it their patriotic duty to join in the struggle against Zionism and the "conspiracy of the Elders of Zion."

13th November

This morning I was taken to see the doctor, which struck me as rather strange; and after dinner I was told my trial would be on the 20th. In just a week's time, that means. So fast. The lawyer will probably be here on Monday.

. . . I have to read all sorts of nonsense here. Frequently, they don't have the books I ordered in the library so they bring me whatever they've got—usually mediocre stuff, written in the 40s and 50s. This week I've been groaning my way through Kochetov's *Brothers Ershov*. He was no ideologist when he wrote it, as he is now, just a yes-man; though even then he was pretentious enough to touch up a few of the Party slogans, when the occasion demanded it and slip in one or two sensible thoughts in the right place. Someone who's obtuse, but thinks he's brilliant, will write down anything that wanders accidentally into his head, whether it be relevant or not. If you have a head full of thoughts can you neglect even the most insignificant?

*** I've just been given the list of "charges" against me. How pathetic and monstrous they are!

14th November

We read that the position of the working class in the USA has deteriorated. What a strange people they are! They always seem to be getting poorer! Their life seems to have been deteriorating for at least 20 years, and that's only as far as I can remember. Education's hardest hit evidently. Ours is free, thank the Lord! Yet, this gives them one reason to stop us emigrating: the government tell us they've spent a fortune on us, and now we're going to give all our knowledge away to our enemies! But why should the master not pay for his slave's education, if the slave isn't allowed to leave him?

It's more profitable to educate your slave, (economically, that is!) Both systems of education have their drawbacks. Free education (as it is here, anyway) opens the gates of higher education to every mediocrity who knows that five years as a student will guarantee him an excellent salary for life with no obstacles of any sort.

The Soviet Union is a paradise for the idler, as long as he's not particularly ambitious. Where else can you get a reasonably good wage for doing nothing? This sort of atmosphere is equally harmful to the average man because it makes him an idler or a loafer even if he wasn't one before. This is not so much because of the educational system as the result of the social-political structure of the state and difference in national temperament.

One year, when I was working as a loader at a textile plant in Strunino, I had four different workmates, one after the other. Two of them had done time for theft, one for assault and battery, and three of them were drunk every single day. So I went to see the manager and said, if he would give me a 50% rise, I would do two men's work (even then, I'd have had a couple of hours left over for reading—I even brought my books to work with me!) but it was all to no avail. It's not surprising that some of those who leave for the West come back.

18th November

I haven't written anything for three days. The value of a diary as a spontaneous register of impressions and events is greatly diminished if you can't make use of it any time you feel like for fear of being found out. You're always scared the "blue-boys"[1] might rush in and take it from you. I'm not afraid they might learn something about my views (I never made any secret of them during the investigation) or find out something new about our case or about any of the others involved, for these are subjects I always avoid. No, I would just grudge them all the time and energy which had been expended not only to no purpose but to my actual detriment.

Today, I'm more optimistic. I've decided to be consistent up to the end, as much as my unfortunate situation requires it. I shall do what I have to do, and what will be . . .

Writing a diary of events which are still fresh in the mind, or writing down conversation, or day-to-day banalities and impressions, affords me the considerable advantage of being able to select my own subject-matter in the way I want. Furthermore, synchronizing events in this manner will give me an abundance of material which I will be able to read later at my own leisure.

It is inevitable that there will be a certain crudeness of style in what I write, a certain hastiness, inconclusiveness, but this is only to be expected. Not so much philosophy, perhaps?

*** Still no lawyer. Strange. Only two days before the trial, yet we only had one half-hour conversation at the end of the investigation, and even then we didn't discuss the case, we simply tried our literary witticisms out on one another. I couldn't care less whether he comes or not, but I would like to find out whether I am allowed by law to have a foreign lawyer represent me; I'm sure no one else could act independently and call things by their *real* names. Why do I not have the right, as Procurator Ponomarev told me, of challenging the court on the grounds that its members are all Communists, and that it's for my anti-Soviet convictions (inter alia) that I'm standing trial?

[1] A reference to the KGB guards' uniforms.

Would you believe it! I'd given up waiting for my lawyer, and been preparing all morning for the trial; I hadn't eaten or drunk from nerves, I sat around, one hour, two hours, three hours . . . and, at last, they told me—in the *evening*: "The trial has been postponed until the 15th December." No reasons, no explanations, nothing but cold indifference!!! Not only that—they told me on the *evening* of the day the trial was due to begin!

The last two days have been full of incident. Yesterday I was moved into cell 239, the second from the end on the sixth floor. It was already occupied by a dark-haired, foppish, youth called Viktor Belkin. He couldn't wait to tell me his whole history, and bored me stiff. After four years in a colony for juveniles he'd been free for just over a year and then got 10 years for raping a girl under 16. He's 21 years old and has served about two years of his sentence. He's from Leningrad, his father's an ex-procurator, with connections; his mother . . .

"My mother's sharp as they come! You should see the way we lived! They were going to put her on trial for bribing and threatening the plaintiff, but the old man got her off the hook."

His father had evidently helped him on several occasions, but he was an "ass" just the same!

"They took me to the police station and the officer there and my father were as thick as thieves. I can see I'm in trouble, I said, let me call my old man. "All right, go on then," said the officer. So I rang my old man and asked him what I should do. But he, instead of telling me to deny everything, told me to say I did it with her consent. But she was a minor! Then my old man started pulling as many strings as he could to get my sentence down to 10 years. But things didn't go very well: Now he and my mother are working on the plaintiff and her mother to get them to make an appeal for clemency. I'm writing to her mother as well: I say I'm in love with her and want to marry her. I think she's fallen for it!"

He was brought here on the 2nd September (the same as

Saltykov) as a witness in a case where an acquaintance of his was released from camp through bribery. He is a nuisance, talks too much, he's a present I can do without! I'd rather be sharing with Saltykov—we weren't even speaking the last two weeks. I'll soon put this so-and-so in his place; it wouldn't be my first fight here. The only trouble is, it's not quite as simple as that: when he was in the camp he worked as a printer, i.e. he was doing a stool-pigeon's job, and now he's here as a witness . . . But first I'll try and live with him as best I can, or we'll be at each other's throats before long.

21st November

Belkin's been ecstatically reading me his letter to his "plaintiff", as he always calls his victim. He writes in an obsequious, flowery style. Then he started composing a message to someone called Valia, a "pen-friend" he's been chasing for a couple of months. He saw her photograph in a newspaper and fell in love with her. The pursuit of "pen-friends" is a very popular hobby among criminals, and takes up a tremendous amount of time and energy. The general idea is to try and get a post-card back from them and then to try and arrange a meeting. Strictly speaking, this is illegal, but the camp authorities, and so of course, the prisoners who collaborate, care very little about what the laws say. When I asked him how he'd be able to send two letters (he's only allowed one per month) he bragged that the investigator himself sent them for him and for no charge. Did he say more than he intended through lack of experience or is he just blowing his own trumpet?

22nd November

Something's just occured to me, but what can I do? The lawyer can't help me; at our one and only tête-à-tête I implied something that could have been quite compromising from his point of view, and he answered me by gazing at the plug-sockets

37

in the wall. It was this that made me see how well and truly he has adapted to life in this country. I'm quite certain he won't take a note for me and how could I get it to him anyway, if they strip me naked every time I meet him? Maybe I'll get an opportunity to whisper it to Iurka[1]. The charge of treason is based on the cast-iron certainty—totally unsubstantiated, of course,—that we would act, if only we had the opportunity, in a hostile manner vis-a-vis the Soviet regime. I may say as proof that I harbour no political ambitions, that I had intended, upon once reaching the capitalist purgatory, that my first step would be to get permission for my mother to follow me. That's the absolute truth. Firstly, however, I have decided to say nothing at all, and, secondly, even if I were to speak, no proof I could give would help me anyway.

Marriages, as we know, are made in heaven, but sentences are made in Moscow.

Yet maybe this could help Iurka or Alik[2], or both together, I don't mean as far as the trial's concerned; but later, if we should live to see the case reviewed. I am sure they will be condemned along with all the others, although, by rights, Alik (for example) should get less than anyone else. Are they not, after all, the only non-Jews amongst us on trial? Soon we shall see how they will be used to proclaim to the world once again that there is no such thing as discrimination in the USSR! It's quite possible they'll call me a Russian as well.

Dymshitz and I will get the same, of course; one Jew, one non-Jew! During the investigation I requested them to ask the Strunino police station for my applications to get the nationality on my passport changed, but, of course, both police and investigators refused. Now it's up to me to convince the court that a man who is "50-50" has the right to call himself a Jew, even though originally he may have been registered as a Russian. ("It's remarkable," the police sergeant had told me, "the first case I've ever met like this. If a man changes from a

[1] Yuri Fedorov.
[2] Aleksei Murzhenko.

Jew to Russian then I can understand it, but the other way round . . . I can't decide this one, write to Moscow!")

Assimilate by all means, become a Russian by all means (as long as the powers that be don't let you forget what race you "really" belong to!—but a Jew? No, thank you very much!

23rd November

Any country characterized by the separation of secular and religious interests is no use to a totalitarian government. For despotism to flourish, the people must be susceptible to monomania.

Possibly the saddest aspect (saddest?—most agonizing, rather!) of being a convict is that one is compelled to associate with the very dregs of society, including those that enjoy power and delight in using it to its fullest advantage.

In 1964, one of my five investigators was Major Kruglov, a conceited wretch who enjoyed telling me over and over again, relevant or not, that he was a graduate in philology from Saransk. We once had the following conversation:

"Why have you forbidden me to correspond with my family?"

"For not attending your political instruction classes: why don't you?"

"They're no use to me—that's why I don't go."

"No use or boring, perhaps?"

"Both."

"So what? I don't always enjoy them either, but I think . . ."

"You are obviously used to making compromises, whereas this is what I'm trying to avoid."

"What do you mean?" he asked indignantly, "I'm not opposed to compromising in principle. Let me give you an example. The first time I was ever asked in school what 2 minus 3 was, I couldn't believe my ears. How could you take 3 from 2? Neither at school, nor at university, nor even now can I accept it. That's what *I* call not compromising."

He was a great big blockhead, but compared with most camp personnel, there's certainly no denying he was a man of principle: if ever he told anyone he was going to send them to prison, he would first, before you could even count up to ten, make them say something they were sorry for, and then starve then in the punishment block for six months: then, and only then, would he send them to prison!

24th November

*** The last time I met Kruglov, (i.e. when he summoned me to his office about the nail they found on me) he poured abuse on the Jews for being bad citizens of the USSR; they themselves were to blame, he told me: if so many of them had died in the War it was because they hadn't shown any resistance to the Germans. I objected strongly, and gave him all the familiar arguments one after another: the Jews are a peaceful race; the peculiarities of mass psychology; the specific role of their religion; death isn't the end of all things; and the most important argument of all—not only didn't they expect any help from the rest of the population but they were sure they would be handed over to the Germans etc. etc.

His answer to this was the following, word for word:

"The Russian people have never surrendered to their enemies and they don't need anybody to make excuses for them!"

"What about the million-strong army of General Vlasov,"[1] I asked, "Who had ever heard of a million men surrendering to the enemy?" But he made me stop "these hostile attacks". No one but a fool would take part in an argument like that. My sense of humour isn't good enough, and I am always cursing myself for showing irritability and bad temper whenever I'm

---

[1] General Vlasov. (1900–1946), Russian anti-Communist leader in Germany during Second World War; subsequently handed over to Soviet authorities and shot.

in the company of fools. I just cannot learn how to negotiate this particular minefield.

Here is Karamzin's description of Edigei's Moscow campaign, which I love gloating over:

"There was not the least resistance. The Russians were like a flock of sheep, torn apart by preying wolves. Citizens and farmers prostrated themselves before the barbarians: they waited for a decision on their fate, while the Mongols cut off their heads or shot them for amusement's sake . . . Many prisoners were taken . . . at time, one Tartar drove 40 men in front of him . . ."

Comrade Kruglov, please be so kind as to avoid generalizations about other peoples who are always inferior to your people in one thing only: they are different! Russian history is conspicuously lacking in respect for any one individual for the very reason that he was only an individual. All a man does is manure the state's cornfields. In the Duma the Boyars pulled each others' beards and spat at one another, and saw no shame in it.

*** Here is Karamzin speaking in court:

"To run away is not always to be a traitor; civil laws cannot be stronger than natural laws: one is permitted to save oneself from one's tormentors . . ."

It would be very interesting indeed to study the history of all Russian fugitives—up to and including the emigrants of the post-revolutionary period. I am convinced you would have to come to the conclusion that they were for the most part not only outstanding people, but exceedingly freedom-loving.

*** Here is another typically Russian scene from Karamzin (as Russian at any rate as the picture of all those people dancing around the prince and exulting, "Thou art our Prince, little sun!" then, the next day, they hang him from a tree—and then sing and dance round another prince). When Ivan the Terrible renounced the throne:

"The capital was stricken with terror: lack of leadership seemed even more terrible to them than tyranny. 'Our sovereign has abandoned us!' lamented the people, 'We shall perish!'. . . How can sheep remain without their shepherd?"

The Opritchnina[1] itself may be regarded as the original Knights' Order—the only Russian knighthood.

*** I don't know why, but today I feel like looking into my mother's side of the family. Sometimes you feel like a good belch after the great-power diet you've been fed on ever since the cradle.

*** Some more yet. From Kurbsky's letter to Ivan the Terrible:

"For thou hast created the kingdom of Russia, and whoever leaves thy land for foreign lands, dost thou call a traitor and punish with death . . ."

25th November

In Byzantium, the basil (king) was not only Tsar but first priest, thereby merging both the government and religious spheres of life. The ideal basil was Koba,[2] both general secretary and head of government rolled into one. As distinct from individualism in ancient days, when personality was generally hero-worshipped, it was the super-personality that prevailed in Byzantium.

In the Soviet state a man becomes an individual only when he falls foul of the courts. Then nothing they can say about his background, or "man's destructive environment" (to employ a phrase so widely used by Marxists even at the turn of the century) is of any use.

Generally speaking, despite the theoretical admission that the individual does play a role in history, you can nonetheless detect an undercurrent whenever you read an account of any Soviet campaign, which seems to imply that victory is more or less automatically guaranteed provided that one retains one's trust in the divine precepts of Marxism-Leninism. I am sure, however, that this is fundamentally nothing more than a tribute

[1] Opritchnina, the secret police force in the time of Ivan the Terrible.
[2] Stalin's pre-revolutionary underground pseudonym.

to the Slavic conception of world affairs, for history (the history of a *people*, that is) is created by *extremely concrete* personalities who are inclined to brag about the creative development of Marxism only when it suits them. They may say they are an impersonal instrument, but what avails it whether it be God, Marxism, or anything else for that matter, that presents itself as the will of the people?

This is merely preserving the status quo: while maintaining the (profitable) traditional values in the lower echelons of society a silent struggle for power is being waged in the upper echelons.

In Byzantium, as far as I remember, they executed dissidents, generally observed ideological purity, and took great pains to keep a close check on anybody who journeyed to the West for whatever reason, for the West was in their eyes the source of all heresies.

All these analogies may well appear somewhat insubstantial, but in reality they are quite correct, although it's true that they cannot easily be argued. For they go to the very core of something which remains quite unaffected either by time or by changes of government, i.e. national characteristics. And where these characteristics among different peoples resemble one another closely, my analogies, are, I think, quite justified.

26th November

The Mafia apparently ceased to exist under the Fascists. So indeed it should. Any dictatorship makes short shrift of organized crime. Whether it be a personal dictatorship or an administrative-party obligarchy, it regards organized crime as its own prerogative, it cannot tolerate competition. The somewhat paradoxical conclusion that must be drawn is that the presence of organized crime is—for a while at any rate—an unmistakable barometer as to the degree of democratization in a society if, that is, the adherents of formal logic among us were not forever declaring that the given amount of democracy in a society is in direct proportion to the amount of crime in that society. Organized crime is the income tax you pay for the benefits of democracy, its inexhaustible expenditure, like pornography, for example. The choice is either freedom of the press plus pornography, or "Pravda" minus pornography. The constant task for the democratic society is to keep cutting down its expenses, while at the same time avoiding the perils of dictatorship.

27th November

Berg: "Boris Godunov . . . despatched 18 young noblemen to foreign lands . . . They soon became proficient in the necessary languages, but only one of them returned to Russia . . ."

Nothing here about their motives; was it just a question of individual temperament, the result of some disagreement with the Lord's annointed one, possibly a personal dislike of the Russian system, or purely and simply a question of everyday considerations?

*** Attitudes to the law. At his coronation Vasily Shiusky[1] swore an oath to his people:

"For the new Tsar thought to free the Russian people of the two dreadful evils of that age: passing false information on enemies and unlawful disgrace . . . he thought to give his people that blessing which neither our grandfathers nor our fathers had even known . . . but many people, both the nobility and others, expressed indignation and not gratitude to Vasily, reminding him of the principle that had been established by Ivan III; that only the people could swear an oath to their sovereign, and not the sovereign to his people. These Russians were sincere friends of the Fatherland, and were not slaves or base flatterers . . . they preferred grace to the Law."

Some acquaintances of mine see this as a very touching historic episode, but stories like this merely disgust me. This

[1] Proclaimed Tsar in 1606, during Russia's so-called "Time of Troubles".

kind of attitude to such a law is no worse and no better than any other: each to his own, after all. But if such stories as this alarm you then there is no place for you in this country.

28th November

At the beginning of the century European newspapers were of the following opinion:

"The carnage in Armenia was organized by the Armenians themselves for purposes of political agitation."

It's not only the Zionists, then, that blow up their own ships for propaganda!

*** I have sufficient fortitude of spirit to save a man, but insufficient wisdom to forgive him his ingratitude, ignorance and spite.

*** A youth has a gun and says he is going to commit suicide. But his purpose is really to make himself justify both his own life and that of others; it is the subconscious challenge of the power of logic within him, a final plea, while he draws up his ultimate balance sheet. He would steal up to the very edge of the precipice, peer over the side, and in that terrible moment of fear perceive the true meaning of life. A man often does drive himself to the edge of despair, yet not to hurl himself over the side (although this does happen frequently), but to seek a miracle: it's a cry for help, a hope of finding secret reserves within himself. What of the violent quarrels between a psychopathic husband and his wife? They threaten, cajole, accuse one another till they approach the very edge of passion, that point beyond which divorce must lie, so they can, at the very last moment, drag out of each other hysterical oaths of loyalty and love. The hysteria and the violence are barometers as to the fidelity of their relationship.

29th November

If an unreluctant believer is obsessed by the search for truth,

45

then the more he is tormented by doubts, the more will he defend the rightness of what he believed. Should he be beset by unanswerable questions he will find no difficulty in scoring over the atheist who has never really thought deeply about faith, and whose arguments are therefore likely to be superficial. Whereas the believer has already tormented himself and found the answers, the atheist is incapable of reaching the deeper truths for he will deny that which logic cannot explain. And the believer perforce finds it hard to share his deepest thoughts.

*** I think I have guessed why the trial was so suddenly postponed until December. The 25th Session of the United Nations General Assembly, which met on 25th November, adopted a special resolution on the hijacking of aircraft. What a brilliant manoeuvre! How could I ever have been so naive as to imagine I might have a fair trial! Maybe this is just what they needed to get the firing squad ready. There is no reason to think the investigators were joking when they spoke of the death penalty. Now I have good reason to think that Captain Savelyev, the last of the three investigators who prepared me for the convict's cross, (or administered the last rites?) was not bluffing:

"Nothing is too cruel as far as our enemies are concerned. Our laws prescribe the death penalty: I advise you most strongly not to forget that."

At first they tried to break me by giving me assurances that I'd get no more than 12 years, but then lieutenant-colonel Elesin, the deputy chief of the Leningrad regional KGB investigation department—a conniving, scheming, peasant with a hail-fellow-well-met handshake—twice threatened me with the firing-squad if I didn't come to my senses and start co-operating. I thought of the idea of protesting that psychological torture was being used against me, but changed my mind —what was the use? It has to be clearly understood that these tactics are not flashes of "pique": each step is part of a carefully calculated and co-ordinated plan of campaign, an esoteric sport played according to the rules of their invention.

When I learned Mary[1], Lisa and Julia[2] had been released from custody, any momentary elation I might have felt was clouded over by the suspicion that a humanitarian plot was in the making, in preparation for either my or Dymshitz' execution. But then I consoled myself with the thought that my conclusion was somewhat arbitrary. For under Art. 58 proceedings are not instituted against certain people (even if they are equally guilty—or even guiltier than the accused.) The reasons for this are perhaps not always so clear to those who are uninitiated into the secrets of the Lubianka. Who but the KGB could so lovingly flirt with the law? Only for considerations of national security, of course!

The capriciousness of those who put into effect the laws of the Soviet Union is like a sort of balance that swings now towards humanitarianism (though always very calculated!) now towards repression, and each deviation suggests, provokes and justifies the next. Please do not think I would like to see Mary and the others sitting with the accused—God forbid! No, I have Russia's future at heart; how I long to see the Russian Saul gradually be converted into a Paul!

I would stand up and fight for the law to be observed strictly. For I feel Russia's only salvation from its traditional troubles is respect for the rule of law, and therefore for mankind itself. Insofar as the kingdom of the Smerdyakovs, who murdered all the Dimitris and Alyoshas in 1917 and then again the Ivan Karamazovs in 1937, appears indestructible, I would be so pleased to see someone tear himself away from this ardent Scythian embrace.

One of the most effective measures that could be taken against hijacking would be to destroy serfdom among some of the member-states of the United Nations. But not one word of this in the resolution! True enough, it's not printed in full; maybe there was something in it that the Soviet citizen isn't supposed

[1] Mary Knokh.
[2] Respectively, wife and daughter of Mark Dymshitz.

to know. Most of us have asked the appropriate Soviet organs many times for permission to emigrate to Israel and have been refused on each occasion without any reason being given. What are you supposed to do if they tell you, "You are guaranteed work and living quarters here," when you say you consider Israel your real home, the object of your spiritual and national aspirations, and it is for this reason that you wish to live there? Is hijacking an aircraft a way of defending your rights as a human being? Would you in that case be accused of doing more than was necessary to defend your rights?

It would be most interesting to try and define the responsibilities of a man who had been compelled to pull off a publicity-stunt as a last resort!

Even more so then must an organization like the UN bear the responsibility, for in its 25th November resolution there are certain requirements and appeals so vaguely formulated that even an experienced procurator in the Third Reich could have turned them to his account. Indeed these procurators frequently charged refugees from Hitler's Germany with treason. I know hijacking wasn't in fashion then, but that's only a detail. The only serious part in the resolution is where it expresses anxiety for the life of the crew and passengers in the aircraft. But in our case there were no threats to the lives of anyone else. But I forgot, that's not what we're being tried for . . . what does the Soviet regime care for an aeroplane and a crew that happen to be in it? Treason—yes, *that* it *does* care about! . . . I can hear my cell-mate coming back from his walk.

30th November

The celebrated writer in this country is the one who writes of banalities in a grandiose style, does not see any difference between thought and popular discussion, seriously believes in the uniqueness of his own views and experiences and is not ashamed of his own stupidity.

48

1st December

Here comes the winter. A couple of weeks yet before my cosy little trial, provided they don't postpone it again. I feel almost sorry for them—so many trials all at the same time! I must find some way to cheat them, to guess in what order they're likely to put us on trial . . . To judge by the list of charges, Sylva[1] can't possibly get less than eight years. But if I or Dymshitz get the death penalty they might make a "humanitarian gesture" and let her go under Article 83. If only she weren't such a simple, kindhearted soul! It's easy to see all the mistakes she's made simply by looking at the investigators' report—she's so human, Sylva!

A first meeting with the KGB is extremely hard on anyone, let alone a woman. One could hardly credit their tricks with originality, but they have the same effect on the unwary as the blow of a club on a naked skull. When I signed that I'd seen the record of the case, I noticed, for example, that Yurka gave them hardly any evidence at all, whereas the very first week I was arrested, they were reading me sections from his "confession".

When grown men in decorations are looking you straight in the eye, it's difficult to believe they're lying to you. But then, you know, it doesn't mean a thing to them, it's only one part of their duties!

When my mother came to the camp to see me, she couldn't help but believe all the slander these accused liars piled on my head; she cried bitterly and nearly had a heart attack.

2nd December

Those who fight for freedom would appear to be extremely intolerant, particularly towards those in their own circle. I once read the programme of one of the pre-revolutionary societies—the one to which D. Karakozov[2] belonged, I think—

[1] Kuznetsov's wife.
[2] Made unsuccessful attempt on life of Tsar Alexander II.

and their most important task as they saw it, after destroying the Tsar and the landowners, was the destruction of any dissidence among themselves. The struggle for freedom itself, therefore, is, due to one of life's ironies, in itself bound up with intolerance—as are all struggles for a radically new order.

*** From time to time you come across pre-revolutionary books here. On the cover, in old-style print, you read the following: "Take care of this book; do not tear out the pages, do not bend the back, do not cover it with pots of hot food, etc. This book is easily spoiled and your prison comrades will be deprived of the opportunity of reading it." Soviet books bear a somewhat drier message: "If this book should be spoiled, its cost will be exacted from the culprit and his cell will be deprived of the right to use the library." In the first case you are asked to have some thought for the other prisoners; in the second, no only are you yourself threatened, but the *whole* cell is made responsible, which, in effect, encourages you to spy on your cell-mates.

*** According to pre-revolutionary foreign observers, only the "old believers" in Russia were known as business people, and to them were attributed all the characteristics common to persecuted peoples: they were called landlords, misers, usurers, etc. i.e. they had to buy their way out of persecution.

*** How long is it since Gödel demonstrated the truth of the theorem that in any reasonably wide system of concepts there are necessarily questions that can be solved only by widening that system of concepts, and consequently, an absolutely logically closed system is impossible in principle. But who is guided by theorems when it is an issue of areas of competence, and when any attempt at widening the system of popular conceptions is met by the bayonet?

The founders of religious and social movements are generally people of great originality and daring, both in condemning the old and in affirming the new.

One finds many brilliant men among their followers until the new movement is victorious, when they are replaced by

50

mediocrities who support the fossilized status quo. The latter always persecute originality and daring; in the beginning the aim of every movement is truth and justice, irrespective of any interpretation that may be put upon them, but after victory is achieved, the aim is to cling to power at all costs. Now it is the persecutors who raise the standard of their prophets.

*** Panin (a bigwig in the time of Catherine the Great): "Russia is ruled by God's grace and man's stupidity."

*** Objectivity is disinterested subjectivity.

3rd December

However gloomy the world may appear to you, life can give you such humiliating kicks that it can have you wriggling about like a clown. I know how inconsequential it is for them to sentence me to death; what they really want is to have me in the necessary frame of mind to entertain the public as well. Never! If only I were Spanish like Unamuno and not afraid to defy them: "You may kill me, but you can't convince me!"

4th December

Lenin spoke of bourgeois democracy like St. Augustine of paganism—its virtues, he said, only served to camouflage its vices.

*** Leskov—"No Way Out": "Just remember who your're dealing with!" said Nikon Rodionovich. The simple folk realized this only too well and not only did they not wear a hat whenever they passed by the Maslennikovs' mansion but were proud of it:

"We've got a merchant living among us now," boasted one petty-bourgeois to a visitor from out of town. "What a fellow he is! Whatever you ask him he'll do it for you; if you want to go to jail, he'll get you in jail; if you want a good flogging or a birching from the police, he'll fix it for you. All he has to say is one word to the town governor or write you a little note, then

you go along and present your note and you'll be all right! . . .
But just to look at him—he's like one of us."

*** Persecution of dissidents is more terrible than genocide:
genocide deprives people of their life, whereas if you destroy
peoples' freedom of thought you are destroying the very essence
of life—its spirit and its development through diversity.

5th December

Soviet heroes have no faults—let alone vices—to overcome.

*** Belkin is intolerably talkative, but I've decided to wait
until the trial, which, thankfully, won't be too long now.

*** Subject: two people somewhere in the mountains. One
of them is constantly addressing silence in the most high-flown
terms imaginable: "Oh silence! thou art the highest bliss . . .
balm to a weary, injured heart . . ." and so on. Then the other
hits him over the head with a stone just so he can *hear* the
silence.

*** Frequently, a man on trial for anti-Soviet activities will
plead guilty to criminal activities and repent his misdeeds: they
say this is caused by his brain which has been worked on ever
since his childhood in a totally determined manner.

The fully matured dissident, capable of thinking for himself
and of listening to the voice of his conscience, will at first be
filled with indignation at the hiatus between what is said to be
and what is, and later will watch this hiatus grow . . . his
greatest sense of outrage will at first be occasioned by the
illegalities from which he is suffering, only extremely indirectly
(mostly because his youth shelters him from the more severe
blows). So long as he personally has acquired no bruises, his
distaste for reality is theoretical rather than practical and this is
the reason why reverence towards the authorities, which has
long been stirring in his subconscious, gains the upper hand at
the moment of crisis.

I once knew an Estonian in a camp who had no faith whatever
in non-violent resistance to the Soviet regime: "They killed

my father, my two brothers and my fiancée," he would tell me, "There's no turning back for me now. Just you carry on playing your little game of opposition."

The logic of repression is such: you push a man into social-political activity—with all its innocence, childishness and puerile theorizing—and once you get him into a camp he is either broken straightaway or swiftly develops a grudge against the government, for he knows better than anybody that he is serving time for nothing: for a childish game he once played, youthful romanticism and an emotional outburst.

*** When a man is stronger than another he will not do away with him quickly, as punishment for any actions (or crimes) he may have committed, but will punish him condescendingly, in his own time. A regime that is strong, yet just, does not punish hysterically or cruelly.

6th December

I got my first two weeks in the punishment block for a witticism of somewhat dubious content. It was the noise of conversation in the barracks that woke me from my slumber; the unit officer was taking a political instruction class on the theme, "Work Ennobles Man". A devil gets into me frequently and on this occasion it prompted me to acquaint the whole of my audience with a delightful new epigram I'd thought up for the occasion: "Work created a Communist out of a monkey."

*** To learn how to state the truth truthfully—that is the problem.

*** You can open the eyes of the people to the truth of one specific fact, but you can never teach them the whole of the truth. All the people can do is stagger from one delusion to the next. The process of developing one's capacity for thought (other than stereotyped patterns of thinking) is a long and extremely individual one, and one that does not lend itself to development "en masse".

*** Whereas I have an unfortunate tendency to make everyday observations in my notes, I intend, for the moment at least, to avoid anything that appertains to the trial (i.e. to keep well away from anything that worries me far more than anything else at this moment, and is therefore worthy of noting down).

*** Obsessed with the need for social experimentation on the masses, "our" leaders work out stereotyped systems of governing people, not as they are, but as they would like them to be, thereby creating the necessary conditions for violence.

*** Robespierre compared a revolutionary tribunal to an ecclesiastical court: each judges you for the ultimate crime—that of speaking your mind.

*** Political religion, founded according to the revelations of its leader, permits the existence of religious establishments and ideological squabbles only when it is still engaged in the struggle for power. Upon its accession to power, however, the new political theology, which supplies dogmatized answers to all questions and threatens the heretic with the stake, is decreed and sanctified.

10th December

At last I met my lawyer. He insists I say as little as possible during the trial, and play the role of the confessed, if not repentant, criminal. I will be neither the one nor the other.

*** If ever you are judging a man's success in this life, don't forget that, provided he believes in the after-life, he could make a career for himself in heaven. If his life here is a "vale of tears", then maybe in the life to come he will be envied for his magnificent career. I knew one such—a Jesuit (by nature) and an informer, by the name of Bakhrov. He was quite frank about it: "If I do a good deed, I do it not for the man who may benefit from it, but for the Lord, and for the salvation of my soul!" In other words, he was really making a path for himself, paying his way, as it were, to the Kingdom of Heaven. (As a matter of interest, he had bruises on his knees from praying so much, whereas the rest of the time he spent preaching and spying.) For Kant this was not a virtue, but a duty, a "conditional imperative". It's symptomatic that nothing is quite so repugnant about religion as personal contact—especially in a cell—with those who practice it. But this goes for the overwhelming majority of the hangers-on of any political idea. People, like Russia, are more attractive from a distance.

*** Do you, in the West, still talk of alienation? We aren't mature enough for this yet, or even for complaining publicly about it, (such forms as occur under Soviet state-capitalism are unknown in the West!) Bread is our major concern—the meat's still far away! I think alienation is an inevitable stage in the spiritual growth of mankind. He who wishes to avoid it is like the man who prefers castration to the pains of adolescence. Do not forget Hamlet's "madness" or Faust's soul, the torture of an alienated consciousness . . .

*** I'm writing almost continuously now. I told my cellmate I was getting ready for my trial.

After dinner we had a visit from the deputy-governor of the prison, Lieutenant Veselov, a long, slim Chekist of about 35, who blushes at the least embarrassment. He's such an angel, just like a thief with wings! He revealed (why did he, I wonder?) that the West has been giving us the full glare of publicity. This won't make the slightest difference, of course, but it's still good to know. There is nothing more terrible than the silent reprisal. Veselov was keen to know whether I would appear before the court in a yarmulka (skullcap) like Mendelevich, who "only pretends he believes". I was outraged that he should dare to make such an unsubstantiated statement, but then he took me into his confidence, "I have never seen any practising Jews. The only thing they ever think about is money." I answered him as deferentially as I could: "Esteemed citizen deputy-governor, the Jew lay on a sheepskin gazing at the heavens and thinking about God when you were still dangling from the branches of a tree by your tail!"

Prison life is so devoid of interest that even the most idiotic of conversations attains the proportions of an "occasion" you simply cannot shake out of your mind. However much you poke fun at such a man he is still the personification of all the forces that are hostile to you. It is not easy for the convict whose self-esteem is hammered daily to be objective about it, any more than you would expect objectivity or peace of mind from a man whose genitals have been wedged in the door. All the same I feel no bitterness, no blind hatred for the Chekist, as long as I think he is one by conviction. There's nothing I loathe more than the treacherous conformist, the indifferent, little man, the victim of the regime and yet its accomplice.

11th December

Asia: "Genghis Khan, wolves, their eyes shining in the darkness, snow and vodka, the knout, Schlüsselburg and Christianity." (T. Mann.) But was not the Third Reich the Western World's Asia? We're all from Asia—some have left, some have remained behind. The only thing of any significance is how far away we are from it. Asia is man's subconscious. Our emergence from the continent is the symbol of our historical development towards the dominance of the consciousness. Asia is the mob, the lynch-party. It's quite in character that Asia should have remained not long in power in Germany, whose external defects were the result of its internal lawlessness. It is as though it strove to conquer the world to prove—to others as well as to itself—its right to exist (see T. Mann's article on the duality of the German psyche) and so it perished, unlike the proper Asia, which has no firm ground in the West. The West is the ancient Gauls firing arrows in the air, or Voltaire, protesting in the name of the spirit and reason against the Lisbon earthquake. And what is the East?—an Asian on his knees before an idol!

*** Instead of the traditional plaint, "there is no happiness in life", I will tattoo on my chest the proud, "life is a means of existence for albuminous bodies—Engels". Criminals sometimes tattoo on their chest or their back a "USSR-Turkey" frontier-post, together with a picture of a man with a knapsack crossing into Turkey, and the inscription, "I am going where I don't have to work." This is how many seem to imagine the West (though Turkey is nothing but the gateway to it).

*** It sounds as if there is a row going on in one of the cells—I can hear the stamping of feet, someone shouting, though I can't make out what they're saying. One of the voices I can hear clearly belongs to "Adenauer". I recognize his wheezing.

"Adenauer" is the nickname of one of the convicts. (I can't remember his real name.) He looks like the devil himself. He's already done a total of 30 years in prison, and wasted away to almost nothing. Now he's more or less a total cretin. He used to start off each morning by masturbating near the slop-bucket, in full view of everyone else and carried on all through the day until he began fetching blood. Then he got so scared, he would burst into tears and make such an uproar they had to send the doctor in. Every day he would yell through his cell window down to the yard: "Freedom for Manolis Glazos!"[1] or "The Germans murdered my brother Yedka—who can I drink with now?" Not one week passed when the guards didn't beat him till he was black and blue. Even his cell-mates sometimes couldn't stand him any longer and frequently took it out of him for torturing them till their very nerves were frayed. Then he would shut up for a day or so, but soon it would start all over again. The very first time I came across him was at Potma transit point in 1962, as I first made my way to the camp just after my trial, a foolhardy prey yet to all those popular illusions about prisoners in general and political prisoners in particular. (In Russian literature politicals are always idealized, held up as a shining example of courage and saintliness.)

They put me in a tiny cell, three yards square. I looked around me; on a plank-bed a couple of men were lying, both covered head to foot in filthy scabs; the cell was covered in

[1] Imprisoned Greek Communist.

rags, cigarette butts, spittle. So, they've thrown me in among the criminals, someone's made a mistake I thought. Silence. I asked them:

"I suppose I'm in the wrong place, am I not?"

"I'm Adenauer," wheezed the dirtier of the two, "This is Kalia-the-Fool; you need pay no attention to him. Sit down, young man."

"No, I don't think. . . I'm under Art. 58^1 . . . It's probably all a mistake . . . they'll soon realize . . ."

"We're 58 as well," said Adenauer, to put me at my ease.

Kalia's name I cannot recollect; I know only that the day they released him after serving his 15 years, he was admitted to a lunatic asylum. He proved indeed to be a fool, a silent manic-depressive, under the impression he was being persecuted by the "New Bolsheviks, who were out to poison him".

What could I do? Somehow I cleaned away a narrow strip on the bed and lay down between the first politicals I had ever encountered. I felt so sad. My mind was a prey to so many suspicions . . .

I turned to Adenauer, "What's wrong?—your ear's gone blue."

"The Chekists gave me a beating yesterday."

I watched him copy something out of a newspaper into his jotter. He used capitals but I couldn't make out what he was writing. Seeing my curiosity he snorted:

"I'm studying politics, and I advise you to do the same or you'll finish up like Kalia-the-Fool here."

Adenauer was copying out the whole of "Pravda" word for word. I was stunned: the idea of becoming like Kalia or Adenauer repelled me and I swiftly came to the conclusion that the camp was evidently so constructed as to leave me no alternative to such a fate. For the first time in my life I contemplated suicide but the following day they threw me into another cell, and to my great relief, I found no more Adenauers or victims of Zionist persecution.

[1] Article 58: used to commit dissidents as mental cases.

*** Choking with joy Belkin tells me about his sheepdog, and how it used to obey every order he gave it. A dog gives people like him the opportunity of giving orders: he loved the dog's unconditional, slavish, trust. But are not many people like this? It's quite another matter when a child not only "rides" on a dog, but tries to make the dog ride on him. According to Tsvetaeva,[1] the normal child is more likely to kill its governess than a dog. I myself was a normal child, though I never had a dog, and certainly never a governess, so far as I know. And who was it that said his last wish was that the affectionate and devoted eyes of his dog should watch him as he passed from this life to the next?

*** Total freedom in this life is impossible; we can speak only of degrees of freedom, and even these are illusory. The best of all societies is the one in which the man who is in pursuit of freedom is not forever banging his head against a wall of social and political slavery. I know you can find this wall anywhere but it does not have to be any more durable than is necessary for those who need it to set up a dictatorship. The majority of people are quite happy to give in. Let them. You cannot force everybody to enter the paradise(!) of freedom. And how can you guarantee that you won't use the man-in-the-street to the detriment of the free man?

*** From "liberty as a conscious necessity" is but one step to T. Mann's ironical "liberty is voluntary slavery". A quick step in the other direction leads to anarchistic rebellion and romantic nihilism . . .

*** Why would Herzen[2] today have been ashamed of the seriousness of the tone of the narrative in *Biliye i Dumi* ("I blessed my suffering and I accepted it . . .")

Herzen, like most of those who create legends about them-

[1] Soviet poet (1892–1941). She returned to the USSR after many years abroad, just before the War; hanged herself shortly afterwards.

[2] Alexander Herzen (1812–1870), Russian writer and revolutionary, wrote "Memoirs", settled in London in 1851, from which his periodical, Kolokol (Bell), was smuggled into Russia.

selves by writing memoirs, took himself too seriously (this was a characteristic of that epoch), and we know that, in the final outcome, it was fully justified. But why should this have been and what consequences did it entail? That century was a lot younger than ours, the whole of the Soviet period included. Revolutionaries, and particularly those who believed in God, had something worth dying for.

I, an ordinary citizen of the second half of the twentieth century, proclaim that there is no cause worth dying for, and even less worth slaughtering others for. How many just causes have there been, and how many have died on their account? Now, with the passing of time, we can see all those ideas are not what we once thought they were, and we are unable to bring all who died back to life.

*** We have our original sin as well—the sin of national and social origin!

*** Herzen was certainly not the icon type. His life was full of high and low points, yet he always remained human. Lenin (the "sacred") had no human weaknesses, no low points, suffered no defeats, made no mistakes. Herzen had Ogariov, whom did Lenin have? He had Koba (Stalin), one of his most trusted disciples, who needed only time to show his true mettle.

*** Nietzsche (and judged not only by his writings) would surely have died in a concentration camp, however much his aphorisms may have been the most popular ideological currency of those who initiated the national-proletarian-petty-bourgeois movement. Would not Herzen also?—"Any crimes that may be committed on this plot of land by the people against their executioners are henceforth justified!"

13th December

The trial is the day after tomorrow. Yesterday morning I changed my mind and began to write out a draft for my speech in court, in case I should decide to use it, after all. I've been scribbling non-stop for two days and I've only just now finished (10 o'clock). I haven't yet determined how I shall act in court. The fact that I have prepared something could very well be the decisive factor.

14th December

I have decided to copy my speech into this diary. While I am doing this I will be able to remove all the sharper political edges, and thus keep it down to a bare minimum. Here it is:

"Before recounting the circumstances leading up to my attempt to leave the confines of the USSR illegally, I should like to draw the attention of the court to an exact description of the offence committed by myself and my friends. We were a prey to quite abnormal passions, and without a detailed analysis of all the motives that led to our being at the airport on the morning of 15th June, it is quite impossible to understand our case.

I ask the court to be patient, for I intend to be as thorough as I can.

So as not to digress, I shall keep to the text of the charges made against me:

"*Being* of anti-Soviet disposition, Kuznetsov entered, during the years 1969–70, into a criminal conspiracy with Butman . . .," then a little lower down: "Being convicted of anti-Soviet activities in 1962 and upon the termination of his punishment, he again began to involve himself in anti-Soviet activities . . ."

Concerning this sham invocation, "being . . .", which is used not unintentionally by those who have compiled these charges against me, I would like to reveal, albeit imperfectly, my true state of mind, which is here described with such ominous significance.

I was born in 1939; in 1956 I finished school, worked at a plant as a turner, served in the army, then studied at the Moscow University faculty of philosophy; in 1961 the KGB, considering that my social activities went beyond the bounds of those laid down by law, arrested me and estimated that the degree of digression of my behaviour from that required was seven years. At first, on account of my naivety and youthful inability to comprehend the needs of the state, I was, I must confess, extremely taken aback by such a severe appraisal of the danger I was considered to represent to the state. A product of Soviet education, I had never gone farther than criticizing the Soviet regime within its own terms. A victim of youthful day-dreaming, of searching for my own identity, and to some extent a prey to my own stormy passions and the schoolboy's understanding of ideology, I was still the tragic-comic victim of a system of myths. In no other way can I explain my lack of understanding of the severity of my sentence. A feeling that I had been wronged *in principle* by the injustice of this sentence played a not insignificant role in the formation of the views which I admit to being anti-Soviet.

But even in the concentration camp the ever-vigilant eye of "justice" did not leave me in peace. I do not mean the innumerable punishment cells and bi-annual sojourns at Vladimir prison; I refer to the breaking of the principle which is the corner-stone of any legislation, namely, that one cannot be tried twice for one and the same crime. In the Spring of 1963, the Moscow City Court, for some reason which I do not know, reviewed my case and, "taking into account the prisoner's personality," sentenced me to be kept until the end of my term in a special regime camp, although, according to my first sentence, I had been sentenced to a restricted regime. A substantial difference, permit me to point out. Perhaps nine months later I discovered that this was an infringement of practically half-a-dozen articles. The decision of the court was quashed and I was given strict regime, which was again an infringement of those same half-dozen articles. But by this time I no longer looked for human logic in the action of the organs of repression.

Here it may be in order to characterize briefly my views,

which I explained thoroughly during the investigation; the court may learn of them by reading the case documentation. I long ago grew out of active dislike of the existing regime. I think that the essential characteristics of the structure of the regime are to all intents and purposes immutable, and that the particular political culture of the Russian people may be classed as despotic. There are not many variations in this type of power-structure, the framework of which was erected by Ivan the Terrible and by Peter the Great. I think that the Soviet regime is the lawful heir of these widely differing Russian rulers. A Jew, with neither any inclination towards the wielding of power, not with any love for meek resignation, nor nourishing any hope of seeing a radical democratization of an essentially repressive regime in the foreseeable future, and considering myself responsible—however indirectly—as a citizen of this country, for all of its abominations, I decided to leave the Soviet Union. I consider it not only impossible but unnecessary to fight against the Soviet regime. It fully answers the heartfelt wishes of a significant—but alas not the better—part of its population.

My mother, Zinaida Vasilyevna Kuznetsova, is a Russian, my father, Samuil Gerson, died in 1941 and was a Jew. It's very curious, but it was in 1953 precisely that my mother changed our family name—and therefore mine as well since I was a minor and under her tutelage—and took her maiden name, Kuznetsova.

Could I, a 16-year old brainless Young Communist foresee how double-edged my yielding to my mother's insistence that I register (on receiving my internal passport) as a Russian would prove to be? Having observed the symptoms of anti-semitism endemic among the people, and sometimes even foreseeing how these symptoms coincided with government policy in certain respects, I grew mature enough to form my own opinions and felt it essential that I personally join the ranks of the oppressed.

I grew up in a Russian family and had practically no knowledge whatsoever of Jewish culture, not did I know anything of the influence it had had on nearly every culture in the world. Therefore, my choice to live and be a Jew was dictated in the early stages by emotional considerations rather than by a conscious feeling of physical identity. Tsvetaeva says something of this: "Is it not a hundred times more worthy to be a wandering Jew? For the pogrom is as life itself to any human being who is worthy of the name."

About two months before I was freed from Vladimir prison I put in an application to the prison governor that I be registered as a Jew in the documents I would receive on leaving the prison. But my application was rejected on the grounds that my internal passport had been withdrawn upon my arrest. Later I asked the police to change the note in the paragraph on nationality, but at first they refused because I was under special surveillance, and then because I still had a criminal record and this could only be done after eight years had elapsed. It fully suited the assimilators, of course, to treat me as a Jew, but nevertheless to count me as a Russian.

I will not conceal the fact that during the seven years I spent in confinement, I had become mentally exhausted, and when I was released my only wish was to be left alone. But then what? I was followed, supervised, summoned by the KGB, by the police, forced to take shelter where I could . . . I was registered in Strunino, Vladimir district. Sometimes the Strunino police gave me written permission to go and see my mother on Sundays, whereas the Moscow police advised me "not to be seen anywhere near her." So during these infrequent, though apparently quite legal, visits home I was compelled to hide myself and stay the night with friends. This was supposed to last eight years. Do not the motives behind my attempted emigration, which, with such crude tendentiousness are described in the charges against me as, "Being of an anti-Soviet disposition," now appear a great deal clearer?

In January, 1970 I went over to Riga to see my wife. In February we received our invitation from Israel, and we had to

Edward Kuznetsov

Sylva Zalmanson

set about collecting the necessary documents to hand in to the Ovir[1] for obtaining permission to leave the country. The greatest problem of all was obtaining the employment reference: (can (not) cope with work, does (not) participate in communal life, morally (un)stable, ideologically (un)sound . . .) I know not whether this was an unconscious effort to humiliate us on the part of the great bureaucratic state machine or whether it was simply the fruit of the labour of one particular Party official. Whatever it was, every alternate word uttered by a specific number of the most sullen of Soviet citizens was to be my reference.

There are many different reasons for withholding this reference. One man is refused because he is in the army (Wulf)[2]; a second—because he is studying at the VUZ[3], (Israel)[4], and if he just so much as mentions this reference, he is likely to be expelled and packed off into the army, and neither during his military service nor for at least three years afterwards dare he bring up this subject; a third (Sylva) is refused—because she's just finished studying; a fourth—is just refused and no reason given. The most frequent method is that, in the absence of a written request for the reference from the Ovir, they cannot help you, and the Ovir refuses to send you this since, "it's you that need the reference not us". I personally know of a considerable number of people for whom the very word "reference" has become almost a vulgarism. But an even larger number of people who wish to emigrate do not have sufficient courage to let it be known publicly. I am not speaking now of the inevitable dangers of such a course of action, for these remain only too clearly in people's minds and they are afraid of a repetition of those dark and dreadful pages of history.

Everybody knows well enough the inevitablity—even though next time it may not be so overt—of repressive measures against

[1] Soviet department of emigration.
[2] Vulf Zalmanson.
[3] VUZ—Institute of Higher Education.
[4] Israel Zalmanson.

the potential "traitor" (the men to whom you may bellow the length of a train compartment, "Why the hell don't you get off to your bloody Israel!" while everybody in the compartment looks on, and smiles their approval). As soon as your desire to emigrate becomes common knowledge, whether at work or in your apartment block, or in the police station, they don't let you forget it. Someone will say the word "Israel" and make an obscene gesture, or wedge a pencil into the dial of your telephone. How people split their sides whenever they hear the old joke: "Jews leaving for Israel, your train will depart from the *northern station!*"

At my place of work in Riga I could not get the reference I needed: I hadn't been working there long enough, they told me. I went to Moscow, then to Strunino, as I thought I had surely worked there long enough by now to be eligible for this necessary bit of paper. When I told the chief personnel officer I had come all the way from Riga especially for this reference, he was dumbfounded and said they could easily have sent it to me by post. "The trouble is that the institution which is asking for a reference insists it should say on it, 'For emigration and permanent residence in Israel'." (The reason for this incidentally is quite simple—the reference as such is not particularly difficult to obtain.) I shall not bother to describe the reaction of the personnel officer to this, only that I was ordered to appear the next day before the chairman of the factory committee, who, after asking me a whole series of stupid questions like, "Why are you going to Israel?" and, "What are you going to do when you get there?" suddenly caught me unawares when he asked me, "What would happen if tomorrow my son was sent to fight for the Arabs: what would you do – shoot him?" I felt there was nothing I could do but answer him in kind: "Oh, has your son come back from Czechoslovakia already?" I didn't get the reference, need I say.

What do you do when you are everywhere so blatantly humiliated? You can wait year after year—which many people do—living in your suitcase and going through all the difficulties of trying to obtain the necessary documents, give them to the Ovir, and then explain in writing how you have relatives in Israel, Israel is your real homeland, that you have spiritual—national aspirations—and then receive answers like: "You are guaranteed living-quarters and work here, you are materially independent of your relatives who live in Israel, and therefore you have no grounds for permission to emigrate."

I was not prepared to accept this. In my opinion I had been denied my right to emigrate and felt I had the moral right to reply to a sequence of illegal acts by my infraction of the law as expressed in Art. 83, Criminal Code of the RSFSR. I have in mind illegal emigration, punishable by a term of up to three years. I declare that we have been falsely charged. We are charged with *premeditated* activities to the detriment of the security of the USSR. It is quite evident that the intention of each of us was emigration. During the preliminary investigation I attempted to explain as clearly as I could to each of my three investigators in turn, and to Procurator Ponomarev, exactly what the security of the USSR meant in this *specific situation*. Despite all their fantasies, I realized that their major concern was the harm that might be caused to the prestige of the USSR, for our escape might have been seized upon and made use of by hostile propaganda. Well, firstly, to be influenced in one's mode of conduct by attempting to forestall the slanderous propaganda of one's so-called enemies is not a very worthwhile occupation; and secondly, had any single one of us ever contemplated that the prestige of the USSR might have been increased by our actions, not one of us would have wavered for one moment. Neither the USSR nor its prestige ever had the slightest bearing on our activities or our intentions.

I have very little knowledge of jurisprudence (this is only my second trial, after all!) and when I was held in isolation during the investigation I was categorically refused any legal literature (I cannot even obtain the Constitution of the USSR!) and, therefore, I cannot give you any references or quotations. I would, however, like to direct the attention of

67

the court to the book, "Especially Dangerous State Crimes", which was published in 1965 (its place of publication I do not know), in which it is stated that treason can be accomplished only with the express intention of causing detriment to the national security of the USSR. The investigation did not establish any such purpose in our case.

As far as our situation is concerned one can speak only of the eventual intent which, in my opinion, precludes treason.

Any government that has ratified the "Universal Declaration of Human Rights" (as the USSR has done) is obliged to guarantee these rights to each of its citizens in realistic terms, including Arts. 13, 14 and 15. It was only because my human rights were flagrantly denied me that I decided to flee abroad. It was above all an act of desperation.

We have not collected any information about the military potential of the USSR, nor have we stolen any state secrets . . . I maintain that we should not be tried on any supposition as to how we might have acted abroad and as to how the propaganda of any foreign governments might have treated our flight. If one must speak of the prestige of the USSR then I have no doubt that any responsibility for impairing this must be borne by those who, having deprived us of the possibility of emigrating legally, provoked our attempt to emigrate illegally, and who now accuse us of treason. It is they who, by the very act of accusing us, must bear the weight of responsibility for any loss of prestige to their country. For in all civilized countries those who cross the frontier illegally are not considered as anything other than minor criminals. There can be no doubt that every government has the right to inflict punishment for any activity it considers hostile to itself, but to inflict punishment only as the result of concretely incriminating acts and irrespective of how those acts may be termed at some future date.

In the book *The Nuremburg Trial of the Nazi Judges*, published in 1970 by "Legal Literature", it is apparent that the officials of Hitler's judicial and legislative apparatus were tried, among other things, for sentencing to death people who

68

attempted to flee from the Third Reich. Walter Brehm, ex-vice procurator-general, "People's Tribunal", admitted they had tried people who had attempted to flee abroad, solely on the supposition that they might, once having attained their destination, engage in military operations harmful to the Reich. And this was in time of war! These people were tried on the supposition that they would act hostilely towards the Reich as soon as they had the opportunity of doing so.

The Military Tribunal recognized that the wide definition of treason operative in the Third Reich gave Nazi judges the opportunity of pronouncing death sentences for actions constituting only a minor offence in the eyes of the rest of mankind; the Military Tribunal recognized that such a definition of treason was a military crime and a crime against mankind.

Without denying the fact that we attempted to flee the country, I categorically declare that we cannot be considered traitors and I affirm that such an accusation is the result of an illegally widened definition of treasonable activities.

Concerning Art. 93–1 of the Criminal Code of the RSFSR (on large-scale misappropriation of state property). Not one of us had the intention of misappropriating the aircraft. We were convinced that it would have been returned to its rightful owner. Therefore there can be no question of misappropriation! The crime in question was the attempted temporary removal of state property, and this is certainly not misappropriation. If somebody in a rush to attend a Komsomol[1] meeting were to take possession of another person's motor vehicle and then, on attaining his destination, were to leave it in the middle of a square on the presumption that it would soon be discovered and returned to its owner, then this does not constitute stealing. Although until recently this was considered stealing, a special article appeared in the Criminal Code concerning responsibility for taking possession of another person's car.

[1] Communist Youth Organization.

In our case the hijacking of an aircraft can be considered a similar action if one takes into consideration the relationship of the subject of the crime to the object. One might object that up to now there has been no article about hijacking aircraft, but it must surely appear soon . . . And what about steamships, steam engines and small space rockets? Yes, so far there is no relevant article. But this does not mean one can apply an article by analogy, for this was recently forbidden by Soviet legislation. To be specific, it was recognized that the practice of condemning car-hijackers as misappropriators was a mistake. Our case is analogous. It is true that there are no articles about hijacking aircraft. This means that there operates in effect the well-known Roman principle, "Where there is no law there can be no crime."

I demand that we be tried for what we did—attempting to hijack an aircraft—and not for stealing, which we never even contemplated.

In order to illustrate my approach to the matter I will be so bold as to impose upon the court a little parable I have invented, though bearing in mind that fact that, while it cannot possibly exhaust all aspects of the case under discussion, it may nevertheless help to throw a little light on it:

A man was told that he had the right to receive a certain sum of money, but that he would never be allowed to even wish to lay his hand upon it. Be that as it may, he once came to the bank. The cashier rudely reprimanded him as though he were some impudent villain and promptly slammed the window shut in his face. This happened seven times. The man was not, however, imbued with the correct measure of Christian humility and forgiveness and, still hoping to receive the money owed to him, made an attempt to break into the cashier's office and finally broke his door down, with the assistance of, shall we say, the office door handle, the property of the establishment in question. Just when he was at that stage in his crime, he felt his hands being forced behind his back. He, poor wretch, had never imagined, and certainly couldn't have cared less if he had, that the accountant in the office next door had been plotting against the cashier and might turn any insignificant scandal to his own advantage. The criminal considers himself guilty only of being over-credulous, of taking too seriously any rumours he might have heard concerning his right to receive a certain sum of money, and of being annoyed when he discovered that this right was merely fictitious, as long as he were not prepared to show the necessary humility. He is, however, charged with aiding and abetting the hostile accountant, treason towards the establishment, and stealing an office door-handle. When he is tried he does his best to defend himself, but, of course, is unable to.

For myself, I am charged, in addition to keeping and duplicating anti-Soviet literature, with intent to subvert the political regime of the country. Well, I have spoken already of my attitude towards the Soviet regime and of the reasons why I never had any intentions of trying to subvert it. I will add only the following. The regime of this country is, in my view, a tyrannical religion with the state as its God. It would not be fitting for me to speak now of the possibility of secularizing Russia. I can speak only of the mixture of pagan cults which exist in this primarily religious atmosphere. For every religion is characterized by violence at the very dawn of its existence: later it matures and is content only with burning its heretics, in a figurative sense. It is unintelligent to encourage the substitution of a younger religion for an already decadent one.

A handful of intellectual oppositionists—a phenomenon as characteristic of Russia as it is alien to her national traditions—cannot and will not change things.

The number of rebels will grow, or diminish, as the political barometer changes. These may be mostly young people, attempting to compensate for something they feel is lacking in their lives and who finally find fulfilment in marriage or a suitable reservoir into which they can drain all their languishing energies. Or old men, gone grey on the field of battle. One simply cannot prevent people loving freedom. If today a man looks down at those who read "Samizdat", (underground writing), then tomorrow, if he knows his friends can be locked up for reading it, he will also take to reading it . . . For that part of society which thinks looks with disgust at the prostitution of talent and ability.

Should anyone ever have told me he had similar views on the existing situation I would have quite understood his desire to leave holy Russia. Do you really understand me? I am a Jew and I want to live in Israel, in the land of my forefathers, in the land of the greatest of all nations. This does not mean Russia is not my homeland, but Israel is my homeland too, and it is Israel I have chosen. For, you see, in my hierarchical system of values, the question of which is my homeland is not uppermost. Uppermost is freedom, and this is why Israel draws me—it is my *Homeland* and my *Freedom*.

I am accused of keeping and propagating two books: *Memoirs* by Litvinov,[1] and *Russian Political Leaders*, by Shub.[2] But I had Lenin in my library too. Yet for some reason I am not accused of propogating Leninism in order to consolidate the regime. I have read Lenin, I have read Litvinov and Shub and many more besides. I have read them because I like reading, because I have by nature an inquiring mind; I have read them neither to subvert nor to consolidate anything. Therefore, if you consider these books to be slanderous, then you must try me for keeping, reading and propagating them only under Article 190–1. Although I have never seen any list of forbidden books, I readily agree that Shub's book is anti-Soviet, but only to the extent that any book on the apostles and saints of the Revolution is bound to be such.

I am inclined to refer Litvinov's *Memoirs* to that category of books which are "not recommended" (apparently such do exist) to be read by the loyal Soviet subject; in which case I would recommend the court to apply only the Lithuanian equivalent of Art. 190–1, Criminal Code of the RSFSR, which

[1] Forged "Memoirs" of Maxim Litvinov, published in the West.
[2] David Shub, "Portraits of Political Leaders . . .", New York, 1969.

differs from Art. 70 only in its inclusion of eventual intent to subvert the Soviet regime.

I do not regard these books as truly anti-Soviet, and this is partially borne out by the fact that I printed them on a machine, an example of the print of which was secretly taken on the orders of the KGB Lieutenant Fedotov by A. V. Prokhorov (agent's designation—"the student"), who was resident up to November, 1969 in Apartment 4, Ordzhonikidze Street, Strunino.

Permit me to sum up briefly:

I can only regard it as just if I be charged under Articles 83 and 72 of the RSFSR Criminal Code, and under the relevant article in the Lithuanian Code, which is equivalent to Art. 190–1 RSFSR Criminal Code.

How can one not approve the UN's demand that hijacking be combatted—on the condition that all member-states do not stand in the way of those citizens who wish to leave their country, even in times of peace?

The generally accepted definition of air piracy is that of an action in which an aircraft is seized in mid-air thereby creating an extremely dangerous situation for crew and passengers. Our intention was to seize the aeroplane on the ground, remove the pilot from the controls and take off with no outsiders on board—only "traitors", only our own people.

My only real fault is that I do not want to live in the USSR. Why do you need me here? Why do you need me to gather in your wonderful harvests, to reap the gains of your brilliant successes, to share in your heroic exploits in outer space! Let me go, let me go!

I am sure the cement of Communism is sufficiently tainted with my blood (figuratively speaking, of course!); nor could I possibly object if you gave me a place in any detailed history of Russia that was to be printed.

Karamzin, in his *History of the Russian State*, gives passing mention to some exceedingly conscientious but powerless historical individuals, "Prince V. Ya. Borovsky, who did not wish to remain in Russia after such a disaster, left for the land of Lithuania."

Much of what I have said is perhaps verbose, confused and beside the point. I am sure there is much in it that is unnecessary, superfluous, perhaps there are too many literary allusions . . . At the moment I cannot criticize what I've written—the umbilical cord tying me to my notes still throbs painfully. There's no point in worrying too much. Lights out.

15th December

The first day of the trial is over. Today's comedy lasted from nine in the morning until seven in the evening, and we didn't get back to our cages until after nine. I'm completely exhausted. Dymshitz, Iosif and Sylva spoke today. Tomorrow it's my turn first. They say officially it's an open trial but its open only for relatives and those with special passes—the fat-faced representatives of the public!

Lury said Bela came but she couldn't get in. Tomorrow I'm going to ask for a pass for her to be admitted as my cousin. Lucia[1] will evidently be present at every session as will Iosif D. and Semka. It's amazing how different you feel when you see faces you know. Dymshitz spoke well, tersely, but with feeling. But he really upset me by insisting hysterically that Butman was our accomplice and by telling them that he knew of our plans to escape. Settling old scores? Surely not in the middle of a trial! But he agreed with me; he was convinced, as I was, that we failed because some members of the "Committee" had talked too much. Iosif[2] is a good fellow; cheerful, frank and carefree, but he doesn't lose his head.

Most of all I'm happy for Sylva; she's regained her composure and refuses, to plead guilty to every single charge. Same

[1] Lucia (Elena) Bonner, aunt of Kuznetsov, married to Soviet nuclear physicist, Andrei Sakharov.
[2] Iosif Mendelevich.

as everyone except Izi[1] and Bodni[2]. During the investigation, Dymshitz and Sylva admitted their guilt all round. It's wonderful not to be alone, as when you're in the investigator's office, but with the people you know, even if the guards shout and threaten you every time you steal a word. Maybe *I* had something to do with it; I used every device during the investigation to get my argument about our being tried wrongly under Article 64 written up in detail in the protocols of the interrogation. I had calculated that everyone would know what my position would be—whether they joined me or not was their business.

The Procurator is an absolute idiot. He knows hardly anything at all about the case: every so often Katukova (his assistant) has to come to his aid. After the session I complained to Lury that the Procurator's face, not to mention what he actually said, was putting me off, "That's his job," Lury told me, "he doesn't have to be fully acquainted with your case. He rather symbolizes the will of the state, shall we say. Do you think Karenin[3] was any better?" "I don't know. That Katukova next to him is a clever woman. Did you see how she kept digging him in the side every time he said something stupid? You can see, she's embarrassed for him . . ."

We had agreed beforehand that we would shield the women any way we could, should the need arise. We had agreed to put forward a united front: the women hadn't known what they were doing and had blindly obeyed the will of the men.

16th December

I woke early this morning. I can't eat or sleep . . . It must be about 5 a.m.

[1] Israel Zalmanson.
[2] Mendel Bodnya.
[3] A reference to the narrow-minded husband of Tolstoy's "Anna Karenina".

Before we left for Riga, our apartment was in a state, clothes and belongings spread all over the place, as we laughed and joked with one another. Sylva had asked me:

"What will become of us?"

"Well, if they get their way and manage to hush it up, I might get the death penalty," I replied, not entirely without vanity. But I saw her eyes and I was ashamed and quickly regretted what I'd said, "But, of course, they won't shoot me. Even if they give me the death penalty, it'll only be as a warning to others. All *you'll* get is about three years, just as we arranged."

"I don't want to. I'd rather get the same sentence as everyone else."

I would have spoken to her softly and put our departure off for a little while, but I shouted at her . . . Now she thinks she'll be able to make things easier for us by sharing the burden of responsibility. She would sacrifice herself for us . . .

As I thought, they fooled her well and truly. She'd had one second to whisper in my ear:

"They deceived me; they said you'd broken ages ago and told me they'd shoot you . . ."

Dymshitz related part of a conversation between Khrushchev and Nasser when the latter came to Moscow after the Suez crisis. The Procurator cut in: "Did you hear this conversation? Were you there?" The unexpectedness of the question struck Mark dumb. He should have made some sort of pungent reply: for example—Marxist methods of finding out information are much more extensive than eavesdropping. If that blockhead Soloviov is as impudent tomorrow I might be the worse for it . . .

Here is yesterday's conversation with Lury (in the presence of the escort commander), or rather two conversations: one during the dinner interval, the other after the session. In the morning I told him I thought I would speak my mind tomorrow as far as I could. He was overjoyed at first but then became suspicious: maybe it were better if I kept silent? What I said confirmed his suspicions, but I didn't have time to explain. The trial had begun.

Lury: Well, are you going to carry on behaving like that?

E.K.: What do you mean?

Lury: As you did with the passport. (What he meant was: when the Judge had asked me about my nationality, I had answered "Jewish". When the Procurator had asked, "You said Jewish, whereas your passport says 'Russian'. Why is this?" I had replied, "I was asked about my nationality and not about what it says on my passport.") I hope your're not going to turn the trial into a propaganda platform.

E.K.: Would I succeed, even if I were intending to?

Lury: Precisely.

E.K.: I have no intention of doing so, I'm too old to have any illusions.

Lury: Well then, thank God for that!

E.K.: However—I will express my opinions insofar as I am offered the opportunity.

Lury: Why can't you keep your views to yourself? If they do ask you, then be a little more diplomatic about it, if you can't keep them to yourself.

E.K.: I can keep them to myself but I can't see any need to hide them. But I'll try not to overdo it, all the same.

Lury: Good, good. Remember the parable about casting pearls before swine? The best thing is to keep calm.

E.K.: I don't think that you have any conception whatsoever of what it feels like to be on trial, Yuri Iosifovich. I am not a cold-blooded rogue, trying to wriggle out of my punishment. Knowing how to keep cool has never struck me as being a virtue anyway. It's the indignity of the whole thing. And no appeals to keep clam are any good. I agree

77

that my aversion to Sovietized Byzantinism sometimes borders on the paranoic, but this is precisely because I always keep my opinions to myself.

Lury: Let me offer you a compromise. I don't insist that you should repent and say you're sorry, but just see things as they are. Today's not the last day of the trial, so there's no point in losing your head. A trial is a tactical battle to be won by minimal losses, while you preserve your strength for the future.

E.K.: No, that is a strategy, not a tactic. How many times have I compromised for reasons like this! And I've always lost . . . always.

Lury: Well, it's up to you.

Evening Conversation

Lury: It's your turn tomorrow. Please show as much restraint as you can.

E.K.: I'm afraid I may not be able to . . . not for anything.

Lury: You think you're bound to get 15 years?

E.K.: Not a shadow of doubt. So you don't have to exert yourself overmuch.

Lury: We may be able to get a year off, that's all. That's about it.

They'll be coming for me quite soon.

16th December—Evening

This morning I thought it would be a better idea if I were to leave my jotter with my "speech" in it in my cell and refuse to say anything at all during the trial, other than that I should not be tried under Art. 64 at all. Here is my conversation with Lury both before and after my oratory.

Before

Lury:	You're intending to say what you've written, then? I can see you've got your jotter with you.
E.K.:	It's the only way I can be sure of not overdoing it.
Lury:	All right, then.

After

Lury:	You cut me off! What can I do now?
E.K.:	I'm very sorry. It's better not to say anything at all—not just me, but all of us, if they're going to shut us up like that!
Lury:	If you speak like that . . .!
E.K.:	How else can I speak? I assure you, I'm ashamed of many of the things I said.

What's it all for?

Can I not be forgiven for hoping I would be able to finish, if it were my turn to speak first? But no! I should have said what I did at the beginning of the investigation: "You're going to give me the maximum penalty whatever happens, so what do you need me here for?"

I would like to write up every stage of the trial, but I have neither time nor strength. I'll put it all down in full later. My jotter with the "speech" in it was taken from me and consigned to the court as Lieutenant Veselev told me would happen. So whatever I was unable to say publicly will be known to the court. Isai, like Sylva, is trying to share the responsibility by taking some of my sins on his back, They asked me what Federov had been intending to do when he got abroad. I tried my best to help him out by indicating he wanted to obtain the necessary permission for his wife to follow him. (He did actually mention this to me.) But he didn't catch on. Surely his lawyer will use this later on.

Got up early again. Walked over three miles already . . . God, how ashamed I feel of all that wrangling with the Procurator yesterday! Have business with a fool and you get like one yourself! What's the point of arguing about helicopters and aeroplanes? I'll try and reproduce it all. I did manage to say practically all I had prepared though Ermakov must have tried his best to stop me a good dozen times. It was only after the first time he interrupted me, ("We know what Western trials are like. Keep to the facts!"), that I got confused and jumped a page—the one about the Nuremburg trial. But then, as it was the "facts" they wanted I continued more or less coolly and self-confidently, and only paused once to interject: "It's terrible to think you can be interrupted at any moment!"

Procurator:	You told us, Kuznetsov, that your mother forced you to register as a Russian. How did she *force* you?
E.K.:	I did not use that word. I said, she insisted.
Proc:	Well, insisted, then—it's the same thing.
E.K.:	I don't think it is.
Proc:	In your long speech you referred several times to the law. Are you a lawyer?
E.K.:	No.
Proc:	Tell me, then, what is the last legal book you read?
E.K.:	What difference does that make? I'm not a lawyer.
Proc:	It doesn't matter—which is the last legal book you read?
E.K.:	I ask the court's permission not only to name this book, but to recount briefly the content of two paragraphs in it . . .
Proc:	Why? Just name it.
E.K.:	It is relevant to this trial and I would like to say just a few words.
Proc:	Its title, its title!

Wulf Zalmanson

Yuri Fedorov

Hillel Butman

Israel Zalmanson

Anatoly Altman

Leib Khnokh

Boris Penson

Yosif Mendelevich

Alexei Murzhenko

Mark Dymshitz

E.K.:	All right. *The Nuremburg Trial of the Nazi Judges.* This sort of trial, it says . . .
Proc:	That is enough! Whatever the book says we can all read it for ourselves. I asked you only its name—you told me . . . Good. We can see that you know something about legal literature. You were complaining that you were constantly being followed and not permitted, so to speak, to live your life after you were released. Well, what do *you* think? You committed a crime against the state as serious as that and you want us to take you back into our Soviet society immediately? Indeed! How can we *not* watch you? You who raised your hand against us!
E.K.:	You should not confuse reasons and consequences!
Proc:	You are a Soviet citizen and are therefore subject to Soviet jurisidiction: you committed a crime—you must answer for it.
E.K.:	As long as the punishment corresponds to the crime!
Proc:	If only you had reformed when you had served your term of imprisonment . . . But listen to this character-reference the camp administration gave you: "During his stay in the ITU[1] Kuznetsov behaved in a negative manner, always retaining his inveterate anti-Soviet views. His reaction to educative measures was hostile, he did not attend political-instruction classes, and he conducted himself superciliously in conversations with camp personnel. He was several times placed in the punishment block and in 1967 was sent to prison for refusing to work. He beat up prisoners who were beginning to reform, insulted hospital staff . . ." Well now! Is this true?

[1] Corrective Labour Institution.

E.K.:	Approximately. In any case there could be no question of my insulting hospital staff, as I never came into contact with them.
Proc:	Why were you sent to prison?
E.K.:	For refusing to work, it says there . . .
Proc:	You mean, you didn't want to work?
E.K.:	I simply wanted to go to prison.
Proc:	Just so as not to work?
E.K.:	Yes. Like Murzhenko and Fedorov before me, I preferred prison, if only so I could have some time for books.
Proc:	I see now. And you say you reformed!
E.K.:	(indignantly) I never said that! I have no reason to reform—in the way you mean it, anyway.
Proc:	So, did you receive a fair trial in 1962 or did you not? As a Soviet citizen, who had committed a serious crime, a particularly dangerous crime, against the State? Yes or no?
E.K.:	(quietly) No.
Proc:	That means—yes?
E.K.:	No.
Proc:	Well then, it's good that you admit . . .
E.K.:	(almost shouting) I said *NO*!
Proc:	Ah, no? So that's what you say. When you'd got to Sweden, you were going to speak at a press-conference—so Butman testified during the preliminary investigation. Was he correct?
E.K.:	I don't remember any such testimony. It doesn't exist. We never discussed what would happen abroad.
Proc:	But you do not deny that you have anti-Soviet views?
E.K.:	I have explained my views. You may regard them as anti-Soviet, though I myself would not necessarily categorize them as such.
Proc:	During the investigation you stated that you did

	not consider yourself a Soviet citizen. Is this so?
E.K.:	I said I was a Soviet citizen in the formal sense only.
Proc:	Have you ever read any Zionist literature?
E.K.:	In the way you understand Zionism—no.
Proc:	There is only one way of understanding Zionism —that is the Marxist-Leninist way.
E.K.:	We've heard it all before—world power, tool of imperialism . . . Zionism's your scapegoat to frighten all your Moscow merchants.
Proc:	Let's leave this. When you spoke about seizing the aircraft you compared it with hijacking a car. A car is not an aircraft. You can drive a car from one street to another, but you cannot fly from one street to another, can you?
E.K.:	(long confused silence) Why? You can . . . in a helicopter, for example . . .
Proc:	Yes, in a helicopter, but not in an aeroplane!
E.K.:	But what *is* a helicopter?
Proc:	It's not an aeroplane . . . Did you personally prepare the bludgeon and knuckle-duster?
E.K.:	Yes.
Proc:	By yourself?
E.K.:	By myself.
Proc:	Sylva Zalmanson, did you help Kuznetsov make the knuckle-duster?
Sylva:	Yes.
Proc:	Well, Kuznetsov?
E.K.:	She was only there at the time. Do you call that helping . . . I made the knuckle-duster myself— alone.
Proc:	And the bludgeon?
E.K.:	Also.
Proc:	Israel Zalmanson, who made the bludgeon?
Isai:	I did, and Edward only helped me.

Proc: So, and for what purpose did you make it, Kuznetsov?

E.K.:   It's not quite so simple as that . . . I'll try and explain. The idea of leaving the country was thought up without me, just as all the details of the first plan were discussed without my being there—in the first stages, at any rate. When they told me all the details of the plan they said we might use a bludgeon as a weapon. There was still a long way to go before we could put the plan into operation. The bludgeon was a detail, but somebody had to see to it. Definite steps had been taken. It's not so simple to obtain the material you need. Making this bludgeon was nothing more than finishing off something that had already been started; obviously, not essential, but it had to be done, nevertheless. The knuckle-duster came about differently: it was the result of a quarrel between myself and Israel: he insisted it couldn't be made by hand—I showed him it could.

Proc: You mean then you did not intend to use it when you attacked the pilots?

E.K.:   While we didn't have it, we never intended to, but when we did have it . . . weapons have an attraction all of their own. So insofar as I had to assault the first pilot, I decided to keep the knuckle-duster on me, although I was simply to seize the first pilot by the collar and pull him into the plane, where I'd have been helped to bind him. I decided to keep my knuckle-duster on me whatever happened.

Proc: Make a knuckle-duster, take it with you, but not use it on anyone—is that it?

E.K.:   Exactly. The problem of what we should do with the crew worried me at every stage of our preparations. Even in March, when we were discussing our so-called "Plan 1", we decided that ideally we wouldn't like the pilots to suffer even one scratch on their bodies. (Cries of indignation and ironical shouts from the onlookers in court.) Of course, not so much because we disliked brutality, but because we had neither the desire to be thought of as common criminals, nor the intention of providing the Soviet Government with a good reason for extraditing us. My intention to take the pilots' papers from them, in case the Soviet organs should declare that we had murdered them, proved that we never intended to cause them any physical harm; such a possibility could not be discounted . . . And in that case they would easily have been able to prove their identity . . .

Proc: You made a knuckle-duster, and were, in your words, to use it when you would attack these Soviet pilots—but Israel Zalmanson had it in his possession when he was arrested. Why is that?

E.K.: I left Riga nearly 24 hours earlier than Israel. With the speed of our preparations and the fact that we didn't really need the knuckle-duster, I forgot all about it, and consequently left it at home. Israel came across it accidentally and brought it with him to Leningrad to give to me, but neither of us obviously attached any importance to it in our plans. I forgot it in Riga and he forgot to give it to me.

Proc: Israel Zalmanson, who was to attack the first pilot with the knuckle-duster?

Isai: I was.

Proc: Ah! Kuznetsov, how did you prepare Shub's book, *Russian Political Leaders*, for printing, and for what reason?

85

E.K.:	I printed it from a microfilm.
Proc:	And who gave you this film, and to whom did you then give it and the book?
E.K.:	This is not the investigator's office, and I refuse to answer that question.
Proc:	With whom did you print this slanderous book?
E.K.:	With nobody. I was by myself.
Proc:	Sylva Zalmanson, did you help Kuznetsov?
Sylva:	Yes, I did.
Proc:	Well, Kuznetsov, did you print it alone or were you helped?
E.K.:	Sylva showed me some of her own photographs at the same time. I did not conceal my work from her and she may have read a few pages, I'm not sure. I am, however, quite sure that I printed it without her help.
Proc:	When you suggested to Fedorov that he should take part in your criminal attack on the Soviet aircraft, did you tell him who exactly were the members of your group? I am referring to the nationality of your accomplices.
E.K.:	Yes, I did.
Proc:	And how did he then react?
E.K.:	In a normal manner . . . as is characteristic of him.
Rusalinov: (People's Assessor)	Why, whenever you came to Leningrad or Moscow, did you always bring anti-Soviet literature with you?
E.K.:	What, for example?
Rusalinov:	Well, Solzhenitsyn . . .
E.K.:	What a catholic taste you have . . . Solzhenitsyn, as is well-known, is not anti-Soviet, he writes "non-recommended" literature.

(This was followed by even more rubbish, so I'll leave it out. It's a waste of time anyway. I'll carry on from where Toporova, Fedorov's lawyer, took up the questioning.)

86

Toporova:	How long have you known Fedorov, and where did you meet him?
E.K.:	I first met him and Murzhenko in 1962 in camp 7, in Mordovia.
Topo:	In the preliminary investigation you stated that Fedorov refused to have any part in your flight across the border and that you used blackmail and psychological tactics to make him agree to join in. Tell us about this.
E.K.:	Since I knew Fedorov very well, I made use of some of his idiosyncrasies. I do not think it is possible to explain here exactly how I did this.
Topo:	Tell us in more detail what Fedorov's psychological idiosyncrasies were?
E.K.:	He suffers from frequent periods of emotional stress. He always felt that he was being followed and this feeling was rapidly becoming an obsession with him, as those close to him know. I know that for a long time he really was followed by the KGB and it was this which was the basis for his present state of mind, which I think is a sort of persecution complex.
Topo:	In the preliminary investigation, you said that Fedorov was intending to ask for political asylum when he got to Sweden, but when Art. 201, Code of Criminal Procedure, was implemented, you withdrew your statement. What actually happened?
E.K.:	We didn't discuss what actions we would take abroad as a rule. I did not attribute any illegality to his request for political asylum, in the sense it was used by the investigators, but regarded this merely as the ritual of someone who, having crossed the border not quite legally, wanted to become a person unable to be extradited. I never guessed my words (what I said was, "I intended to act

according to circumstances. Perhaps I also might have asked for political asylum") would be interpreted as proof of any planned action hostile to the USSR. Since I did not regard requesting political asylum—the right of which is stated in Art. 15 of the Declaration of Human Rights—as an act hostile to the Soviet Government, when asked about Fedorov's intentions, I replied thoughtlessly that he might have asked for political asylum had the situation demanded it. At the end of the investigation, when I realized how ambiguous the investigator's game was, I specified that, strictly speaking, Fedorov never told me of his intended actions abroad, although he confided in me his ideas about the steps he would have to take in order to obtain permission for his wife to emigrate.

Proc: And why should you, if you knew about Fedorov's psychological illness, have wished to compel him to flee abroad, to a foreign country, far away from his family and friends?

E.K.:   I do not know a great deal about psychiatry, but I do know that a change of residence can often benefit a person's state of mind . . .

I'll write the rest later—it's 8 o'clock already . . .

Evening

The interrogation is now finished, and it's the witnesses' turn to testify. Dymshitz insists on making Butman one of the accomplices. I can't understand this. Maybe he's too inflexibly honest. He speaks the truth without any semblance of embellishment whatsover; he refused to choose his words, whether he's talking about accomplices or the Soviet regime. Really, in a trial like this, how can truthfulness always be moral, how can you choose now of all times to settle an account with someone?

Sylva looks ill to me. It's quite impossible to get a word with her. They've placed us so far apart on purpose. And we each have a guard who watches every glance. Yesterday Lucia and Bela smiled at me every now and then from the hall. Today Bela left for Moscow and she'll only return for the sentencing.

This morning Lury dashed in; "Congratulations, you spoke with such gusto the secretary couldn't get half of what you said down." "Unfortunately," I replied, "they took my jotter from me and turned it over to the court . . ."

Alik and I have been trying to show up some of Yurka's eccentricities in the light of psychological disorders and thereby show diminished responsibility on his part. But our efforts to get him into a hospital instead of a camp are too clumsy and ridiculous to have any hope of success. More important: I would imagine this contradicts the KGB's intentions, for otherwise all we would need to do would be just to hint at psychopathy. Why does he not catch our bait? Is he afraid of being labelled "psychologically abnormal"? It's not like him. Earlier on, some idiosyncrasies in his behaviour led one to believe he wasn't quite normal. This didn't appear to worry him in the least. Has he decided he will not humiliate himself by seeking the indulgence of the court—particularly in such a manner? I fear he may get the same as me.

18th December

Sometimes the witnesses are so comical. Yurka's mother, Pelageya Stepanovna, nearly gave me heart failure, her face was so sad, yet her words were so artless and simple:

> "He used to tell me again and again they were following him. Don't you pay any attention to them, son, I said, if you think they are following you. Who *don't* they follow? They've been following me all my life and who am *I*, what have I ever done? . . . So I went along to the Lubianka, and some officer there spoke to me. I

	told him to stop persecuting my boy, he's never done anybody any harm . . ."
Proc:	And why did you go to the Lubianka, and nowwhere else? What made you decide it was the KGB that was following your son?
Pela:	Who else would it have been? Do you think I'm stupid altogether?

The trial has been adjourned till Monday.

Lury:	The supplementary interrogation is due to start now. Can you not possibly condemn the particular method of "repatriation" you attempted?
E.K.:	Not at all. All I can say is that I regret what happened, but I'm afraid that could well sound very ambiguous indeed.
Lury:	I'm thinking of casting some doubt over the experts' conclusion about your knuckle-duster's being a dangerous weapon. It *did* have a thick layer of rubber around it, didn't it?
E.K.:	I'm sure you remember Major Revald, who first described it, wrote of it as a "weapon of stunning impact", and then . . . But this is irrelevant. I'm sorry to have to say this, Yuri Iosifovich, but I think it's about time you realized just how ineffective you really are . . . not just you personally but all the other lawyers; you all have some bookish ideas in your heads about political trials . . .
Lury:	Do you think this is my first political trial?
E.K.:	I know, I know, but it makes no difference . . . It's only because you know, and won't admit it, that all you can do is concern yourself with trivialities, or with nuances, or psychology, or whatever, and ignore the really important matters. What use is it if you leave out the most important thing of all?
Lury:	And what is that?

E.K.:   That a man has the right to live in any state that corresponds to his views, his preferences or anything else. Otherwise he is nothing but a slave. The real criminals are those who prevent free emigration and by so doing provoke the crimes they accuse us of. The time has come for us to break as clearly as possible with the customs of the past, where you could be thrown into prison for even daring to suggest publicly that the American worker gets a better wage than his Soviet counterpart. Have you ever heard what they say in the camp: "They put me in here for anti-Soviet agitation—I called a kolkhoz[1] cow a whore!"

Lury: We mustn't neglect the minor things either. Times change, the climate improves; they may have your case reviewed. Then every word you said will count.

When it was Sylva's turn to testify, Lury asked her if I had ever expressed any anti-Soviet views in her presence. She said not. The Procurator indignantly pointed out to her the inconsistency between this "no" and her "yes" during the investigation. She then launched into a quite truthful description of how she had been tricked by the Chekists, but unfortunately she was not convincing enough for those present. Here is what she said as far as I can remember:

"I kept on repeating I had never heard him express any anti-Soviet opinions. Then the investigator told me Edward had long since confessed to everything including his anti-Soviet convictions which he had expressed right and left. And all the others, I was told, had confirmed he had never made any secret of them. "Are you the only one he never confided in— *you, his wife?*' And I didn't want to create the impression that he'd told everyone except me, so I said I knew all about his

---

[1] Collective farm.

anti-Soviet views, and he'd often told me about them. In fact, this was not so."

This trial has absolutely worn me out. I've slept half the day already, and I'm still tired. On Monday it's the Procurator's turn.

Towards the end of February or the beginning of March—no, in February—I remember, I wasn't working, I wanted two or three months off, so I wouldn't need the employment reference when I had to hand my papers into the Ovir. But I'd only had a couple of weeks of the dolce vita when I was summoned to the police station and ordered to get myself a job within five days or else they'd be forced, so they said, to put me under supervision and then I'd be compelled to do a labouring job.

It was at the end of February then, when I came home, and Sylva introduced me to Butman, a small stocky, perhaps even ostentatiously, energetic man. Butman was over five years older than I, and for two whole months I denied outright that I knew or had even heard of him; but when I finally was convinced he was testifying—not only that, but telling the "so-called" truth—I shielded him as best I could. But how these people cling to every careless word, every breath, and curl of your lip, even if you don't speak they know what you're thinking . . . they play games with you, disturb your equanimity and reduce you to the depths of despair, even to insanity . . . May God have mercy on your soul if you have a secret vice, or a hair out of place—they'll find it! . . . It nearly broke my heart to read the evidence some of these "committee members" gave.

He and I then went to Rumbula, to that modest stone that stands where a thousand Jews were shot. Through the forests, between the snowdrifts, that lay grey in the Spring, till we found the glade. Was it our step, silent as the martyrs that slept beneath us, or their lust which deafened them to our approach? She murmured gently, straightened herself and patted the back of her coat into shape. "Here of all places!" I exclaimed. But they were already far away from us, their knees hidden in the snow. This scene long remained in my mind as a symbol.

As we returned Butman kept glancing over his shoulder too often for me to think his customary nervousness could explain all the polite questions he was asking me. I knew he was driving at something. "What chance do you think you have of success?" he asked at length. "At the moment, none at all—and it looks as if it'll continue like that for a long time yet. Unless . . ."

"What?" he looked at me impatiently,

"Unless there is a big scandal they can't hush up. At the moment each of us is thinking only of himself—our only concern is to get ourselves out. This is not a question of individuals. It's a problem of free emigrating for all those who wish to leave—this is what we should be thinking about. This is our only chance—tearful messages to the Kremlin or the United Nations are no good. This is what you, me, all of us are doing. Just sitting in corners and acting separately. As far as I'm concerned, I'll get myself out. I think I will anyway."

"First, let's discuss all those who want to leave. What exactly do you propose?"

"I'm afraid I have no concrete remedy: I've no idea what things are like in Riga now and I don't know the people here. Talking about creating a scandal, I certainly do not mean an artificial or provoked one. Everything must be as pure as the air. The situation as I see it is like this. Many are desperate, ready to explode, their applications are rejected with no reasons given, and they go from humiliation to humiliation. They spend years in and out of their suitcases, their whole life, whether it be personal relationships, or their job or their apartment, and all the rest of it, at the mercy of others, as you know only too well yourself. Can't you see it? Maybe today or tomorrow a group of people, united in desperation, will take the fateful step forward. They themselves may suffer greatly but by their actions they will break the dam through which many others will pass. My good sense tells me, "Wait, wait, wait, and you'll get there without undue difficulty". But my conscience says, "Yes, but over someone's else's dead body." My temperament despises waiting, yet, united with my conscience and my impatience, it urges me to take my part in every stage of the way forward."

"What can you suggest that's concrete, though?"

"God only knows! Surely we could scrape together 30 or 40 people and declare a hunger-strike and demand that Articles 13 and 15 of the Declaration of Human Rights should cease to be just empty words! Only we mustn't cheapen it, we mustn't treat it as though we were only whetting our appetites before dinner, or be like those that fast for a day and think it's a great event—we must fast as they do in prison—even for a year, if necessary."

"A year?" he looked at me suspiciously.

"Yes, of course. Certainly they'll force-feed us . . ."

"Well, and what else?" he didn't wait for me to finish.

"We could always burn our dearly-beloved mothers-in-law in Red Square as a sign of protest!"

"Seriously though?" he burst out laughing,

"I'm not ready for serious conversation on this subject yet. As far as *I'm* concerned, I am storing up all my venom and when I feel I'm absolutely bursting at the seams, then I'll lash out!"

"Not so loud," he begged me, and lowering his voice almost to a whisper, he asked, "What do you think of the idea of running away?"

"In terms of individual success—a waste of time, but on a more profound level, it could work. It would have to be a unique case in which personal and communal interests coincide."

"Of course, it's risky . . ."

"Naturally," I agreed, "but the only thing I don't like is being in the dark. I'd like to determine the element of risk for myself."

"Let's go over to that square," he suggested, "it's quieter there . . . All right then," he began, when we'd made a little room for ourselves on the edge of a wet bench, "I confess, I made enquiries about you in Leningrad and here, in Riga. I'll talk freely: we have an experienced pilot. We need people. We have to make our numbers up."

"You have a group—how many? Two or 20?"

"About 50 people," he laughed proudly.

"What!" I was amazed, "this isn't a hunger-strike we're discussing! . . . You said there was a good chance for all who took part themselves . . . So I understood you, anyway."

"I would swear for every one of them!" Butman seemed quite offended.

"In what sense?"

"That there are no informers among them."

"That's only half the story."

We continued talking for another couple of hours, until we began to shiver with cold.

Although I accepted Butman's suggestion that I should take part in principle, I didn't really believe it would ever see the light of day.

"Just you listen to me!" I said angrily, "you'll have to give me the opportunity of having a chat with every one of those taking part now—right at the beginning—before it's too late. If I tell you that at this very moment I could swear for only a couple of people, then I mean these people really could be trusted! We must take each one by his collar, drag him off into the corner, knock his vanity out of him, give him a good shake-up and make sure he knows just how much the fate of a dozen people is going to depend on his being able to keep his mouth shut. You have to understand, it's not intentional treachery that scares me, although this cannot be discounted either . . . No, if on the night before our projected escape, someone

95

should let his imagination get the better of him, and start bragging about his escapades of the morrow; if his girl-friend were to wound his vanity in some way or other, he may take offence, "Come now, who do you think you are? Never mind, just you wait till tomorrow!" And this could be just enough to put a spoke in the wheel. You know what this country's like? You've got to talk to each one of them until his eyes pop out of his head—and then, and only then, can you be sure of him!"

Butman swore I need have no worries as far as his people were concerned.

I felt that the possibility of a leak in information was what we, who were living in a police state, had to worry about most. This was all the more urgent in that many of us had already managed to make ourselves known in one or more spheres under the jurisdiction of the KGB.

At a meeting in Leningrad attended by Butman, Dymshitz, Korenblit and myself, I tried once again to draw the attention of my accomplices to the need to hammer out a professional approach to the problem of secrecy:

"Friends" I said, "we are too much concerned with being shot down from the air or with the matter of who attacks whom. If we should fail it will be at the airport, and not in the aeroplane. Our first priority is our own people—after that we can attend to all the rest."

What can one say? We really should have been able to rid ourselves of all this cowboy-and-indian type of thinking. There is no way I could possibly justify it. Particularly as far as I am concerned, because it was I alone who really appreciated our weaknesses. (I don't know of one case where five people were involved and there wasn't one informer. We did not have one. This fills me with pride now . . .) I know it's ridiculous, but if someone close enough to me to forgive me my stupidity were to ask me, would you do it all again, if you had the chance, I would say this: "Guarantee me three conditions: (1) No one else but the pilot should know about the intended flight. (2) I should not have to have the need to build Communism for each of 365 days. (3) I should be provided with sufficient money for freedom of movement, which is so necessary."

When Butman told me on 1st May that neither he nor any of his people would take part, I pestered him once again to see his friends kept their mouths shut, irrespective of whether Dymshitz and I should go through with the plan or not. If they had been afraid to speak out loud earlier, what was to stop them boasting about it now all over the place? Butman said no one except the "Committee" itself knew anything, and he would swear blind for their reliability.

That evening I suggested to Dymshitz: "Let's postpone it for a year. Let everything quieten down and be forgotten. Then let's free one of us from the necessity of working, guarantee him enough money to live on and for freedom of movement, and then, a year later, we'll ask him for the best plan of escape he can work out plus the names of a dozen people whose best quality is that they know how to keep their mouths shut." The reply he gave me, "It's now or never," tended to cast doubt on his strength of mind.

To me strength of mind is something time-worn, which will not disappear however well-to-do you become, or whatever happens to you in life. His resolution, I suspected, was of a rather hysterical type, the kind that grasps at a straw; here was his chance to rid himself once-and-for-all of the multitude of troubles that weighed upon him from all sides. And I gave in once again. Though I told everyone that they would need courage to change their minds if the plan was clearly doomed to failure. I was already in the grip of my own inertia, after spending so much time and energy, and it would be a great pity if it all had to come to nothing; and I myself was now the slave of the impatience of those on whose behalf I was negotiating. There was one person, from whom I drew information about Butman and his background, whom it was absolutely essential to include in our plans—as a possible partner at first, but later, when he turned me down, as an advisor. On the 14th June, the day before "X-Day", he bade me farewell:

"Well, what do you think?"

"They'll get us at the airport!"

"It's not too late to change your mind?"

"It's too late for me, but I'll tell the rest of them today—they may be able to get out of it more easily than I."

That evening, near "Smolny" airport in the forest, I told everyone that we were being followed. It's just your nerves, they said. I realized that everyone felt such forebodings, but wouldn't admit it, either to themselves, or, for that matter, to anyone else. What a curious state of mind this was: maybe one day I will understand it!

Even when the three of us—Sylva, Boris and I—were on the Riga-Leningrad train, Boris confided in me: "I don't care what happens, so long as I don't have to come back here." This is how we all felt. Such was the grip of all our day-to-day trivialities, our petty, not to mention, important, problems, that the hope of ripping asunder with one thrust the web that stuck them close completely mesmerized us. Whatever was to be our fate, nothing could be worse than the life we were leading. For the most terrible thing that could possibly happen was only problematical, whereas the daily diet of evil we were being fed stuck fast in our gullets. It was Bodnya who gave voice to the general feeling: "They'll put us in prison and then they'll probably let us go to Israel."

One was fleeing from his college exams, another from his unit, a third had parted with his mistress, and had already posted a letter of farewell to his wife . . .

How could we return? What if the miracle were to happen and the following midday we were in Sweden? How could we return to what we had left behind? To a life with which we had broken every tie? They're always watching someone or other—maybe they didn't know about our plot, maybe they'd follow us to the airport, we would get in the plane and they would be left far behind . . .?

What tortured me most of all was thinking about my wife and her father, but I could say a lot more about this particular subject . . . I'll try and come back to it, when I have some time.

I have read over the last few pages. It is possible I may be giving the impression of shielding myself and blaming Dymshitz and Butman alone. This is not so. If they were less than attentive to every suggestion I made, then I did not attach sufficient weight to everything they said. Our worst fault was our incredibly infantile underestimation of the might of the secret police of our beloved Homeland.

When we were released, Alik was pressurized just as much as I was. I have never been able to decide whether ex-prisoners are really persecuted consciously and deliberately, or whether it's the soulless programming of some computer or machine that cannot foresee any of the side-effects of what it does. I don't mean what they do to the countless thieves and petty-criminals that get lost in the crowd at a factory or plant: these are given short shrift indeed. No, what of those who may have shown the slightest lack of confidence in Big Brother's divinity and refuse to betray themselves or their friends under the spreading chestnut-tree? For in the camps treatment of the recalcitrant convict falls basically into two categories: loss of rations or the punishment cell, both of which abandon him to the whim of as many levers of persecution as you could possibly imagine: registration, apartment, work, family, neighbours, friends . . . In the camps a man either holds out, prepared not to be released before his term is ended, if the price he must pay is collaboration—or he breaks. And when he's freed he either goes straight downhill or he is soon imprisoned again. Should he meet a girl more than once, she's hauled off to the KGB, interrogated, warned off . . . in the end he keeps his distance from everybody, full of his own suspicions yet torturing himself with the knowledge that they are unfounded; he refuses to play this game that's forced on him, yet he plays it just the same . . . (and should you really be a person of distinction, a real threat to the security of the state, they have special conditions for you, too!) But if all he wants is to be left alone, how soon—how soon!—will he weary of his Chekist guardians and sob his heart out, "Even the camp was better than this!" In the outside world a man does not break, he goes swiftly downhill or is again imprisoned, should he dare to voice his views as openly as he did in the camp. Yes, Russia has its Speakers' Corner too—in Mordovia! There, behind the barbed wire you can say what you like—all you'll get is two weeks' punishment cell or a year in isolation or two or three years in prison. This is social-democracy: you are free to say what you like and they are free to lock you up for saying it. If they've marked you down on their lists of opponents to the regime, they won't try and "correct" you but kill the personality inside you—which is what "correcting" you means anyway. *They* don't need you to become a Marxist-Leninist—why should they? God preserve us from anything that smacks of any sort of principle! They don't need you to admit $2 \times 2 = 5$, only to agree that 2×2 equals as many as the Party wants it to equal! And how they make you agree is their business! There's a metaphorical, though not very appetising, saying that illustrates one of the most popular methods of re-educating the dissidents that they have, "They beat you till you shit yourself, and then they beat you for shitting yourself!"

*** Yuri stated in court that he had long considered fleeing from the USSR. It was I who unintentionally provoked this admission for he made it after the Procurator had caught us out "contradicting one another":

Proc:	Kuznetsov, how did this state of affairs come about? You told the court Fedorov did not wish to take part in your criminal activities and he only gave way after you applied a great deal of psychological pressure. He says all you did was to tell him about your intended treason and he asked to join you. Which of you is speaking the truth?
E.K.:	Fedorov has either forgotten what happened or he is trying to protect me.

Fedo: I have not forgotten and it is Kuznetsov who is trying to protect *me*. I had been thinking of fleeing from the USSR a long time before.

Not one week after the gates of Vladimir prison had slammed shut behind me, then I already spent night after night unable to sleep, my eyes misting over at the thought of a ravishing mini-skirt; with the vocabulary of the camp so deeply embedded in my subconscious I still called Communists Bolsheviks and KGB-men Chekists, or the USSR a "Democratic Utopia", or addressed a policeman as "guard". No longer did I care if no one believed me when I told them what prison life was like; I still jumped like a madman and protested my innocence, ready for the old admonition; "No sleeping, no sleeping during the day!" And I still bought meatpies around every corner; how hungry I was then . . .

Yuri Subbotin had swallowed a set of dominoes to satisfy the curiosity of a new guard who had promised him a loaf of black bread. Then the domino-players had beaten him up because two pieces had got lost and the rest stank to high heaven. After three months of prison on strict regime I hear the old question asked, "What would you choose—a pound of sausage or a woman?" There was no argument—they all preferred the sausage. When I said "half a pound and a young girl", everyone started swearing at one another and we made a resolution not to mention food any more. Once I forgot: "Just think, in Moscow you can get hot meatcakes in nearly every street." It sounded so wistful that an Estonian whom everyone called Fevral burst into tears. I never forgot this or the Estonian we nicknamed Fevral, because he was so dense. For hours on end he stood by his food-hatch: "What you standing there for?" someone asked him sarcastically, "do you think they're going to give you some bread?" "Perhaps they will," this pathetic soul would answer humbly.

We were allowed five roubles per month. I would buy meatcakes even when I was so full I couldn't eat another thing . . .

"We must break out of this hell-hole," Yurka had said.

"It wouldn't be a bad idea," I agreed, munching my next meatcake, "but how?"

"However we can."

"I thought you had an idea!"

"I can't think of anything," he admitted.

"Maybe we could cross the border on foot?"

"Don't be so stupid. Didn't you know people who tried that in the camp? It's not all that bad here at the moment."

"Just you wait," he said morosely, "in a year or two you'll be ready to hobble all the way from Moscow to the border on crutches."

The first month after I left Vladimir I too was in a state of bliss.

20th December

Everything happened too short a time ago for me to be able to juggle the facts with any confidence and separate the wheat from the chaff. Everything seems important. I am haunted by the hopes and fears I once had . . . The words will not yield and permit themselves to be squeezed into a recognizable order, not one word will sacrifice even a tenth of its muddled truth or its clarity of expression, preferring that all should remain an inarticulate mass of events, predictions, and premonitions. How can you avoid this if you are seeking the truth, and turning it over and over again in your mind . . .? Is there some latent need to find a reason for it all, a rational explanation of the world? . . . Every thought is stretched to its limit of expressibility, brought forth only at the price of sacrificing some of its quality, by breaking its many links with the reality it pretends to express. I have put my thoughts on paper—the plain unvarnished facts, no beating about the bush, every word approximate, yet in its approximation tending to clarify its meaning all the more . . .

How puzzled Lury was the day before yesterday, during the

dinner interval: "What made you do it, if you knew what was going to happen?" he asked me. Flattered by this opening he had given me, I launched into a discussion of so-called "tactical analysis", explaining how I saw our flight as a sort of childish "search for the last mystical city on earth", and God knows what else. Have I made things any clearer? Hardly, not even one little bit? I always get carried away when I'm explaining something, but I soon get bogged down in the details and lose interest. I know I ought to explain more than I do. But what can you do if you're on tenterhooks, expecting to be interrupted at any moment?

How easy it is to be wise after the event, particularly when you're sitting in a cell. If you'd asked me a couple of years ago: "Would you do anything illegal if a dozen others knew about it as well?" I would have said the same as I would today, "No". Firstly, I would have doubtless made some witticism to the effect that, what a glorious baker's dozen we would have made; secondly, if you have a large number of accomplices it's practically impossible to prevent a leak of information, not to mention spies and informers. Thirdly, they won't only follow me—an ex-criminal, unreformed after seven years of imprisonment—they will follow most of these 12 people. They were not born, but became dissidents. And while they were in the act of becoming "counter-revolutionaries", they most probably drew the attention of, at first, just one ordinary Soviet citizen, and then of their dear authorities (this is one reason why cases of "treason" are comparatively rare among those who go abroad, or among occupying troops).

With the number of participants we had, only a specifically illegal act, which of course is quite immoral, could ever have been successful. It's one thing to make a financial profit illegally, but quite another matter if the actions of the people involved are motivated by considerations which, in the last century, would have received the high-falutin' title of idealistic. If the former acknowledge clearly the reprehensibility of their intentions and know how to keep quiet about them, then the latter, who have ideas of their own and unflinchingly demand that they be put into effect, regard their actions (which grow gradually, more often than not) as unselfish and noble and heavily spiced with romantic self-sacrifice. Noble intentions are difficult to contain. Extremely so. The inequality of conditions of departure from this blessed country is such that criminal tendencies and manifestations are very widespread indeed, and any institution whose function it is to diagnose, treat and cure such maladies as these must be an institution of unassailable credentials. In this respect the KGB is on firm ground indeed.

One's experiences of the world are not come by easily. If they were you wouldn't be happy about it. It's better to be a murderer, a thief or a rapist than a man who does not vacillate with the Party line. It's a miracle anyone ever realizes how essential it is to preserve one's own, independent views. By the time they're finished with you they have you squeaking something like:

"I am a little boy,
Always playing a game,
Uncle Lenin I never did meet,
But I love him just the same!"

Then your enquiring mind is funnelled off into a pen set aside and sheltered from the world by a high fence of expendable Marxist wisdom while they teach you how to bow down before their personifications of truth, justice and holiness. A unified system of education provides the opportunity of manipulating minds, and producing in the masses one single, united reflex-action to events.

This type of education, far from encouraging a creative and critical attitude towards the world of ideas, serves only to prepare citizens for the spread of propaganda by those who work the machine. Do not forget also the difficulties that stand in the way of one who wishes to have access to foreign information. You will not be surprised then by the gratitude with which you learn from company political officer, Captain Zhuchkov, that "a Soviet fool is more intelligent than any American intellectual". But if in spite of everything, and by some miracle, you are able to penetrate beyond what you're told—beware! You will not find it easy to come by an independent philosophy, or even to choose one from among the great philosophies of the world. You will be beset by doubts, arguments, and by the time you are old enough to be a heretic an asterisk will be pencilled in by the side of your name. From now on you're like a suspiciously deft concubine watched by the faithful eunuch, who is afraid of the greatest of all crimes, adultery. "Why do you not pant with delight whenever your sovereign takes you to his bed? Why do you turn your eyes away? Why do you glance surreptitiously beyond your sheik's garden, to where you can see only gloom and misery? Are you sure you haven't acquired a lover." "Ah", she answers sadly, "freedom beckons to me." The eunuch can understand the role of a lover—not forgive, but understand—the yearning for freedom he cannot understand and therefore hates it all the more.

Often a man is unable to resist the political order because he has lost his soul—to those that watch over him daily and observe the political-ideological purity of the state.

This is not the end of the story by a long shot, but it's enough to puzzle you into asking, why ever did I agree to take part in such a plot if I knew how impossible it was to fight the powers-that-be? Could I really have thought I would win? My logic and my experience told me, no—a miracle was needed. And if suicide is often a cri de cœur, then so was my participation a sort of suicide, the cry of the persecuted for salvation. This is it. Whatever I said, I could never give a satisfactory explanation for what I did. Has not the whole of my life been a constant search for escape? Perhaps I never really grew up. Maybe I felt I could release my inner tension by travelling in "outer space"! Or was it my desire to resolve the so-called eternal problems of conflict with the society into which one happens to be born? A political protest in exchange for a revolt of the spirit? But cannot the logic of accusing society of intentionally obstructing your search for unofficial types of self-expression not prove a delusion in the final count? This explanation, for example, would appear to be based solidly on firm ground. Puzzled by the eternal questions, you reject the concept of life as a biological entity. You cannot brush these questions aside and you do not know how to solve them. The only worthwhile retreat left you is to blame the social-political structure of the state for intentionally preventing you solving these problems. The younger you are, the more forgivable your desire to change the world (which is one way of escaping your problems); a few years later you attempt to run away to another country, sure that its climate will suit you better . . . but when you're old you realize that your problems are just as insoluble wherever you are—the structure of the state is quite irrelevant. This explanation, and many others besides, is only half the truth. There's no need to hurry to draw any firm conclusions; suffice it to say that, towards the summer of 1970, the theory and practice of so-called "Marxism" repelled and nauseated me, I was absolutely convinced they were inextricably tied up with the camp barracks, and I dreamt of settling in Israel, and I knew that my inability to receive permission for a visa was not accidential. The 20 months from my release from jail until the time I was arrested again were one continuous spiritual turmoil.

*** I would prefer to see more agreement between us all regarding our behaviour in court. I know each person has the right to make the best of his own situation, and it woldnn't be fair to rebuke anyone for this. But I don't see how more agreement could possibly infringe upon the fate of another person. But it's all an illusion. You see, something more significant than my fate is being played out here today, and I am resolved to be ready for whatever may befall me. If anyone thinks otherwise, then they must act as they see fit. What if our group had been selected on the basis of their probable behaviour in court? I'm sure this would have been more reliable a method than any other devices we thought of. Those that fall into the hands of the KGB all have one curious thing in common—they cannot believe they will ever really be put on trial; and only when the cruelty, the indifference and soullessness that are the real faces of the state, yet so cleverly masked; only when brainwashing is so wide-spread; only when, for the over-whelming majority of the citizens of this state, the earth—quite seriously —begins and ends at the Kremlin: then only blow after blow into the solar plexus can sober up a person and help rid him of the social-political myths that cloud his brain. It has been your lot to lift the stage curtain just that little bit to enable you to peer into the darkness that lies behind the scenes, and, aghast, to discover how little it corresponds to the hoardings outside, you are filled with the fervour to expose everything. You think you have understood everything now and have parted forever with the life of the law-abiding blockhead. But you are a romantic and you can withstand nobly all the power of the state, cruel as it is, but three times crueller to him who sees it in all its hypocrisy. And so when they tell you they're going to execute you, you don't believe it. For too long they've stuffed you with declarations of how humane, democratic, just, they are, for you to believe that you've really been found to be an enemy of the state and are going to be punished by death. Now here indeed is a paradox: to them you are a most dangerous political criminal, but to yourself—in the depths of your soul you believe everything they've ever told you! Only later, when you find yourself in the very heartbeat of the state machine—its camps— where the representatives of the state don't bother to wear anything so tiresome as a mask, where the principles on which the state is founded stand out in their purest form, do you begin to shamefacedly realize just how servile your protests were. A man who has not been in a camp cannot possibly appreciate how implacable, hypocritical and unprincipled is the enemy, punishing him in the most cruel fashion for ever daring to be an adolescent rebel. If you love liberty, prison is your school. If they don't break you or bend you into conformism when your back is still straight and delicate, you will be ashamed of your former complacency. There comes a time when you can no longer escape all their kicks yet remain an individual, for any effort to soften the impact of the blows means you are betraying yourself. You must either take them stoically and unflinchingly or answer each blow with an even harder one.

Your submission is not enough, they will demand ever more and more until you have nothing left to give. Major Nikulushkin, my second investigator, lost his patience with me, "Once a prisoner comes into contact with you, nothing can be done with him." Really what a poor selection of instruments you have: "plants" in cells, tape-recorders behind the wall, falsification of friends' testimony, distortion of their recorded words, toying with the intimate details of your life, promises to mitigate your sentence and threats to execute you . . . and a dozen no less banal tricks.

But why do they need your confession and repentance if they can put you away for as long as they like? This is because, if you are not brought to the stage where you are a repentant sinner, then the matter loses much of its completed character. It would seem to leave the question of the morality of trying dissidents poised in mid-air. Or is this an unconscious tribute to the popular mediaeval conviction that the only real criminal is the one who confesses? Only one such confession was sufficient for conviction. Vyshinsky[1] can be regarded as the theoretician and inquisitor of the Soviet middle ages. The religious essence of the totalitarian state is that the political opponent is a greater heretic than the common criminal!

*** Yes, in my more sober moments I would tell myself that such a plan was suicide. This is not to say I did not do everything I could to get away with it. After my unsuccessful attempt to get Dymshitz to put it off I tried the two people closest to me. Everything I did and thought arose from that cry of desperation and indignation, "One more year, one more

[1] Andrei Vyshinsky (1883–1955) Procurator-General and chief prosecutor during the Stalinist show-trials of the 1930s.

long year!" Now I put the blame on my own head—my too scrupulous adherence to democracy, my reluctance to grumble that, if the greater part of the burden of preparation was mine, then the powers and rights that went with it, should have been mine also. This is where I was at fault. In a state like this, democracy is out of place. Nobody shuddered at the thought of being arrested because all had agreed to die; we decided that even if an intercepting aeroplane had tried to bring us down by threatening to fire at us, we would never, never, land.

I remember how Iosif and Isai once had a violent quarrel over methods of recruiting participants for our escape. Iosif's "amor fati" impelled him to over-emphasize the perilous nature of our venture. Whilst Israel insisted on success as a principal in life, Iosif felt that everyone should be told that "our chances of success are practically nil, the likelihood of our dying is as great as the likelihood of our ending up in prison". Israel regarded our success as guaranteed and feared we might put off intending recruits. Iosif won this particular argument. But we spent too much energy on reconciling all the different opinions and searching for compromises. However acceptable or customary this may be in everyday situations, it is debilitating and dissipating, whatever energy one has, whereas an order is what is needed. A bad dictatorship is sometimes better than a good democracy—when you have neither the time nor the will to make this democracy organizationally flexible.

*** Dymshitz spoke in court of an antisemitic outburst by a bus driver: "Hitler didn't kill enough of you!" The Procurator Soloviov did his best to make a joke of it and, with truly bureaucratic pathos, went to great lengths to find excuses for the Soviet people, who, he said, were incapable of anti-semitism. God, how proud of their democracy they are as long as they're not pushing you into the gas-oven! You're not beaten up every day, and you're *still* not satisfied, is the undercurrent of their reasoning. They no longer (for the moment at any rate!) put this trembling creature up against the wall, whenever they feel the urge; they have lightened his yoke and he dares to think he's free! Remember how sad and indignant Maliuta Skuratov[1] was when the holy Tsar suggested he take it easy with his axe for the time being! . . .

Why is it this bus incident was treated as a joke, as an irrelevance? Is it because it wasn't pregnant with social-political significance, as this sort of thing can happen in almost any country and is therefore only a matter of degree? Only by acknowledging that Soviet society is permeated at every level with anti-semitism can we have no excuse to be surprised if ever we experience it; only by appreciating how subtly it is interwoven into the very fabric of this society, and how ,consequently, every official platitude about equality and brotherhood is to be scrupulously ignored, can we hope that what we say will have any effect. Is this the traditional religious hatred of the Jews? Yes! The primitive fear of the alien and hostility towards him as the embodiment of the unknown, and therefore of the potentially dangerous? Of course! The projection of all that is evil in you onto another person? Naturally! The most accessible scapegoat? Indeed! And a hundred other reasons. But the most specific reason, I think, is the anti-intellectual prejudices of the people, for in their minds the Jew and the intellectual are synonymous. (When I was a child I frequently heard curses directed both at intellectual non-Jews and Jewish non-intellectuals.) If, as Lenin asserted, the Russian proletariat crowns world history, then artists' hands and spectacles and hats may legitimately be despised! But the most important factor of all is the dislike felt for those who don't fit in, neither in the camp, nor in the community, nor in the splendid palaces of the future.

Dymshitz recounted this incident in the bus with unaffected emotion. In other words, it's good enough for him: he doesn't need to analyse his reasons for wishing to emigrate. Let me stand the question on its head. When does this sort of incident make an impression on you? Only when you are secure in the knowledge that if people are not friendly, at least they're not

[1] Head of Opritchnina (secret police) in the reign of Ivan the Terrible.

prejudiced; when you haven't thrown up the diet of propaganda you've been prescribed and not yet learned to distinguish the facade of the house from its backyard. Then this incident would affect you, then you would see how monstrous it really is. But if you are acquainted with the attitude of all layers of society and, not only that but *share it yourself*, then what is so dreadful about this sympathy for Hitler? Who has not heard this remark a dozen times, and who has not seen how condescending (if you're lucky!) can be the reaction of those who had the good fortune to be born non-Jews? The mentality that produces the pogrom is not limited in time or space; the violence perhaps has faded, but it is not gone. The masses are still imbued with a feeling that accumulates little by little, until it is ready one day to break out in all its primaeval barbarity. There is not one other country in the world where conditions are more favourable to the pogrom—whether it be provoked from above or whether it be spontaneous—than Russia. The Russian regime is hardly a barrier. On the contrary. All it does is try and fit it with an unrecognizable form (for itself it is afraid lest the masses become emotional and burst the bounds of the simulated enthusiasm of the 1st of May demonstrations!).

And what of anti-semitism within the elite of the Party itself? It's a strange fact that overt anti-semitism only began to be encouraged when the original and genuine expectations of the Revolution were forgotten. Only when the emphasis on the class solidarity of the world proletariat turned out to be an empty promise, did the leaders realize that their only prop was their own people, who required but a few profferred sweetmeats from time to time to keep them happy.

22nd December

I had no desire to write yesterday: the Procurator demanded the death penalty for Dymshitz and myself, 15 years each for Yurka and Iosif, 14 years for Alik and so on. He even asked for a 10 year sentence for Sylva. I am left in no doubt that the court will reply to his wishes in full measure. For this is nothing but a great political game in which our fate does not count one iota; it is the judges and the Procurator that are the pawns—we are nothing. Insofar as I—a lowly Soviet citizen—am deprived of access to objective political information of any kind, all I can do is guess the factors determining our fate. There is as much chance that the death sentence will be carried out as that it will be commuted at the last moment . . .

Today I am ready to "come back to the world again". Yesterday I was, to put it mildly, unsettled. All the irritation towards Belkin that had so long piled up inside me suddenly exploded and I took it all out on him. When they brought me back in the evening, I wanted to be alone more than at any time in my life; I needed to be able to cope with the skeleton face of the Procurator (my friend, the skeleton, still has many parts to play: the day after tomorrow I see him speak through the judge's lips, then he grins at me from between the pages of a pile of official documents, and lastly he will be barking orders through the well-fed snout of the camp-guard!).

When Belkin found out the "wishes" of the Procurator he told me how dreadfully shocked he was that anybody could be so bloodthirsty and then proceeded to read me a letter from a girl he knew called Valia. I tramped up and down in a vain effort to collect my thoughts and adjust to my new situation . . . but I could not. My head was spinning; all I could think was, "It's better than 15 years, it's all finished in one go," "Does it make any difference when you die?", "We shall see what happens," etc. and I felt more and more oppressed by a feeling of perplexity, of mental confusion. All I wanted was to be left alone in darkness and in silence. When at last he laid his letter aside and attempted to draw me into a discussion about its contents, it was the last straw:

"Can't you leave me in peace even on this day?" I yelled, and banged his head against the wall three times. (In the cell next to us they must have thought this was a signal, for they replied with three taps of their own—in morse code!) After this I didn't hear one more word from him and when I returned from court today he wasn't there. At last, at last, I'm alone! I doubt whether I can ever make mankind happy with my diary and its value seems dubious. I decided to burn it. But then I changed my mind (hope springs eternal . . . in spite of all logic). After all, I have no desire for clinically analysing the trepidition of a soul on the edge of non-existence (or after-life). I'll keep to trivialities. But that is enough today.

23rd December

The comedy is over—now for the sentence. Tomorrow at 6 in the evening. I have all evening and tomorrow at my disposal. I am by myself: I've heard nothing more about Belkin and it looks as if they won't punish me.

At first Mednonogov the public prosecutor (I call him "copperhead") demanded the "supreme measure of punishment" for all of us, but I thought the manner in which he used this set expression did not indicate that he meant it in its specifically bloody sense. I thought he drew the line there. A curious, yet typical point: even during the investigation Mednonogov kept trying to find out for what purpose we had picked the 2nd May. We told him this was because it would give us the opportunity to come to Leningrad in a group, remain unnoticed and then disperse to people's houses in case we needed to postpone our plan, and so forth. But the day before yesterday he piped up: "Not for nothing did they plan their vile crime for 2nd May—they wanted to spoil the world proletarian holiday! Not for nothing did they choose a Jubilee year, when the whole world is celebrating the 100th anniversary of Lenin's birth!"

When he had finished, Lury came up to me:

Lury:	Well, how is it going?
E.K.:	What an absolute idiot. I hope he didn't mean execution when he demanded the supreme measure?

Lury:	No, of course not.
E.K.:	How did you like all this rubbish about 2nd May and the Jubilee year? Last year it was the Party Congress—also a festival for the world's proletariat. You just never know which is the best year to betray your country—there's always some festival going on!
Lury:	You chose a bad time—Kurchenko's death and the UN assembly.
E.K.:	How interesting that the UN passed a resolution on hijacking just at that time! Until there were cases of hijacking in the USSR the UN did hardly anything. And now they've brought pressure to bear . . .
Lury:	Who said there weren't any cases before? This very year . . .
E.K.:	Yes, of course, there were some even before this year, but they always managed to keep it quiet. There was never such a scandal as there was with us. Anyway, in spite of all the bloodshed, as far as I know, one got 15 years, and the other, a woman, 14 years.

After the Procurator's speech

Lury:	I never expected that . . . Nobody did. This is without precedent! But don't despair. I'm sure it won't come to the death sentence. It would be too much of a scandal.
E.K.:	I'm afraid that now the Procurator has asked for it—we'll be sentenced to death.
Lury:	I won't hide it from you . . . it's not impossible that you may be sentenced to death. But I assure you, all they want to do is take you step-by-step all the way—and then spare you at the last minute.
E.K.:	Let's hope so. But I will not ask for clemency. Not now, anyway, later perhaps, when I'm

	absolutely desperate, then . . . But I wouldn't like to lose my human face.
Lury:	Perhaps it won't come to that. Why do I say "perhaps"—I'm sure!
E.K.:	You don't know them. What happens to us doesn't mean a thing to them—they've got something else in mind. But for this very reason they might well do it.
Lury:	Such a thing has never happened before.
E.K.:	What do you mean? Don't you remember, in the case of Rokotov and Faibishenko—they were tried retroactively and shot!
Lury:	That is a case for specialists, but yours is different.
E.K.:	In 1963–64 they shot people on special regime for nothing at all. You don't believe me? Of course, it was all done very, very quietly. And particularly for tattooing anti-Soviet slogans on their face . . . This was also done by widening the scope of the article—they were tried under 77–1. And is it so long ago that people were tried under Art. 58–14 for escaping from a camp—as well as for sabotage and economic crimes? They were sentenced to 25 years each.
Lury:	Those times have passed. What's your last word going to be? This is very important now.
E.K.:	I will not repent and of course I refuse to admit guilt—except under Art. 83. Did you notice that the Procurator called me a Russian? Do you think they do anything for academic reasons? I'm sure that was not done for nothing. It's one thing to sentence two Jews to death, but an entirely different matter if one's a Jew and the other's a non-Jew: no discrimination you see. I shall mention this.
Lury:	You could not do anything more idiotic than that! It's only conjecture on your part. Did he give

	you reason to think that? Then why do it? Don't you think you've got enough problems to try and be clever in the position you're in! Although I am quite certain that neither this court nor the court of appeal will sentence you to physical annihilation, I think that for the future, you should be prepared to reject militancy which, in your position, would be extremely out of place.
E.K.:	It's out of place in the sense that it's stylistically bad taste to disregard the rules of the game you're forced to play. I'm not going to say one more word in court from now on.
Lury:	Do you think you're going to get the opportunity to speak again? You're an optimist—or a pessimist, depending on which way you look at it. Why?
E.K.:	Why what?
Lury:	Why do you think silence is the best means of defence?
E.K.:	You and I have a different approach. It's not a defence, but a more worthy expression of my attitude to this judicial farce. I would be ashamed to have to lower myself to explaining my motives in primitive slogans, but that is all that could be done. I would rather go into it in detail, with all the psychological nuances—but they shut me up . . . If I were to limit myself to a dry, thesis-like account of my objectives, state of mind and what I would call my "pre-criminal" situation, I would be giving the prosecution an excellent opportunity to make good use of all of these and turn them against me.

Yesterday evening

Lury:	You don't seem to be very pleased with my speech?

E.K.:	Why? What difference does it make?
Lury:	It's so much easier for Pevsner to defend Dymshitz than for me to defend you—and *you* do not consider it necessary to conceal your opinions or your conviction for anti-Soviet activities! I think you have damaged your case from the very beginning by this attitude of yours: "You're going to give me 15 years whatever I do, so to hell with the lot of you!"
E.K.:	Do you not think it rather strange that the Procurator has been asking them to give me 10 years each for a couple of books? I think it's quite a lot, don't you? They get two or three years for that at the most, nowadays.
Lury:	What rubbish you talk. What difference is it to you whether they give you 10 years or three years compared with the death sentence?
E.K.:	All this nonsense is driving me mad. Is there no end to it?

24th December

Yesterday Sylva spoke better than any of us: like a woman she went straight to the heart of the matter; first in Hebrew she said it and then in Russian: "If I forget thee, O Jerusalem, may my right hand lose its cunning!"

Dymshitz threatened them. "If you think that by shooting us you will frighten the fugitives of the future, you are mistaken. They will come, not with a bludgeon as we did, but with guns, for they will have nothing to lose." (In my opinion he went too far: he makes it appear as if we would have taken to the gun had we known they were prepared to condemn us to death. But he's a good man, just the same. He's right in the sense that what is at stake here is the invincibility of the spirit.) Then he thanked all of us, "I'm grateful to my unfortunate friends. I saw most of them for the first time the day we were arrested at the airport, but we have never descended to blaming one another in defeat."

Of the rest of the speeches I liked Altman's best. If it were me, though, I would have spoken about the Constitution and given nothing away about myself. I'm always afraid of lapsing into pathos.

This evening cannot come too quickly. It's more than a week since I exchanged views with Belkin on the so-called last wish of a man condemned to death. I doubt whether such a relic from the feudal-bourgeois-humanist past would suit the Soviet prison guards and executioners. More and more often I find myself reflecting over such nerve-racking problems as where, when and how the death penalty is actually carried out. I've heard so many variations on this theme, but never anything definite. Legal murder is shrouded in secrecy.

With regret, I must report that I am not original; Morozov recalls that it was the thought of how worthily he would conduct himself while they read out the sentence that worried him more than anything else. The same with me. At such a moment as this to worry about how others see you! I know I would have to suppress these fears somehow, but how can you control the host of bizarre ridiculous questions you ask yourself? I am sure Dymshitz is not tortured by such exquisite problems, for his courage is less literary and more natural than mine. (There you are, a slip of the tongue—I consider my behaviour to be courageous too.) It would be good if I had no reason to worry about him, to seek to warn him to prepare himself for the death sentence.

Not counting clemency I still have $1\frac{1}{2}$–2 months before I hear from the court of appeal. Sometime in the second half of February, then. I think February will not be too happy a month.

Part 2—1971

I have a deep layer of obstinacy in me, as you can see. On the 30th April we had the pre-May Day search and I lost all my papers or, to be more accurate, they sank without trace. One of the guards, a young Party zealot seething with enthusiasm, discovered my hiding-place and relieved me of a whole pile of my papers. I made a dive for him, grabbed the bundle out of his hands, then I jumped on to the water closet, tore the papers into little pieces and flushed them down the Neva, or Fontanka, or Moika, or wherever the pipes lead to down there.

A couple of guards thereupon gave me a good beating and even now, nearly a week later, my face is still covered in bruises, my neck and arms are black and blue and my left shoulder feels as if it has been dislocated. That's how I destroyed four month's notes. What became of my first two jotters (for November and December) I don't know. When they put me in the death cell they wrapped all my papers, notes on the trial, drafts and diary in a newspaper and said they would store them away with my personal belongings. I'll find out whether they did so when I get transferred, which apparently won't be long now.

The trouble is I had got used to the weekly searches and had confidence in my good fortune and my cunningly contrived hiding-place. If during the first two or three months I kept well away from certain subjects that might have been of use to those who maintain constant watch over our souls, then later I became bolder, my internal censor grew slacker and more liberal and allowed me to write whatever I wished, like one of those fuddy-duddy Party historians.

If I let the first two jotters go comparatively easily, knowing as I did that nobody could possibly be harmed by them, my attitude to the others was somewhat different, and I suffered for it. They contained nothing out of the ordinary but even a psychological analysis of my friends (a subject I've been into very thoroughly over the last few months) might have been valuable enough ammunition for those who will have us in their power for many years to come.

For those who are not here for long, camp life is an unnatural way of life. They see it as a dangerous adventure which is soon passed, a journey to a land of exceptional spiritual and physical stress. And he who in ordinary circumstances would never dream of putting pen to paper, here uses up page after page of notepaper depicting the prisoner's way of life. You can catch him writing away furtively in his cosy little corner before even getting his breath back from the "ennobling" work he's been doing and pretending he's writing a complaint or a letter to his family. If for one man this is a form of self-realization under the most relentless persecution, then for another it's simply a matter of describing the "exotic" conditions he's found himself in: the horrors of the outside world tempt the budding author to see himself as an extraordinary person living an extraordinary life. A third who describes the people here in all their emotions, opinions, customs, plans for the future, is actually presenting the authorities with information about them, for this is what becomes of anything written about any living person in a police state.

I ought to be more careful; I myself am no guest passing through the prisoners' kingdom; this little cage will be my life yet awhile. I write only to stay human. This is a diabolical place, its purpose—to drive a man deeper and deeper into despair, to make him doubt whether truth after all is sacrosanct.

Perhaps the only truth is a biological truth, one of adaptation; first self-preservation and then life as an end in itself.

During my first period of imprisonment, I instinctively resisted the impact camp "life" was having on me. Now I find it considerably more difficult; I'm older, the punishment cell is no longer a novel experience, I no longer feel the desire to use my fists, the academic illusions I once had about suffering being a means of attaining the higher truths are all dead and gone, I have shed the tender down of romanticism that once covered my soul . . .

A diary is for me a way of consciously opposing an impossible way of life. The very act of writing down the features of prison camp existence, as it were objectifies them, allows me to stand back and every so often stick my tongue out at them! Between January and May I wrote over 50 sheets in my little handwriting; I tried moreover to reproduce the protocols of the trial as exactly as I knew and even wrote a little story entitled, "Next Door to Lenin". For seven days before my death sentence was commuted I shared with Aleksei Ilich Liapchenko himself under sentence of death, in cell 194, next door to the celebrated former address of the leader of the Revolution.

Practically every morning, as soon as he got up, and every evening after lights-out, Liapchenko would hammer on the wall with his fists, "Greetings, Uncle Lenin; how are you getting on you bald-headed bastard? . . ." (This was no irony or sneer: it was the reproach of an aggrieved man. In all fairness, one can hardly blame Lenin for what the Soviet system has become; one cannot really blame anybody or anything but fate itself.) I wrote about myself, about Liapchenko, about what it's like in the death cell. But when I read it through, I realized I had not really come to grips with my subject. Not wishing to keep it even for a rough draft, I destroyed it.

I will try and reproduce in general terms the most significant events of this year, insofar as I remember them. The main thing is to omit nothing, but to write it as it was; fire is all-consuming, and the Chekists are not great stylists . . .

6th May

On the 31st December about 10 o'clock in the evening, I was informed that my death sentence had been commuted, and I was moved to cell 199. On the 13th January, I was told that, according to the decree of the Leningrad City Court, I was to remain in the remand prison until the trial of Butman and the rest at which I was to give evidence. At the beginning of April I was removed to cell 197, where I am now.

During the investigation I would always try to keep to the simple rule: say what you like about yourself, but never say anything about anyone else. But this rule isn't perfect. For example, if someone I regard as an intelligent and resourceful man is telling the so-called "truth", then I, who may be hearing only an incomplete version of what he's said, am prey to the gravest doubts: is this a repentant criminal speaking or the manoeuvring of a man with his back to the wall, a man not yet fully demoralized, but wandering along the thorny path of half-confession towards the concealment of something more important, which I cannot hope to know? In cases such as this I can see nothing wrong in confirming other people's evidence as long as it does not harm a third party. I have heard extracts of testimony given by Butman and M. Korenblit, and although, in some respects, I thought their confessions were more of an incantation than was necessary, I did manage to catch indirect hints which related only to them and myself, and I therefore confirmed what they had said, as much as I could. Only after I learned of all the details of the case did I find out they really had repented. And now I must testify. Rather strange, I think. Indeed, if Dymshitz confirms that Butman and Korenblit knew of our attempted flight then I shall insist on the contrary.

Am I really a witness for the defence? This is fantastic. Precisely because a "witness for the defence" has no more to do with a trial of political criminals than has a verdict of "not guilty" under Art. 58, camp etiquette unconditionally equates the witness with the active collaborator. A witness is as odious as an informer, or "team-leader" or a collaborator, or even a "trusty". For myself, I have never been a collaborator in any sense of the word. Yet I am to be called as a witness! It's like some bad joke!

Only our closest relatives were allowed into the trial; (God this is nothing but a silent vendetta, and only our gnawed bones will ever bear witness to this "justice" of theirs!— no shrieks from the victims, no bleeding wounds, no fountains of hot blood!. . .)

Maybe I can hang on here in the "Mansion" a little while yet—before me lies work, work and more work still, the aggressive idiocy of cell-mates, rotten herring, the arbitrariness of the authorities and other Soviet delights. Here I've been now for five months in solitary (I'm on special regime and therefore permitted to come into contact only with prisoners of equal danger to the state and hardened criminals, of which there are none here); reading from morning till night, receiving my monthly five-kologram parcel, and smoking cigarettes. The convict's Utopia! Every day outside a camp is a day won from the Soviet regime! So close are my relations with the Socialist camp that life and prison have now become synonymous, and the days I am not persecuted are days of joy, transient yet deeply heart-felt. It is as though those times and countries, where imprisonment in itself was the greatest of misfortunes are wrapped in a rosy distant haze. But here imprisonment is so many ways of torturing a man that non-freedom, in the sense of withdrawal from normal life, seems not even a misfortune. For this very reason the remand prison has been like a sanitorium for me, particularly this year, when I have been deprived of the daily torture of contact with any other prisoners. Was it not Sartre who said hell was other people? Dostoyevsky also said that the most diabolical characteristic of the hard-labour camp was having to live in close contact with others, and the impossibility of finding a little corner to yourself, even for a short while.

Nowadays, the arsenal of instruments of torture is infinitely richer. Its foremost weapons—so appropriate to that inhuman spirit of social experimentation which is known to us as building paradise on earth (always in the *next* five-year plan, of course!) —are the continuous oppression of a man's soul, conscience and intellect, an oppression that never shrinks from the vilest methods, and the so-called "corrective measures", which are nothing but an attempt to turn him into a moral and spiritual zero.

No, as long as they don't starve you half to death, or keep playing that loathsome gibberish radio, which, in Vladimir Central, you have no means of switching off, prison is a luxury—almost like being at home!

In the heat of the moment I was going to sign a declaration stating that I would not participate in the judicial reprisals against Butman and the rest; but when I cooled down, I realized I was in no hurry to get sent off to camp, and anyway I might be able to help Butman and Korenblit in terms of the part they played in our case.

7th May

At dinner today I heard Liapchenko's voice. Evidently they'd just been giving him his food when one of the bosses happened to be walking past: "Citizen Warden, what about 'Novy Mir',[1] No. 5?", was all I could distinguish. I might not have recognized his voice, had it not been for this "Novy Mir", which is an unmistakable sign. I'd had it from him, day in, day out. The Procurator had demanded the death penalty for him and Morozov, and on the day the sentence was to be passed, in those few moments before the court rises for the judges, a man had approached him and asked if he'd read the story about himself in "Novy Mir", "No, I haven't", he growled. The man, who thereupon introduced himself as the author of the story, warmly recommended him to read it. But Aleksei Ilich was not feeling in an ambitious mood at that moment and had other things on his mind than stories and so he sent the author to that well-known place where so many Russians go. It was only afterwards that he regretted not asking the stranger for a copy of the magazine. Whether in fact there was a story, or anything at all of this nature, I never got to find out. I shared a cell with him for a week and there wasn't a day he did not mention this

[1] The article was "Sotnikov" by V. Bykov, Novy Mir, 5. 1970.

124

magazine, directly or indirectly. He's not a bad fellow, like most wartime collaborators, of which I've seen no small number. His is a pathetic story I've heard a thousand times before; he is one of those low-lives who preferred the role of the executioner to that of the victim. In this world there are three basic roles one can play: the executioner, the victim or the spectator. By nature he is a spectator, but when passions get charged and executioners and victims begin being forcibly recruited from the ranks of the spectators, he had to make his choice, and of course, chose to be an executioner. The spectator, of course, is most often a potential executioner.

In spite of this he's not really a bad fellow, he's absolutely honest—in a worldly way—and quite sentimental. I am quite prepared to believe all the stories he tells me about how he helped the partisans and their families when there was no threat to his life. It's quite understandable. They would never have sentenced him to death had it not been for the "scissors". (investigation slang—Liapchenko has already served 10 years in a camp and now, if he got 15 years, those 10 years would be taken into account—indeed, he was tried for the same crime. "Five years is much too little for you," the investigator told him.) I have read one or two articles about these "scissors" and I think the praise that was heaped on the heads of the ever-vigilant Chekists—who are supposed to have searched for Liapchenko—was, to put it mildly, exaggerated. After his release in 1955, he lived in his native city, refused to change his name and every so often was summoned to the KGB. He attended the appropriate political lectures and more than once spoke as a witness in collaborator trials. In the autumn of 1969 he and four others were arrested and brought to Leningrad, where they had once worked for the Germans. (He might have been taken to Estonia as well, since he took part in the occupation— I beg your pardon—liberation, of 1940! Though to be fair, he was only an annexationist then, but now he's a traitor!) "What a fool I was—for nearly 15 years I worked like the devil for them. I had a house, a family, a young son . . . I became assistant manager of a mill. Would they have made me assistant manager if I hadn't worked 16 hours a day with a serious disability? I did my best! I didn't put a foot wrong . . . every time I saw a policeman I broke out in a cold sweat—just leave me alone, that's all I wanted from them. Then they confronted me with a fellow. "You swine," I said, "what are you telling lies for? Wait till your turn comes." "I've already done my time," he said, "and the people have pardoned me." "Well, I've served my time too," I said, "and they've pardoned me, but now . . ."

They hadn't been looking for him, of course, but quietly gathering the information, fattening the calf for the purifying sacrifice that would come when the time was ripe. Every so often, you see, you need a bit of publicity, a few more trials to whip up a bit of patriotism to publicly encourage and justify all the spying that goes on, to pay off old scores on your secret enemies and to make sure the Soviet man-in-the-street fully appreciates the need for all the apparatus; but most important of all you need the mass demonstrations, the "Cuba-yes! Yankee-no!" type, (God forbid, the crowd should ever take leave of its senses and chant "Cuba-yes! Meat-no!") I have heard of people who had done 15 or 20 years being taken straight out of the camp, put on trial again, and then shot.

War-time collaborators are loathsome and mediocre, and how much more so when you know their past! It's not their bloodthirstiness so much as the fact that they are the living personification of the gloomiest forces of soullessness, conformism, and obedience to any and every master . . . But it's the state that is the most terrible of all: its past, present and future are bathed in blood, reared in lies, built of impenetrable stone—the state, before whose nightmarish face a man is nothing. Here the criminal is not tried that justice may prevail but solely in accordance with the political and economic dictates of the moment. No wonder the state cannot tolerate such humanitarian concepts as justice, humanity, love and honour being taken out of their social-political context.

126

8th May

Liapchenko told me in confidence he had always respected Jews; even his wife was Jewish. This latter fact was evidently supposed to be to his credit. I have invariably noticed that as soon as you become the least bit friendly with an anti-semite— or give him a fright!—he immediately tells you he's always had a secret liking for the Jews. Too much blood on the conscience, perhaps? He wanted sympathy and justification from me but even in the face of death I could not bring myself to give him one or the other, for in his every word and gesture I see the face I hate so much, the face of the "little man", (O sancta simplicitas! O, this saintly, touching simplicity—with the eternal bundle of brushwood in his hands!) who roars "sieg heil!" amidst millions of stinking voices in sports stadiums and herds fighting their way into the parties of Hitler or Stalin, (when they are already in power, of course!) This "little" man-in-the-street is not the victim of repressive regimes, he is their support.

I had no desire to hear him out. But on the 31st December I couldn't prevent him from turning the cell into a confessional. It was I who set the ball rolling by calling him a coward. All I had to do was clank his food-hatch and he began trembling; then he staggered to the farthest corner of the cell and froze there, his hands tight to his chest, his eyes goggling the door in fright. That New Year's Eve he kept returning to the subject of death: he was hoping to die during the night from a heart attack and begging me not to call the doctor, or he was poking fun at the stupidity of those who had built the death cells ("Just think, they covered it with planks," he nodded at the water-closet, "I could climb on the window-sill and split my head open on the floor, or when I'm in the bathroom, I could hang myself on a towel . . ."), or he was thinking aloud, where, how, who, would perform the execution. I was used to it already as I was to his nightly screaming. All of a sudden the guard banged his food-hatch, probably just to see if it was open. Aleksei Ilich fled to the corner, his eyes rolling in insane terror. For a split second I thought I saw the barrel of a gun protruding from the black surface of the food-hatch behind me. I shivered, and turned round—there was nothing there. I flung myself at him with a curse.

"Oh, Edward, Edward," he moaned, "if only I could describe my life to you in a novel—how you would weep!"

"Oh, Aleksei Ilich, Aleksei Ilich," I mocked him, "why should any of us want to be the hero of a novel or a film? We are only simple working men, not without faults, but with lots of good points; and whereas our faults are the tragic result of circumstances, our virtues are our own work . . ."

"I understand. What you really think is it's about time they shot me and had done with it!"

"Am I not in the same position as you?" I retorted angrily, "How could I wish anyone to be shot? I don't even know anything about you. Not only do I not ask you any questions about yourself, I have no wish to hear you talk at all . . . it just so happens we're in the same cell . . . I'm not your judge, let alone your procurator. Life, unfortunately, long ago denied me the opportunity of being too fussy about my companions. I cannot choose solitude, so what can I do? I am a convict, whether I like it or not, and my attitude towards any other man is that of someone to whom silence is the most important thing: can my cell-mate observe it or can he not observe it? I would much prefer an informer, or even someone who devours babes-in-arms to an honest man who can't keep his mouth shut. I don't care who you are, as long as you keep quiet. The only time I ever want to change the world or people, is when I'm fast asleep."

I went on and on about what a fine, objective and fair fellow I was, and how sick I was of everything in this damned world. But he's one of those people who can't wait for you to stop talking so that they can start themselves:

"You remarked a long time ago and quite rightly, that I am a downtrodden man." He spoke as he always does, sadly and slowly, while I sat smoking a cigarette. "I was a prisoner

128

in a German hard labour camp and in a Soviet concentration camp . . . When they arrested me, on the 2nd October, they banged on the door, and I stood there, just stood there, for three hours, without moving. I only had one thought in my head, 'I'm going to be robbed and beaten up!' You know what it was like in those days? Do you think I joined the Germans because I wanted to? I was so hungry I was eating human flesh . . . The French and the English got food parcels and chocolate, and we were dying of starvation. Stalin said he had no prisoners-of-war, only traitors. And in 1941 when we were driven through the countryside, barefoot and wounded, old men and women and children threw stones at us; 'Shoot Stalin's protectors' they were screaming. There were all sorts of partisans; this was later when the Germans reintroduced the collective farm system, whereas at first they had greeted us with hospitality . . ."

This is a country of appearances, of dummies in shop-windows, of swollen statistics and bogus declarations; a country of fiction and of pretence . . . The repeal of the death sentence on Dymshitz and myself was of course planned. It was on the 26th December that I saw most clearly how predetermined was our fate; though I suspected it had been predetermined somewhat differently.

About 8 o'clock on Saturday the 26th December four guards came for me and took me to the office of the prison governor Major Kruglov. He and Lury greeted me with marked cheerfulness:

"Come on now, write your request to the Court of Appeal," Lury was grinning. It was straight down to business. I think I must have gone as white as a sheet. No doubt, about it, I thought, they're in it together. There's obviously been too much publicity about us and we have to be shot as soon as possible—in accordance with the well-known Machiavellian maxim: "punish decisively and immediately, and give out few sweetmeats, but often".

The healthy man who sympathises with the sick man and is

amazed at the latter's propensity for suffering, is the victim of a psychological miscalculation, for he is measuring by his own yardstick. The sick man thinks differently, his organism adapts to ill health in terms of weaknesses, its frequent fainting, its lowering of the threshold at which pain can be felt . . . The man who is under sentence of death takes refuge in madness, in hoping for a miracle, in playing hide-and-seek with time: he will do anything in this world but remain alone with the thought of how inevitable and how close is his death!

I had been pretending I still had a couple of months left. So little, so hideously little, but sufficient not to have to think of the end just yet; there was still time left for me to gather my thoughts, look within myself, prepare myself for the state of non-existence that was to overtake me . . . But now, so suddenly, so immediately? . . .

After lights-out that evening I smoked a dozen cigarettes, I laughed at the terrifying logic of the conclusions I had reached so quickly. All the rest of the time I had somehow or other succeeded in restraining my thoughts from wandering too far along their horrific path. Though, I must admit that afterwards, when the death penalty had been commuted to 15 years and I'd been moved to cell 199, I again fell sudden prey to the most fearsome suspicions. What scared me most was that cell 199 was the death-cell; the letters I was getting from Lucia and Bela appeared to me to have been forged, the slightest break in prison life routine became a monstrous symbol of ambiguity, the most inoffensive reality seemed out of joint, submerged in surrealistic terror and secrecy, a concealed threat, an implied horror.

This, thankfully, did not continue very long, for my sense of humour gained the upper hand, and never allowed me, even for one moment, to become the trembling creature they wanted:

"Come on now, write your petition to the court of appeal." Lury was pressing me, as soon as I entered the office.

"Why should I?" I asked, "only yesterday, I was given a copy of the sentence—I still have a week, if I'm not mistaken."

"Listen," Lury said, "today is Saturday, it's not a working day, yet the whole court's waiting. Does that mean anything to you?"

Lury, forgive me, I did not appreciate what you meant. If you were lying, you would never have dared to say a thing like that in the presence of a Chekist! I asked no further questions and said I would write the petition on the Monday.

"What did you say?" the Major snarled at me, "I'm not waiting here all night for you. It's got to be done by 9! Dymshitz and all the rest of you have done it already—it's up to you now."

For some reason I can't explain I was impressed, I began to feel cheerful. They seemed in such a hurry for me to write this all-important document, it must be a mere formality. I sat there in the office for half an hour, wrote out a couple of pages and handed them over.

There is a minor detail which I think is worth recording. Since I had all along insisted that I should never have been charged with treason, but only with attempting to cross the border illegally, I began my appeal, "While I do not contest the gravity of my crime—an attempt to cross the border illegally—I nevertheless . . .", as ironically as I could, ironically, that is, if you read it within its context and remember that such a crime as this merits only three years at the very most, whereas I had been sentenced to death. In the decision of the court of appeal, however, this phrase had a repentant ring about it, "Kuznetsov does not contest the gravity of his crime . . ." There is a big difference. For it was our repentance that they had really been seeking.

B. Barsov and A. Fedoseyev, in their article, "The Criminals Have Been Punished", (Izvestia, 1st January, 1971) informed their wide Soviet readership that "the accused answered one by one, 'Yes, I confess I am guilty' ". Myself, Yurka and Alik, of course, were ex-criminals too. Well, what difference does it make? There are no political prisoners in the Soviet Union—didn't Khrushchev say so himself? What interests me is, how did the authors of this article find out that "they had even determined the point at which they were going to fire—they would have fired at the back," if neither we, nor the investigators, nor the court, knew this?

10th May

In "Izvestia" 30th December, 1970, there appeared an item about the reprisals on 16 Basque patriots. "You may imagine," squealed the correspondent, "the hatred of the murderers for these patriots, if they took such an unprecedented decision: they twice sentenced three of the Basques to death."

I don't know whether this is unprecedented or not (maybe I have heard of such cases), but the correspondent had evidently decided that *our* trial at any rate could not be regarded as a precedent for Spanish law: were *we* not sentenced, not twice, but three times, to be shot, under Arts. 64, 72 and 93-1? Vive la Vérité!

Aleksei Ilich and I decided to celebrate the New Year at 9 o'clock in the evening. We knew, of course, that 12 o'clock is the appropriate time, but if we have a "party" at that time of night we would be committing the most dreadful offence. Even a man condemned to death has something to lose—his $1\frac{1}{2}$-rouble shopping spree, for instance. I had thought that, as a man shortly to be executed, I might have been permitted to forget the regulations—what a hope! $1\frac{1}{2}$ roubles a month—just enough for tobacco. And your last wish before dying? Oh, no, no public squares, none of that bourgeois publicity for *you*—here you're done away with on the quiet! . . . But I'm beginning to stray from my subject.

Having obtained our meagre rations, we asked the guard if we could have a mug—only for a moment, please don't worry, word of honour, we're not going to bash one another on the head with it! Then we sweetened a drop of warm water and sipped from it, in turn, each making a wish: I, that this shouldn't be the last year of our lives: Aleksei Ilich, that we might at least live until the following spring.

I tried my best to cheer him up:

"Aleksei Ilich, you and I will meet in Mordovia in the Summer, on special regime, and we'll have a good laugh at your pessimism! I'll bet you two packets of tea."

"The only trouble is your tea won't be any good when they put handcuffs on our wrists, and gags in our mouths and take us out into the woods. They may well take us both together. And why Mordovia, Mordovia all the time?" he suddenly shrieked, "Do you think there are no other camps but in Mordovia? There are camps all over Russia!"

When I tried to convince him there were no more than 2,000 political prisoners at the present time, he looked at me more suspiciously than ever. He reminded me of the Strunino police inspector who was convinced there were at least one million politicals. It was like my mother asking me in disbelief: "Surely they can't have been beating you, can they?" I was about to ask him if there was any reason why I should paint a rosy picture of the Soviets, but didn't.

I only remarked that the present number of political prisoners was of no importance: the only thing that mattered was that our leaders had the potential to build millions of concentration camps whenever they might consider it necessary. At that very moment the door opened quietly and a senior warden, behind whom loomed the faces of several guards, ordered: "Kuznetsov, put your hands behind your back and follow me," and then in the same gruff tones to one of the guards in the corridor, "Get his things together."

I shoved a packet of cigarettes into my pocket and strode towards the door. I turned towards Aleksei Ilich: "Well—whatever happens—goodbye." He didn't say a word, didn't even nod his head. It flashed through my mind that it was all some gigantic nightmare: the vaulted roof, the New Year's Eve, that lump of terrified flesh that clung to the wall, the fingers that stuck fast to the collar of its white vest, the fearful anticipation behind the spectacle lenses on its fleshy nose, the pinkish blotches on this senior warden's square cheeks... But where were the handcuffs?

I cannot remember my heart beating, I cannot remember what thoughts were in my head—it was someone else this was happening to. It wasn't I who slowly stepped down that corridor with my hands behind my back, it wasn't I who so painstakingly avoided stepping on the heels of the guard in front of me or bumping into the guards on either side or treading on the feet of the guards behind me. Fourth floor, third floor, what if we miss the second floor—what then? We halted at the second, we turned left towards the prison governor's office. Major Kruglov rose heavily from behind his desk and announced majestically: "A humanitarian gesture has been made on your behalf: the sentence of death passed against you has been commuted to 15 years on special regime. May I wish you a Happy New Year . . . What's so funny?

But I wasn't laughing; he must have imagined it. I hardly saw him, so thick were the tears of humiliation and hatred that were streaming down my face—hatred for myself, for the whole Chekist comedy of my sentence, for my New Year's gift from this blue-epauletted Father Christmas . . .

"Aren't you pleased?" the major asked sardonically. He must have thought I was putting a show on specially for his benefit. Let me go to my cell and have a cigarette and sit down and think.

"What a filthy trick all this is!" Suddenly I could not restrain myself any longer. "What humanitarian gesture are you talking about? This isn't clemency. All they're doing is admitting the first sentence was unjust . . . What about Dymshitz—him too?"

"Of course."

"May I go?"

"If you wish." He shook his head and looked me over from head to foot. "Even in 20 years time, if they told me Kuznetsov had reformed, I wouldn't believe it!"

"And how right you would be!"

"Here is a telegram for you and you may go."

He was so disappointed, his cheeks were flushed. Did he think I would jump for joy and kiss his feet?

The telegram was from Lucia, "Your sentence commuted. Happy New Year. Mother. Lucia. Friends."

12th May

For two days now, night and day, I've been hearing doors clanging in the corridor and guards rushing backwards and forwards. Sounds like they're dragging some poor souls off on their last journey. If so, tomorrow or the day after they'll be taking me to court as well and then my transit will start round about the 25th.

Karl Frusin's emigrated. Judging by all the nuances I see in my letters, many are now being allowed to leave for Israel. And not only Israel—I hear Nikita[1] is getting ready to go to Paris. Surely this enchanted tsarist palace isn't about to crumble and fall? What sort of a regime is this if anybody can go where he likes? You can't build Communism like that! Perhaps even I could be happy in a state like that . . . For was I not still only a schoolboy when I found out (by accident, of course!) that the world was shut for me, and I began to examine all the slogans in minute detail to see if I could find out what was on the other side? No, even if Russia were like that, my place would still be in Israel. Love Russia by all means—but from a distance! I never cease to be amused that those who have international passports never seem to make full use of them. If ever I should be lucky enough to have one, not only would I run for my life from this Socialist camp I'm in, I wouldn't even go anywhere near any of Russia's neighbours in Eastern Europe. I have met people who came to Poland and Lithuania in 1940— to see their families . . .

You meet all sorts in a camp. It's only fools that say those days

[1] Nikita Krivosheyin, freed summer 1971, left Soviet Union for France.

are gone—fools that read three-copecks worth of history in their daily "Pravda" editorial.

*** So I was right after all in my argument with Butman when I said that our hijacking—or attempted hijacking, should it become public knowledge—wouldn't only be a marvellous kick in the pants for the Kremlin demogogues, who had been denying that such a thing as an emigration problem even existed, but a chance for many thousands of other people to grab their freedom. I was right. Not because my argument was stronger than his, but because for us, as for every lowly Soviet citizen, whatever goes on in the Kremlin goes on behind locked doors. I agreed to the plan because I was sick to death of all the difficulties and uncertainties the would-be emigrant is faced with, whereas he refused to take part for many different reasons, some of which may well have been personal. But who, in such a position as we were in, would not agree for "communal" reasons? We abandoned our prophecies and our predictions and agreed to go. True, our curiosity cost us more than we bargained for. If you cannot live a civilized life legally, legitimate lawlessness can be obtained only by an act of mad self-oblivion, at the price of the greatest effort of will-power, which, unfortunately, is always likely to hurt other peoples' sensitivity. It always seems to go too far, beyond the point where, in a normal state, the limits of normal existence are clearly defined. You can only straighten a stick by bending it. Only a very wise man or a scoundrel could have planned it properly. It's always an act of desperation, just like in a camp (nowhere so well as in a camp can you penetrate into the very core of a country's—any country's—political system) when a convict reaches the outermost limits of despair, when he cuts off his ears, or tattoos on his forehead "CPSU Slave" and then jumps into the firing-zone; if he takes others with him the regime will maybe soften for a time. But not for long, not for long. Soon it will return to the same old unlimited dictatorship, the same repressions and humiliations. Until the next explosion. This country knows of no reforms that are not soaked in blood.

13th May

This morning the new prison governor, Major Gorshkov, and his assistant Veselev made a tour of the prison.

"When will the trial be?", I asked.

"We've no idea," they said.

"What is it—a military secret?"

Gorshkov is a very skilful play-actor, much too clever to allow himself ever to be tied down. After my bloody battle with the guards, he called me into his office, and asked me what papers I had been protecting so assiduously. They were the drafts of some letters I was writing, I said; I was in a nervous mood, I thought it was intolerable that any riff-raff who chose should be able to poke his nose into my business. He had no alternative but to put me in the punishment cell, he said. I still hadn't reconciled myself to the waste: how many times had they searched me and found nothing! What I missed most were the notes I had made during the first days of 1971; the scratches on my face were still bleeding, my shoulder ached. . .
I demanded to be sent off to the camp immediately as they had kept me here, in the remand prison, illegally for five months already. (As a witness they should have brought me from the camp only on the day of the trial.)

"Why must you keep talking about the law all the time? This isn't your first marriage, is it? You're not stupid, you know it's the spirit, not the letter, of the law that counts." He smiled good-naturedly. He certainly knows how to win people over—just a touch of cynicism, just the right measure of confidentiality, the bare minimum of official phrases, the whole mixture spiced with the endearing smile of a man who knows what your relationship to him must be and secretly shares it with you; but still that cold squint when the eyes forget their smile.

"Yes," I said, "that's right—the spirit of the law; which, translated, means—the KGB is outside the law in the sense that it is above it. The KGB is the force which manipulates the law, pulls the strings, you might say . . ."

137

"Not exactly," he smiles, "but something like that. We keep up with life," he says, "but the law always lags behind."

"Yes, you would be quite right", I responded, "if your actions were subject to universal morality and not to Party and bureaucratic interests."

As a result of this intellectual conversation we entered into an agreement: he didn't put me in the punishment cell, and I kept quiet during the trial about the beating I'd received. As a matter of fact I never even intended to mention it. (Don't I, of all people, know what a waste of time that would be?) Camp life has taught me not to lay myself open to a beating for nothing. It was I that started it, after all, and I emerged victorious—they didn't get their hands on my papers!

Veselev also summoned me to his office that day. What a blue-eyed Chekist he is! How he blushes in embarrassment when he carries out his duties! He sees himself as the representative of the younger age-group in the KGB, and the standard-bearer of the new ideas, the essence of which I've never yet managed to understand (for the simple reason that they don't exist!) I could see Veselev hadn't been a Chekist for long: he was full of mythical stories about Cheka exploits, intoxicated with his own impatience, his uniform, and his "notoriety".

(Telephone rings, Veselev picks up the receiver, listens a moment, then blushes and asks politely, "Who did you want?" —the snake coils, pauses, then strikes—"this is the KGB." The majesty of his tone, the absolute certainty that whoever is calling is left speechless—if not from fright, then certainly out of respect; myself I am dumbfounded: before me sits the representative of another world, a priest officiating at a religious ceremony, quite genuinely convinced he is privy to the sacred mysteries of existence.)

Veselev spoke only of trivialities, but I thought I knew what he was after: he was worried I might say something at the trial. He told me they shoot people "automatically" nowadays. In the past only one of the five guns was loaded so the soldiers wouldn't know which one of them was carrying out the death sentence. But now, "you just push a button and that's it!" I told him that in my opinion every time the state sentenced a criminal to death, it was giving birth to an executioner, and the executioner was no better than the criminal. He simply didn't know what I was talking about; his concern for the good of the state did not extend this far.

14th May

This morning, just after I returned from my walk I was loaded into a black maria and driven off to the court. I was able to exchange a few words with Iosif as we rode along, though the guards were bawling at us. There were three of us in the vehicle; I, myself, was in the main compartment, Iosif was in the "box" on the right, and we could see an enormous pair of feet protruding from under the door of the "box" on the left. I think they belonged to Maftser. "Who are you?"—no answer. They must have frightened the giant out of his mind. How courageous, how dependable he used to be, and what a pathetic shrunken milksop it was that testified at our trial. Many lose their way when they enter the investigator's office. The main thing that must be understood is this: that if you have done anything that is in any way prejudicial to the "security" of the state, then you are defenceless. You are as *nothing*. How many can find the strength within them to resist this when it's thrown at them with all the might of the state behind it? It's amazing: the more "respectable" a man in normal life, the more lost he feels when misfortune falls upon him; the more respect he inspired beyond the confines of the camp, the greater the "lickspittle", "toady" and "sponger" is he when arrested. These are the "in-between" people, those without a defined place in the system, those who are unable to comprehend its true essence, nor the bounds of its power (which ends where the human soul begins) and who prefer death to humiliation.

"The three of us put up a good show, don't you think?" Iosif asked me. "Magnificent for a first attempt!" I replied, in all sincerity.

It can be said with certainty that, out of every hundred that pass through the hands of the KGB, there is only one from whom they cannot extract a confession nor reduce to tearful repentance. They try their best, though, you must give them that. On the other hand, the more infamously a man behaves during the investigation and the trial, the more militant he is in the camp (provided of course, the tears he shed were only the weakness of a strong man and not the beginning of a rogue's career). It's as though he were taking his revenge for a "spiritual knockout".

Iosif cheered me up: "I'm not sorry for anything I've ever done," he said, "I knew what I was doing, and I don't regret it. But I'm sorry for Alik and Yurka." He and I disagreed about whether it was their own fault for talking too much. (What a paradox—they suffered for being non-Jews!) I told Iosif that, I had been expecting 15 years, I had decided to declare a hunger-strike in protest against our being tried for treason, and to start straight after the sentence—in the court itself. I was sure someone would join me. But the death sentence had knocked me off balance: was it not clearly futile to declare a hunger-strike when they were going to shoot you?

I had thought out my answers to anything I might be asked as a witness, but I'd not had one single question. Both the Procurators, Ponomarev and Katukova, must have thought it would be better not to have anything to do with me. They didn't even want to let me finish. The judge interrupted me twice to tell me I'd said enough, and twice I had to say, "I have not finished yet."

I could not stop myself reproaching my would-be accomplices, they looked so humble. I hope they realized it was because I was bitter about them. I explained why Butman was not included in our plans:

"I was scared at the idea of having two committees. There's

always trouble when people do something they're not qualified for."

Then one of the lawyers asked me:

"If the first committee was the committee of state security, what was the second?"

"The Leningrad committee," I said, "just the same."

We conducted ourselves as militantly as we could. When I came into the hall I nodded "Shalom" at them, but no reply. *** I've just seen Lucia. We were given one whole hour. One hour with a guard on top of us, making sure we didn't mention anything serious. Lucia will again be upset that we just "gossiped away our meeting". She hasn't yet realized that these meetings can only be a waste of words—they're not for exchanging news or confidences: they're a gesture, a sign and no more: "nothing's changed, everything's as it should be, sit tight, dear comrade, we're thinking of you."

Lucia is sympathy itself, but I find it easy to talk to her.

15th May

On the 6th January I put in a request for a meeting with Sylva— no answer yet.

16th May

I had a funny dream last night. This time, unlike my first stay as a convict, it didn't take me long to stop dreaming about days when I was free. Now I never dream anything except camp faces and camp situations. No, that's not true; even when I was free I couldn't shake off memories about life in camp. Strange how bright and happy were my dreams that first night in prison! I would have forgotten about them, had I not been arrested again.

Occasionally I have what I would call word-dreams; there are no faces, or concrete objects, or events—just words.

Frequently these dreams are a sort of intellectual debate between myself and some real person, who always seems to have a name. For example, I know my opponent's called Ivanov, but I never see him. Last night I had a very interesting discussion with God himself. When I awoke I couldn't take my eyes off the cracks and cobwebs in the ceiling. I tried to go over every single word that had filled my dream with such a special yet puzzling significance. When dawn broke, however, the profundity of my dialogue had drifted away into the early morning. Anyway, here it is, this night-time dialogue with God, tainted neither with the logic of daytime nor with any invented symbolism. I've just added a slight literary touch at the beginning. When you dream everything seems to rise from nowhere and fade away whence it came; when you try and recall it later it needs a little introduction, or it doesn't make sense.

*** Should science ever prove, if indeed it can be proved, that there is no such thing as the after-life . . . we would have banners, illuminations, portraits of the plumpish and wizened old eggheads that work in the laboratories of the Institute of Scientific Research into Atheism; there would be march-pasts and the masses would celebrate with a day of wild rejoicing . . . But on that day I would weep. No, no, it's impossible that there should be no after-life, or Day of Judgment, at least! The world needs its Doomsday Court just as the Third Reich needed its Nuremburg Trial. It *must* exist. If it doesn't, if there *is* no life after death, I cannot go on. I do not necessarily mean the immortality of the soul—just the Day of Judgment. Well, whatever will be . . .

*** Here at last is the Day of Judgment. What did you say! It's devilish clear all the angels that summon the souls into court have wings, and they are white, not blue—something well worth remembering! The souls are quite naked, defence-less. When God, who was laughing into his white beard, questioned me on what had happened to me during the day, his summing-up was loud enough for all to hear: "No, thou art not an angel," I thought to myself: "Did you have to probe so deeply to come to such a conclusion? I could have told you that right at the beginning."

The Lord spoke once again: "Thou art not an angel."

I agreed humbly, "It's true my Lord, but . . ."

"Why art thou then so pretentious?"

"Precisely because I am not an angel, Lord."

"When, then . . ."

They just came and searched me; just managed to get my papers out of the way in time. I've lost the track. I feel more like howling like an animal than writing!

18th May

I meet Sylva today. It will be a miracle if we can speak for any length of time. How well I know this feeling! If I were a younger man, and if it were my first time in prison "How dare you?" I would protest, "How dare you take liberties with such a fine fellow as me?" . . .

The Cheka cannot function without its cheap little tricks. However experienced you may be, they are bound in one way or other to ensnare you in one of their traps. You will believe the greatest rascal that ever lived so long as he pretends he's your best friend.

Major Gorshkov told Sylva, in Veselev's presence, that he would set no limit to our time, on condition that we avoided forbidden subjects (i.e. we must not mention our case—which is such a secret!—nor prison, nor slander the Soviet regime).

Thus, thinking we had all the time in the world, we skipped from subject to subject and we were just about to start on Spinoza's definition of liberty, when the guard, seated high on his stool, wiped the smile of perplexity from his face and grandly announced, "Meeting over!" "But you heard what the Major said, didn't you?" Well, he'd heard and he'd not heard. When the senior warden arrived, he calmed everyone down and explained that he was quite prepared to believe the Major had said something like that but he'd gone home and not left any written orders behind. Therefore all we had was one hour. And that was it!

Prison has made Sylva pale and she smokes non-stop. But she's very cheerful and still militant. Thank God.

The Cheka is nothing like it used to be. I don't mean during the 1930s and 1940s, when the investigators zealously despatched their victims off to their graves, all for the sake of building Communism. But even 10 years ago there was none of the cynicism that exists today—the cynicism of those that until only recently were the servants of the blood-cult that was rampant in the country, but now are merely officials in a temple their God has left deserted. Nowadays you never hear of how fortunate you are to be a Soviet citizen or about the bright future of mankind, for which you can and must suffer, etc. (how sincere this was is another matter!). Now the investigators work on you as if you were in a communal kitchen: "Come on now, you can't chop wood with a penknife, you know!" or; "Why be so ambitious—take things as they come!" and so forth. Captain Totoev was even more outspoken:

"Not so long ago I packed some currency speculators off to jail. One of them was a lad your age: he had too much money and too many girlfriends. But *what* girlfriends! That I can understand; it was worth going to jail for! But you? Just think, you're going to spend the rest of your life in prison. And for what? A man gets an idea in his head, and before he knows where he is, he's torturing himself and not giving anybody else any peace either . . . You don't know how to live, young man, that's why you spend your life half in and half out of jail."

Something is rotten in the state of Denmark. Times have changed. The inquisitor has begun to doubt the God he once served and now his only concern is his material welfare: he's lost his revolutionary ardour, his faith in the Absolute. How can one doubt the religion is entering a new phase, and that the time for a new cult is with us? How are the mighty fallen! The way they once "argued": "If I can't convince you, then you'll go to jail!" is still as popular as ever, but it no longer terrifies heretics. Now you see people smirking at those same idols to which only a short time before they were vowing their lives. This is not nihilism, simply indifference to ideology in general and to official ideology in particular. The tin-god has blundered, self-mutilation has run riot, the whole ritual stands in public view, all its shallowness and boring mediocrity revealed. But there can be no revision of ideology. This is a long way ahead in the future—the people are historically unaccustomed to independent thought. Besides, Russia is not simply Moscow and Leningrad. One may perceive the alarm of the leaders whenever they see any signs that the population are uninterested in ideology, but they will recover and find a way out. Yet they will have to renovate the old idols. What they really need is a burst of patriotism to bring passions up to boiling point, a good purge, an energetic campaign to inspire people with the knowledge that universal bliss is just around the corner. These may be rather unsubtle weapons, but they are so reliable, and so well-tried in the field of battle that you don't have to be a fortune-teller or a connoisseur of the human heart or a prophet to make such predictions.

21st May

I'm in a Stolypin. My itinerary—Gorky, Ruzaevka-Potma-Udarny Settlement.

The "Stolypin[1] Carriage", as they call it, or just the "Stolypin", is the special carriage for transporting convicts from one place to another. If you look at it from the outside, it's just an ordinary railway carriage, but if you were to glance a little more closely at the plastic partition behind the windows you would be surprised to note that the side of the carriage has no aperture whatsoever. Inside, the compartment has been turned into a cell, with doors fitted with iron bars, and alongside the windows a gangway has been left for the guards to pass.

[1] Piotr Stolypin (1862-1911) Conservative Prime Minister of Russia, assassinated by revolutionaries.

Everything's just the same as it was four years ago, the last time I was in transit. When you've spent some time in the "special zone" you stop believing in the reality of prison life, you think things must change, they couldn't possibly be as loathsome as they used to be. Yet all the same . . .

The "Stolypin" is supposed to hold 50 people, though one of the guards said there were 87 of us. But it's not crowded in my compartment—I'm quite alone: firstly, because I'm a political prisoner, and secondly, because I'm on special regime, (though this isn't being strictly observed.) It's three days journey to Gorky from here.

Every so often our carriage is uncoupled and shunted into a siding, where we sometimes have to wait hour after hour. The "Stolypin" has to keep to a tight schedule, and serves all the prisons and camps. Whenever we stop we're not met by crowds of women throwing flowers but by armed guards with sheepdogs, any one of which gets more meat that 50 of us put together.

22nd May

I am writing this while the train is standing still. We've a very good set of guards this time. They go out of their way to help us, never refuse anybody water, let us go to the toilet whenever we wish and only close the windows when we stop. That's why we don't get any of the usual hideous brawls. It's the tow-haired sergeant that's responsible—he's about 25 years old, and no fool by any means. He seems to know how to deal with prisoners. "Well, what can I do for you?" he asks, drumming his fingers on his holster and grinning. "What are you making such a song-and-dance for? Is it water you want? Don't worry, we'll get you some right away!"

About three days ago there was an article in "Izvestia" about our case. Since the sergeant found out that I was that very "Kuznetsov" he's spent every free moment he's had leaning on my door and asking me the details of the case. He doesn't

146

believe what he reads, he told me. I've never ever met such a guard before in all my years as a prisoner.

The guards, who usually came from somewhere in Central Asia, are quite often extremely aggressive and dim-witted. They take liberties with the convicts, and when they see how easily they can get away with it they extort money and possessions at the least provocation. They love showing off their ammunition and are totally unscrupulous.

I have days of rioting and uproar to look forward to. The same old verbal masturbation, the same old exhibitionism and "strip-tease" at the least opportunity. Every two or three hours I hear the sound of someone clearing his throat at the other end of the carriage, then the uproar is gradually dimmed by a dull, rhythmic voice, always with the same story: "Girls, get ready! I'm coming. Girls, wait for me. We'll be taken to the toilet soon, but I'm not going for a piss! Just you show her to me, so I can see what she's like. I just want to see what she's like, I haven't seen one for thirteen years. I've forgotten what it's like . . . Thirteen years without it!" Then someone else chimes in, "What do you want now, you old bastard? What can *you* do for a woman?" "Just you watch me, just you watch me!" he replies, in no way daunted. "If only they gave me the right food, I could manage it once a week, just you watch me!"

In the next compartment some villian decides he'll tell us a little tale:

"I said my goodbyes to the warden, I'd had my share of prison. I ran for my life . . . I got to Leningrad, went from station to station, from girl to girl . . . I got this tart down Shvorinsky alley, there was this bloody policeman who butted in . . . I thought I'd give him a thrashing, but when I woke up . . . there I was again—back in the 'Crosses'!"

The same old irritating, stereotyped stories, the same old sexual and criminal confidences, the same old cynicism. Nothing spared—cynicism and then more cynicism. These are not hard labour convicts from the "House of the Dead", nor rejects of the state, but those that have remained within the bosom of the Church; it hasn't rejected them, nor they it, even in sinning. These are Soviet prisoners, who have been weaned away from Christian morality yet have misunderstood so-called Communist morality and turned to a life of crime, (even if the divine precepts are broken daily by the Clergy themselves, they nevertheless retain their truth for the ordinary parishioner; but moral precepts which have been decreed by a ruling party cannot be broken by the members of that party without their provoking immorality among others).

Here are one or two examples of convicts' stories:

"I went to the cinema. This dark girl sidles up to me. Come on home with me, she says, my husband's out of town on business, he's a colonel (or a Procurator, or a Sea-Captain!— E.K.). She pours me out this brandy and cuts me up some Polish sausage, in great big chunks and some caviar . . . Then she showed me her bank book—60,000 she had! Live with me, she says . . . But what did I want a piece of shit like her for? I'd sooner die in a ditch, my freedom's dearer to me than anything! I got what I could from her, anyway, all sorts of fine clothes she had . . . Just you give me away, I said to her and I'll tell the court your husband knew all about it, and that you, you shit-bag, had led me on all the time!"

"I had a great time for three months," another convict begins, "When I got free, I went straight to the police station. I'm going straight from now on, officer, I said, I'm a reformed man. And he says, how dare you talk to me like that, who the hell do you think you are? Well, what was I supposed to do, talk to him like a good upright citizen and all that sort of rubbish! What do I need you for, he says, what do I want a cunning bastard like you for, when all the police here are simple people, from the country? Let them drink beer during working hours, what do they want to spend their time catching you for! . . . Well, all right then, so I pissed off to Leningrad and this lad and me were working as partners, having a great time . . . One night I was daft enough to go home when I was drunk—there was my wife and two snivelling drips with her! . . . The next day Galka reads me this sermon: 'you should work,' she says, 'live like an honest man, be a comrade and a brother to everybody . . .' 'You bloody tart,' I told her straight! Whose money was it when you sent me all those parcels to the camp? You're like the prison governor, I said; 'work lads, live honourably!' and he was stealing half the factory himself. Yes, I know exactly what you mean by 'honourable'. Plough the fields from morning till night and steal a bit now and again, but don't get caught! Me, I steal the whole lot in one go, you rats, but I steal a thousand times less than you honest people do! . . . Gave her as good as I got, I did, then I gave her one over the table, cracked her one between the eyes, and then I left. Where can I go and drown my sorrows, I think to myself, it was about 2 o'clock in the morning, everything was shut, by the time you get to the station—there's an all-night cafe there— you could walk your bloody legs off. . . So, anyway, I see this fellow walking about, drunk as sin, with a bottle of vodka and some tomatoes in his bag, so I banged him on the head with this brick . . . but I was just going when two policemen stopped me—got ten years for it . . ."

23rd May

The sergeant told me in confidence that they had sent him off to Czechoslovakia when he'd been a Party worker in Kharkov: "When we were half way there we realized we were all in the same outfit . . . They could pick us out from a mile off. . . what a fool I was, I believed everything I was told and now I've seen as much as I want to see—I'm sick of the lot of it!" "So you're against them, are you then?" I was joking, feeling my way. "What do you mean, against them? I'm the victim of red-tape. As I said, I joined the Party regional committee, I was young and green and full of ideals . . . Then I saw what I'd gotten into—it was like one big brothel! Bastards they were, the whole lot of them! But I couldn't get out, no matter how hard I tried. Then, when I'd done my fifth year at the

VUZ they stuck me in the army. That's how I got into this convoy. I don't know who's worse—the guards or the convicts. It's not so bad this time, but you couldn't imagine what kind of things go on sometimes. Last week, for example, we had this load of convicts . . . the idiot in charge gave orders that they shouldn't be given any water. There was this sick old man there, who said he couldn't last out if he didn't go to the toilet. But the officer wouldn't let him go. So he did it in one of his shoes and it all splashed on the floor. 'Don't give them any water, so they won't ask to go to the toilet,' this officer said. But how can you not give them water if they've been guzzling herrings all day? You know how dry the rations are—herring and black bread . . . So they nearly turned the carriage upside down—it was swaying from side to side, and the wheels were starting to come off the rails . . . In the end we managed to calm them down. But this old man ruined the officer's uniform all the same: he slit one of his veins open, and let the blood drip into a mug and then poured it all over him. They nearly murdered him, of course."

Pskov: About 40 prisoners have been set down and about the same number taken on. Two have been put in with me. As soon as I saw their cases and bags I knew they were here under Art. 58. Common criminals rarely carry a bag with them or any sort of bundle. Usually they have a herring-tail sticking out of their pocket or a loaf of black bread, and nothing else. Though not always: at Pskov, two tall Letts, both robbers, and each with a pair of suitcases, joined the train. I thought at first they were "58s", but I was way off the mark. Suitcases are not always a sure sign, you sometimes get Balts, Western Ukrainians and Caucasians carrying them.

My travelling companions are both Lithuanians, going from Vilnius to, of course, Mordovia, but to a strict regime camp. One of them, Boniulis, a six-footer about 50 years old, is serving his 13th year. Not unnaturally, we've met before. The other one, Leikus, a stocky, broad-shouldered, fellow who has preserved his magnificent military bearing in spite of his age, is about 60, I should imagine. He was a captain in the Lithuanian national army and protected his country from the Soviet liberators, yet now he's been sentenced to 15 years for "treason" (oh logic! oh jurisprudence! oh justice!). Boniulis had been taken to Vilnius to identify someone who had taken part in the Lithuanian national movement, but had refused to recognize him.

The Lithuanians generally conduct themselves very steadfastly in camp. Whereas the Letts are usually servile and conformist by nature. It comes as no surprise that, during the war, the Letts worked for both the Germans and the Russians, whereas the Lithuanians fought against them both, and others too, in defence of their independence. The younger Letts are usually honest fellows, but there aren't many of them in the camps. In 1967 one Lithuanian (I can't remember his name but I remember reading about him in the Chronicle of Current Events[1]) who had served 17 out of his 25 years sentence was persuaded by the Cheka to write a request for clemency. He wrote it but nothing happened. His own people had turned their backs on him (if you request clemency you have no choice but to renounce all your ideals and actions and say how much you love the powers-that-be), so he killed himself. In full daylight he jumped into the forbidden zone and made as if he were going to try and climb the fence a few yards from the watch-tower. There could have been nothing simpler than to catch him— there he was, the high fence in front of him, and then the barbed-wire fence, and then one minute's walk from the guard-house which was crowded with soldiers. The sentry stood and fired round after round at him!

When a convict is killed in the forbidden zone, the murderer always receives the gratitude of the authorities and is rewarded with a two-week holiday. I wouldn't say it was for this reason alone that the sentries that guard political prisoners run and bayonet any madman or daredevil as fast as they can.

[1] Underground bi-monthly account of trials, imprisonments and illegal acts of the Soviet authorities.

The authorities tell them the most fantastic and horrifying stories about us and about how cunning and clever we are. It's this which keeps alive in them that vigilance which becomes nervousness at the critical moment and that misinformed comprehension of their duty that turns into the fear that they are committing a crime themselves in allowing a horrible beast to escape, an enemy of the Soviet regime, who, before you know it, will blow up the Kremlin! I know several cases when would-be escapists, surrounded on all sides, and standing with their hands raised, were shot point-blank. This is what happened to Algis Petrosyavichus in 1958—the two men he ran away with were killed—(one of them while climbing up a tree and completely unarmed) while he, twice wounded, was left for dead. This was the only thing that saved him: the camp hospital was too crowded to finish him off, so all they did was amputate his right arm up to the shoulder, though there was nothing wrong with it (the bone was untouched). He later protested against this "operation" after hearing the surgeon say, "Let's make sure he never forgets this as long as he lives!" He was then 18 years old.

In late summer 1964 I saw Romashev bestially murdered before my eyes. He had served two years of his four-year sentence when he was rejected by his Komsomol wife and Communist Party parents on account of his anti-Soviet views. What had happened was that the authorities had written to them saying he refused to praise the Soviet regime and aid it by spying and informing on his friends. So one day he jumped into the forbidden zone and climbed over the fence only 10 yards from the watchtower. The sentry pointed his submachine gun at him and screamed, "I'll kill you, I'll kill you," but he shot twice in the air, unable to bring himself to shoot a man who was just sitting on the fence waiting to be killed, and making no attempt whatsoever to escape.

A minute or two later a few soldiers ran up and one swine among them cold-bloodedly emptied his gun into the living target, who didn't even blink when the barrel was levelled at him. The body, its legs stuck to the barbed-wire of the fence, hung head downwards. Possibly Romashev was still alive but he could well have died in the 10 minutes it took the sergeant (Kiril Yacovlevich Shved) to come. He just tugged one of its arms and the body crashed to the ground. If Romashev had still been alive when he was hanging from the fence, the blow of his head on the ground would have been enough to kill him. The prisoners went wild, nearly rioted and had to be driven back by the guards. Then about 10 of us wrote protests and demanded a public enquiry, but we might as well not have bothered.

And what about Ivan Kochubei and Nikolai Tanashuk, who were slain by soldiers in the very middle of the camp?

Tanashuk had gone out of his mind and so had Kochubei, from all accounts, but this of course didn't prevent them serving out their terms. There was one fellow (I can't remember his name) whom I actually saw jump three times into the forbidden zone; each time he was removed by the guards, who knew he was insane—they never took their eyes off him during exercises and warned the sentry not to fire if the "fool" as they called him, should jump over the wire. In the two weeks I shared with him in the punishment block he jumped over the wire three times. Each time a guard dragged him back from the fence by his feet while the sentry smashed his rifle butt into his forehead. One week after he left the punishment block he was shot down in broad daylight in the forbidden zone. The zone isn't the punishment block, after all—how can you be expected to keep a guard on every "fool"?

30th May

Potma. We stayed five days in Gorkovsky transit prison, spent the Saturday in Ruzayevka, left Ruzayevka this morning, and now we've reached Potma. Gorkovsky transit is a complex of gloomy multi-storied blocks. I always associate its dirty brick-red buildings with those of a factory: it has such a cheerless, woebegone appearance. They call this prison the "Soloviov Villa". Legend has it that its former governor, Soloviov, who once lived and slept in the prison, regarded it almost as his own property. He used the sweat and toil of the prisoners to build as many amenities as possible, and so taken was he with his role of the omnipotent property-owner that, when he won the Stalin prize—the legend says nothing about *why* he won it—he spent all the money on fitting a water closet in every cell.

There are five of us to every three and a half square yards. The whole of Potma transit is crowded end to end. This is why we've been joined by a couple of fellows going to the foreign zone, in camp 5. One of them is a stateless Greek (serving five years for a motor accident) and the other a Persian, about 30 years old, who was a student at Baku Institute of Architecture but got three years for trafficking in foreign currency. In the cell next to us there are, I think, six Chinese, in greasy jackets and each with a colourful bundle which they never part with, even when they go to the toilet. They think someone will steal it, I suppose. They're on their way to the foreigners' zone as well. When I shouted through the window: "What are you in for?" One of them answered, "My wife's a filthy alimony-grabber."

The Persian curses the day he ever decided to come to the Soviet Union, though he admits life wasn't too bad as a foreign student. He agrees with me that a Soviet degree only carries weight in the underdeveloped countries. He could, of course, so he says, have studied a further two years in the West, but it's easier to get a Soviet qualification than any other.

31st May

Night-time—as soon as one person shifted his position it woke everyone else up. The Greek was breathing in my face, the Persian down my neck, the huge carcass of the Lithuanian was keeping my legs warm. Oh, Russia, Oh Russia, how vast and how spacious thou art!

1st June

The Persian and the Greek were taken away yesterday evening. We have to stay here till Wednesday, but there's a little more room anyway. There are four of us now we've been joined by another traitor. I haven't learnt his name yet and he's keeping the charge against him to himself; all he says is he got 11 years under Art. 64, he'd been a colonel, and he's from Moscow.

I think he looks like a rather unpleasant Party functionary with an engineer's training; he speaks as though he were writing a "Pravda" editorial (though I'm not convinced whether he's playing the part of the convinced Communist because he's afraid of informers, or whether he really is what he says). He reminds me of the inventor of a perpetuum-mobile who wasn't fortunate enough to find official favour and tried to foist his invention on some foreign tourist. But it must have been *some* invention, for 11 years is a fair offering under this Article! No, I'm simply letting my imagination run away with me—all he did was imply what a great capacity he has for invention.

3rd June

Here we are at last. Home again. I have fourteen years ahead of me here until I decide to pop off to Vladimir for three years for variety's sake—you get bored after being beaten so often in the same place!

I'm in quarantine: in a cell by myself. Same old wooden two-tiered beds, same old slop bucket—just the same as it was! Even the same dirty-green walls. Same faces: one's gone a bit further downhill, a second's lost his hair, a third's gone round-shouldered: same guards—this one's grown a paunch, that one's become an officer, another a lieutenant . . . It's seven years since I left here. It's as if I'm coming home again.

I feel so inexplicably irritated, despondent, weary in spirit. Over and over again. Do I have the strength this time? Work-cell-work-cell . . . cell-mates! My second day on special regime and the second day I've heard somebody screaming at the top of their voice through their cell window (maybe it's coming from the punishment cell at the far end, near the exercise yard), "Lenin, go and fuck yourself, Lenin go and fuck yourself!" This goes on for 20 minutes, stops an hour or so, then off it goes again. I have to live with these people year after year; night upon night, they are going to breathe in my face, switch on the radio during the day full blast, clatter their dominoes, tell 20-year-old jokes, tell me all the intimate details of their lives, lie to me, argue with me, suck up to me and detest me . . . Sleep on the same bed, turn my soul inside out (whether I wish or no) and tell them its most cherished secrets, year after year, face to face, 24 hours a day. Where will I get the patience and calm I need? I know them all so well—their habits, their gestures, their stupid, little expressions . . . Every thought on every question, exactly as it was 10 years ago. I shout to some people I know through the window, "How's life?" "Just the same, no different," comes the reply through their few remaining teeth. It's hard to keep up morale, they say. This "just the same" of theirs is a frightened glance over their shoulder, a sh, sh, don't rock the boat, a God forbid!

Yesterday, hardly had I been searched or even put on my new prison dress, when I was summoned to the office of Captain Kolgatin, the camp governor. His assistant was there too, Captain Vorobiov, a dark little man with a gammy leg and a shiny face. I remembered him from 1963 when he was a young self-conscious lieutenant, a detachment officer. Now he looks like a hardened administrator who has tasted the sweetness of unlimited power. Maybe it's he who is in command here. I was told what punishments threatened me should I break any minor camp rule: "You'll get the red stripe," Vorobiov said, obviously trying to cheer me up. "What for?" I asked, "There's no evidence I might want to try and escape." "Nor would I advise you to! I'm sure you remember those two men hanging over the fence? Our guards here are all good shots."

He asked me why it was written on Murzhenko's papers that he was a Ukrainian, but on Fedorov's that he was a Russian. "Why not?" I asked. "They're Jews," he said. I sniffed. Our conversation ended with these words of Vorobiov: "We have another Jew here, Berger. If I were you, I wouldn't try and create any of those Zionist groups here, or it'll be 77-1 for you."

5th June

The men brewed me some tea. I didn't realize how much I'd missed it. So far I've only really come into contact with the prisoners here in the little exercise-yard:

"Can't you remember? He was freed, he died, he was shot, he got another sentence . . ."

Mediansk showed me the tattoo on his chest: it says in letters two inches high, "I seek justice, Soviet power and legality! Down with the TsK[1] dictatorship!" "Aren't you afraid they might shoot you?" I asked him. He said he wasn't afraid since it's five years since they'd shot anyone for tattooing. "It's unlikely that they would increase the sentence, they owe me one or two favours—they'll try and hush it up!"

6th June

Sent a letter to Lucia. I'm still keeping up the cheerful facade—you can believe anything, if you try.

[1] Central Committee of the Soviet Communist Party.

The day after I was sentenced I was given one hour to see her in Kruglov's presence. I talked non-stop, the silliest trivialities, anything rather than serious conversation. Was this because I wouldn't swop the beautifully tragic fate that awaited me for the morsel of consolation she could give me? To be executed by Soviet law is fate, whereas to be a Soviet prisoner is a way of thinking, a privilege, which has to be paid for.

*** "Law is a political measure—it is politics itself," said Lenin. This is not just a sad fact of life, but a slogan for all times.

*** At the dawn of its existence, the totalitarian state attempts to intrude into man's spiritual life. This is soon followed by swift industrialization (It's the old, old story: a man is nothing, the state is all, and justification is always found for it) by means of the most pitiless exploitation of the people. But the economic reins, when proved too weak, are followed by the most strident demand for harnessing the internal reserves of the people to stabilize and consolidate the dictatorship. The spiritual realm becomes the object of the coarsest possible manipulation, the aim—to produce the new man, i.e. the man who will respond religiously to any slogans the leaders can think of, who is prepared to participate in all their social and political experiments, who is prepared to make the most backbreaking about-turns for the sake of their theories, a man whose dissatisfaction, however geniune, is easily channelled into the right direction. Experiments are more or less an anachronism nowadays. They only discussed them seriously when they were struggling for the power that would give them the opportunity of turning theory into practice, in extra-laboratory conditions, that is, and on the living human material; but as soon as the theoreticians and the experimenters came to power they were faced with the problem of holding on to it, which most definitely pushed their dreams into the background. To hold on to power was the first and only necessity. Since then any experimenting there may have been has been strictly subordinated to the problem of stabilizing the power of the rulers, and in no way to the attainment of universal bliss.

8th June

I haven't found out yet what they're like with papers here; maybe they're keen, maybe they don't care. When I arrived they took away all my four books and my drafts. I managed to hold on to my diaries though: being in a camp has taught me something at least. The papers that were taken away from me on 24th December I found among the rest of my things. They don't look as if they've been examined. That's a good sign!

I can't see myself able to work out a reliable method of preserving my papers. I'll have to be on constant guard and rely more on luck than anything else, there are so many unforeseeable situations here. Russia, in Kolodia's[1] beloved expression, is a country of wooden shoes and sputniks, a combination of refinement and coarseness. Neither of these unfortunately can be foreseen and every concrete situation has to be judged on its merits.

*** I still retain among my possessions a copy of the declaration I made on 25th December, rejecting Soviet citizenship. Lucia had been so tactful and concerned, and I so intent upon keeping our conversation as trivial as possible that I quite forgot the main thing I had intended. I had been meaning to tell her at the very end of our meeting, when I was no longer worried it might be stopped, that, should my appeal against my sentence fail, I would not ask for clemency but request the Supreme Soviet to deprive me of Soviet citizenship before I died. When the meeting ended so unexpectedly I got confused. I still would have had a few seconds to tell her this, at the very last moment when she got up to leave, but I had grown so accustomed to joking and making small-talk about my situation that I quoted her something from Villon I had specially amended for the occasion:

"I, Edward, am unhappy, alas, a rogue's death awaits me, and whatever this back of mine may weigh, my neck will surely know tomorrow."

[1] Camp name of Vladimir Telnikov, imprisoned 1957–63, left USSR in November, 1971.

Lucia had laughed, rather a contrived laugh, and rejoined: "Well, I'm sure your back is quite heavy," and then she left me.

9th June

I was called in to see Lieutenant Piatkin, who informed me that he was the officer of the unit to which I had been assigned. I would say he was about 25, a rather stupid-looking, cunning devil with a face the shape of a chopping-block; obviously a Mordovian, with an inarticulate misunderstanding of Russian patriotism ("Our great fatherland, where we were all born!") He could find no answer to my question: "If you were the offspring of a Soviet diplomat, and you were born, God forbid, on British territory (for example), which country would you choose as your fatherland?" I can see him writing in my character-reference: "Kuznetsov frequently asked questions of a provocative anti-Soviet nature."

In September of last year, Piatkin told me, he and several other officers and guards had helped the soldiers to put down a rebellion in camp 5, where the criminals are, not the foreigners. They had set the barracks on fire, looted the shop, beaten up the "trusties" and thrown them all into the firing-zone, and then attempted a mass break-out. . . The order had come from Moscow to use force only as a last resort since this was a special regime zone and contained only small-time first offenders. The soldiers' cartridges were removed, and the rebellion was put down without a single shot being fired though, true, the soldiers' rifle-butts were kept fairly busy. About 30 of the prisoners, so Piatkin told me, were to be tried, out of whom perhaps five would be condemned to death under Art. 77-1. Being no naive newspaper reader, I didn't ask how he knew in advance the sentence of a court which hadn't yet sat, but I was nevertheless rather curious as to how relatively harmless minor offenders could be tried under Art. 77-1. But what ridiculous questions I ask! The KGB man is all right for pacifying you or holding on to you, but for anything that requires a little brain-power, the model citizen is dead.

11th June

Out to work today—from cell 9 which I'm sharing with Yurka, Berger (about whom I was warned by Vorobiov) and Stovbunyenko. It's very strange, accomplices are not usually put in the same cell. The censor's office is just next to the wall of our cell; this is the office of the camp KGB man, Captain Kochetkov, whom I haven't yet had the pleasure of meeting.

The work doesn't appear particularly onerous at first glance—I'm sewing gloves—but the norm is fantastic: 75 pairs a day. There must be a trick to it. By law "exceptionally dangerous" prisoners are to be used par excellence in heavy work, but it's not always easy to organize them into a group (i.e. from the economic point of view) and we are not allowed to leave our zone (say for felling trees, or breaking stones, etc.).

12th June

I first met Stovbunyenko during my first term. He did four years under Art. 70, was released and then in 1966 got 12 years for murder (as a common criminal). At that time in the criminal zone, he soon managed to wangle himself out under Art. 70. He says he did it to be with his "friends". It was thanks to him, he told me, that I'd been put in cell 9. Keeps on hinting how influential he is. The others are convinced he's working for the KGB. We shall see. There's no doubt each cell has its informer.

13th June

Stovbunyenko is 28 years old, born in Leningrad; he wears a heavy spectacle frame on his pimply and puffy face, never stops talking but can be tamed by a mere glance or a word in his direction; his pseudo-intellectualism makes me revere silence all the more.

Berger I heard about a long time ago. In 1963 or '64 he was in a cell with his accomplice Liashenko (nicknamed "Snubnose"). Berger has done 28 years already, but still has another seven to do. He had 13 convictions (eight of them he says, were dropped for lack of proof) for armed robbery, "banditry" and murder (five or six times). I was well aware he'd been a thief (nicknamed, of course, the "Yid"), notorious for his audacity and his eloquence, whenever thieves' gatherings took place.

In 1958 he decided to leave the "punishment camp"[1] and join up with "Snubnose" and "Ultra", both of whom had once been "big shots" in the underworld and were not the type that you were likely to get much change from. Then they did something that went against thieves' etiquette—(I remember Snubnose had spent their loot and tried to save himself from their swift vengeance by splitting open the head of the assistant governor of the camp and being kept in the punishment block under surveillance)—they decided to change their "colours" and become politicals. Several months preceding this decision they had found in the forest, where they were supposed to be working, several NTS[2] leaflets, and made a fat profit out of them. Every now and then they would find a new leaflet and sell it to the KGB for a quarter-bottle of vodka or a packet of tea. Now, they say, they have long had connections with the NTS, but refused to discuss them (and not surprisingly—they know nothing whatsoever about it!).

Previously, any contributions, however nonsensical, about "links" with the NTS were gratefully received. After the 20th Congress the position of the KGB was precarious and it had to cling fast to anything at all that looked like counter-revolution, to prove not only how essential it was to the well-being of the Soviet Government (this was beyond dispute!)

[1] Now obsolete.

[2] Popular Labour Alliance (Russian emigré party, based in Frankfurt and Paris).

but how necessary it was to increase its staff, its subsidies and its powers, and to demonstrate how completely unfounded was the fastidiousness sometimes shown by the public in relation to old workers in the Beria apparatus.

Berger is 48, stockily built, robust, talkative. He cleans his shoes 10 times a day until they gleam, is constantly to be seen sweeping the floor with a broom, never stops fussing about, and is always ready for a fight, despite his years.

17th June

A few particulars about the special regime camp at different periods in history:

1964

1. General number of prisoners: about 450.
2. Type of prisoner: 50% ex-criminals, 15% political, 30% wartime collaborators and 5% under Art. 58.
3. Number per cell: 12–15.
4. Soup: couldn't be worse.
5. Monthly purchases in the camp shop: for three roubles— tobacco, toothpaste, soap, cigarettes and shoe polish.
6. Hunger: a beating for stealing rations (sometimes fatal).
7. Visits: four hours per year.
8. Work: enough to go to working zone, so as not to be labelled a "refusal".
9. Stool-pigeons: were beaten.
10. Atmosphere: a spirit of disobedience, rebelliousness and summonses to governor.

1971

1. About 130.
2. 50% ex-criminals, 10% politicals, 35% collaborators, and 5% Art. 58.

3. 4–7.
4. Simply bad.
5. For four roubles—sweets, biscuits, apple jam, vegetable fat.
6. Sufficient bread, but there's no convict who wouldn't, at any time of the day or night, finish off in one swallow, for example, a pound of sausage, however mouldy.
7. Up to three days if there are relations.
8. 100% necessary, or it's the punishment block.
9. Respected and untouchable.
10. Spiritual exhaustion, humility and obsequiousness.

2000 (Not quite Orwellian Communism)

1. Five people.
2. One Jehovah's Witness, One Orthodox Tikhonovite, Three traitors—Fedorov, Murzhenko, Kuznetsov.
3. Five plus t.v. screen, loudspeaker, without off-switch and a bookshelf with latest *Ogoniok* magazine.
4. Excellent, but extremely synthetic.
5. No longer exist (due to liquidation of monetary-trading system).
6. Spiritual only, but making itself felt only at rare moments, when the electronic supervisors of the spiritual-psychological state of mind of the prisoners are non-functioning.
7. None to see: all family and friends long ago rejected us and swore oath of allegiance.
8. As a punishment for non-creative attitude to heavy physical labour (only that which reforms political prisoners—see commentary to speech of General Secretary Savaofev, given a triumphant meeting dedicated to the 40th anniversary of Khrushchev's public statement that we have no political prisoners,) a six-hour lecture on the theme: "Labour has Created a Communist out of a Monkey".
9. Unnecessary—live electrodes, inserted into the brain, transmit all necessary information to the camp detective.

10. Difficult to come to any definite conclusion, but euphoria reigns, of course, ("frame of mind" is that sphere of the spiritual life of the "New Man", which most easily yields to manipulation).

18th June

In 1963 my blue-shouldered guardian at the time, Captain Garushkin, called me to his office on the first day of this chequered period of my life and told me that every one of us in the camp was the vile enemy of the Soviet state; the people demand that we be annihilated and what was a matter of a couple of weeks in the punishment cell in any other camp, here would mean the firing squad under Art. 77-1, which had been created specially for convicts like us.

Prisoners were indeed shot frequently for many reasons, but most of all for cutting their ears off (particularly if they tattooed on them something like, "A gift to the Congress!") and for facial tattoos. In 1963 alone nine people were shot for tattooing themselves. The local radio announced frequently that our education was making excellent progress; it went something like this:

"At the special regime camp in the Urals two prisoners, Ivanov and Sidorov, placed tattoo marks of an anti-Soviet nature on their faces. They were sentenced under Art. 77-1, Criminal Code of the RSFSR, to the supreme measure of punishment. The sentence was duly carried out."

Convicts tattoo all sorts of things on their foreheads, their chins, cheeks and even necks, e.g. "CPSU Slave!" "Bolsheviks give me bread!" "Bread and Freedom!" "Down with the Dictator and Murderer" (usually Khrushchev, Brezhnev, etc. but sometimes the governor of the camp or even the doctors). "Down with the Soviet Buchenwald!" "Death to the Tyrants and Dictators!" "Soviets without Bolsheviks!" "Death to the Jew-Bolsheviks!" and so on and so forth. One man even tattooed several lines of verse on his right cheek, as far as I remember:

"I'm not scared of Khrushchev,
And Furtseva is my wife,
I can't wait to sleep with her,
And live my Marxist life."

Here is Art. 77-1 under which men were tried for tattooing not all that long ago: "Specially dangerous recidivists and those convicted of serious crimes, who terrorize in places of confinement prisoners who have begun to reform, or who assault the administration or who organize for such purposes criminal factions or who actively participate in such factions are punishable by confinement for a period of eight to 15 years or by death."

Although on page 178 of the four-volumed "Course of Soviet Criminal Law" (Moscow, "Nauka", 1970) it says that, "Refusal or disinclination to work in places of confinement and tattooing with tattoos of an anti-Soviet nature may be considered neither terrorization nor an attack on the administration, and therefore do not come within the sphere of Art. 77-1, Criminal Code of the RSFSR," Berger and a good dozen others condemned under the Article for tattooing (either themselves or others) are always given this stereotyped answer every time they complain: "You have been correctly convicted; there are no grounds for reviewing your case."

It's very difficult to get hold of any books here. The library is very poor and we are very limited as to what we can receive through the "post". I swapped my fountain pen for Berger's fourth volume of the "Course", which he only agreed to part with after Captain Vorobiov, to whom he showed the above quotation from (Art. 77-1), made fun of him: "I'm surprised at you, Berger—reading all this rubbish and actually believing it!"

Here is the sentence in Berger's last trial. I have retained its stylistic and orthographic originality: "In the name of the RSFSR, the Judicial Board on Criminal Cases of the Supreme Court of the Mordovian Autonomous Soviet Socialist Republic, composition: President: Kott, People's Assessors Mardakina and Shagneva . . .

Having reviewed in open session in Yavas Settlement, MASSR, on the 15th–16th August, 1963 convictions against: Leizer Niselevich Berger, alias Gert Khasifovich Kolodiozh, born 1922, native of Kishinev, employee, of Jewish nationality, bachelor with secondary education, formerly convicted: 28th May, 1948, under Art. 1-1, Decree of 4th June, 1947, to six years' deprivation of freedom; 22nd August, 1950, under Art. 142-2, CC RSFSR, to 10 years' deprivation of freedom; 14th January, 1956 under Art. 1-2, Decree of 4th June, 1947, and Art. 70, CC RSFSR, jointly to 10 years' deprivation of freedom . . . Nikolai Ivanovich Nefedov, born 1924, native of Naroforminsk, Russian, with fourth form education, bachelor, formerly convicted: 3rd October, 1940 under Art. 74-2, CC RSFSR, to three years deprivation of freedom; 23rd September, 1941 under Art. 58-10 (1), CC RSFSR, to 10 years' deprivation of freedom; 26th September, 1944 under Art. 168, CC RSFSR, to two years deprivation of freedom; 20th May, 1947 under Art. 168-1, CC RSFSR, to six months' deprivation of freedom . . .

The Judicial Board finds: that the accused, Nefedov and Berger, alias Kolodiozh, convicted on several occasions for various crimes, including crimes against the State, and serving their punishments in places of deprivation of freedom, have not shown themselves in any positive light. Over a long period of time they have maliciously infringed the regime of places of confinement, refused to carry out reasonable physical work and continuously led a parasitical way of life . . .

Thus, the aforesaid Nefodov, leading a parasitical way of

life, and refusing to carry out physical work on more than one occasion, perpetrated on visible parts of his body tattoos of a cynical and anti-Soviet nature . . .

On the 23rd March, 1963 in cell no. 32, Nefedov once more perpetrated on himself a tattoo of an anti-Soviet nature and did defame one of the most prominent leaders of the Communist Party ("Khrushchev, we want bread!" "Down with Khrushchevian Democracy!"—E.K.) and of the Soviet Government, as well as a tattoo calling for the overthrow of the social and political order of our country ("Down with the Sovient Buchenwald!"—E.K.) The tattoos of anti-Soviet character on the face of Nefedov have been preserved until the present time.

In addition to this Nefedov, being in places of confinement, wrote many letters and declarations to Soviet Party organs of uncensored and cynical context, which bear witness to his apparent disrespect for the social and political order of our country and his refusal to engage in socially productive labour.

The aforesaid Berger, alias Kolodiozh, being of hostile disposition to the camp authorities and to measures taken by the Party and Government to re-educate convicted citizens, flagrantly disregarded the regulations in places of confinement, provoking prisoners to resist the administration of the camp in its re-educative and corrective work . . .

The sentence of the Judicial Board is as follows: that Nefedov and Berger, alias Kolodiozh, be found guilty and punished under Art. 14-1, USSR Code of 25th December, 1958 (Art. 77–1 CC RSFSR) . . .

Nefedov to receive the supreme measure of punishment— execution by firing squad (he has been shot—E.K.); Berger to receive 13 years deprivation of freedom, the first three years of which to be served in prison, and the remainder in a special regime corrective labour colony, inclusive of the addition of that part of the previous sentence left unserved to the present sentence—15 years deprivation of freedom.

I have many times witnessed some of the most fantastic in-
cidences of self-mutilation. I have seen convicts swallow huge
numbers of nails and quantities of barbed wire; I have seen
them swallow mercury thermometers, pewter tureens (after
first breaking them up into "edible" proportions), chess
pieces, dominoes, needles, ground glass, spoons, knives and
many other similar objects; I have seen convicts sew up their
mouths and eyes with thread or wire; sew rows of buttons to
their bodies; or nail their testicles to a bed, swallow a nail
bent like a hook, and then attach this hook to the door by way
of a thread so that the door cannot be opened without pulling
the "fish" inside out. I have seen convicts cut open the skin on
their arms and legs and peel it off as if it were a stocking; or
cut out lumps of flesh (from their stomach or their legs), roast
them and eat them; or let the blood drip from a slit vein into
a tureen, crumble bread crumbs into it, and then gulp it down
like a bowl of soup; or cover themselves with paper and set
fire to themselves; or cut off their fingers, or their nose, or
ears, or penis . . .

Strangely enough, when you are in close proximity to them,
none of these bloody deeds horrifies you so much as they would
were they narrated by a "Samizdat" (underground) writer,
seething in righteous indignation. Taken out of their prison
context, and their everyday varnish removed, the self-muti-
lators are a symbol of courage, their reward the halo of martyr-
dom. They are the tragic victims of the regime, its hunted and
its persecuted, those who have been reduced to the ultimate
despair. Having tried all other forms of protest against the
lawlessness and caprice of the prison and all other authorities,
they have finally resorted to self-mutilation. They are one-
dimensional martyrs, pathetic cardboard figures. With only
rare exceptions, self-multilation is not a form of protest (in
a conscious sense, that is) but an attempt to "carve a slice out
of life"; to get into the hospital where the nurses swing their
hips, where you get your hospital ration and you're not forced

to work, where you can get drugs, diets, postcards, meetings with "penfriends". Many of these people are masochists, in a permanent state of depression from one blood-letting to the next. Many of them display symptoms of degeneracy (the pain-resistant level of their skin, for example, is lower than the normal).

To be quite honest, I'm not certain whether the fact that most of them have aggressive and predatory natures contradicts in any way the psychological make-up of the masochist. As the destructive element within them boils over in a rage of impotence, and is transformed into fits of hatred and feverish dreams of revenge on the prison governor, as soon as they realize they can't get their teeth into his throat, they finally turn on themselves.

Thus, self-mutilation begins and ends as a dire necessity and, like fits of hysteria, finds its outlet at that precise moment most suitable for carving the "slice out of life". This is the beginning and the end, yet there is also a middle, spread out over a period of years, which many never manage to leave behind them. Those that remain in this "middle" state still have not thought of the advantages of blood-letting; self-mutilation in their case takes the form of a fit. For example, if a self-mutilator in this category receives an unfavourable answer to his request, "You gave everybody a pair of shoes except me: Please give me a pair of shoes too!", he will brood for a week, store up all his anger inside him, and then announce to all and sundry, "I demand that the USSR Constitution be changed", and, as if in order to support this demand, he swallows a couple of spoons. Then they have to slit his stomach open and extract them; but hardly is he down from the operating-table, then he swallows a thermometer, and this state of affairs continues till he gets his new shoes.

21st June

Still on the subject of self-mutilation. For the most part this type of person is not only illiterate, but ill-disposed to any-thing that bears no relationship to his particular form of savagery. It is not surprising that the self-mutilator is most often encountered in prison, or in the punishment cell on special regime, rather than in the open spaces of the camp, with all its cliques and factions, its card games, its drugs and its "extravaganza". The four walls of a cell are an intolerable burden to the extrovert for he is incessantly tortured by the fear that his life is slipping by slowly but steadily, and this thought is worse than any other for the convict. He spends his days dreaming in his cell, still young and agile and energetic, he feels he could achieve whatever he set his mind to . . . But his life is going by, 10 years already, 15 years to go, no hope, no one notices him, it's almost as if he didn't exist: "Guard!" he hammers with his bony knuckles on the food-hatch, "give me a needle, I have to sew my shirt." "Not allowed!" again the pacing up and down the cell, hands behind his back, his eye-balls dilated and biting his lips. "Guard!" he drums on the door, "just go to the cell next door for me—Ivanov owes me an envelope, I've got to send my mother a letter . . .!" "Not allowed!" the same dull, mechanical voice in reply. A few minutes later "Guard! go and get me some tobacco, I've nothing to smoke." "Not allowed!" He rushes to the door, "Call the doctor! To hell with your 'not allowed'!" Then he slits a vein open—and, at last he's the centre of attraction: the doctor comes, a stretcher's brought for him . . . at last he's living! He's the centre of attention, a human being that has to be reckoned with, sworn at, beaten, cured. (In fact, for the last seven or eight years anyone who slits a vein open has gone to the punishment cell after treatment instead of to the hospital, and can now be convicted under that same Art. 77–1.)

Only on the rare occasion is self-mutilation a conscious protest, whether directed against the spirit of lawlessness and capriciousness that prevails in the prison-camp atmosphere, or against a specific injustice. Generally speaking, nearly every infringement of the regime is a form of protest, some-

171

times savage or hideous, it's true, but no more so than that against which it is directed.

Life is easier for the introvert who never feels quite so oppressed by the walls of his cell. Not everybody can raise himself above the level of each insult he receives, not everybody can protest and yet at the same time preserve his human dignity. However trivial or ridiculous a man's reason for rebelling, it is the years of continual oppression, the incessant trampling over his personality that lie at its basis. I can see this clearly from the view-point of someone who craves for silence and who loves books, as if this were the only possible point of view. If you are compelled to live amongst other people, unpleasantness—to put it mildly—is bound to exist. Meet a man outside once a week and you're friends, but in a cell that man is your worst enemy, more dreadful even than the Chekist, for the Chekist you do not see nearly so often, and your cell-mate is there every second of every day.

Watch him, pacing the cell muttering under his breath, "Right, you Bolsheviks, I'll show you!. . . I'll show you!. . ." Watch him make a rope out of his sheet: "Well," he says, speaking to no one in particular but to everyone in general, "I'll show you, I'll show you! . . ." Watch him fasten his rope to the window-bars, pin his ear to the door and wait till he hears the guard coming—and then quick, before the peephole opens, put the noose round his neck and jump off his bed hoping the guard will come in time to save him! And what if the guard doesn't look through the peephole? *You* sit there quietly, watching him and thinking, "For God's sake, you bastard, hang yourself and have done with it!"

22nd June

. . . I could shed a tear of sympathy for martyrs only from a good, long-and abstract-distance. But when I'm with them . . . I cannot forget the triviality, the vileness, of their objectives!

But It's not this alone: the great majority of prisoners are only the inadvertent victims of the regime, the flesh of its flesh; they do not basically oppose it. They have been ruled by circumstance. They could have been guards but they became prisoners. When the guards torment them they look for someone who's weaker than themselves; the law of the jungle all over again. Should you help a man who is weak, if only yesterday he was persecuting someone even weaker than himself? They're like wild animals, these people . . . if only I could be on the other side of those bars, like in the zoo! But there's nothing to enjoy here! God preserve me from ever making a martyr of anyone! You can't help feeling sympathetic all the same, you try and help him, and hope you can tame him . . . but you never can, all you are doing is deceiving yourself . . . You never know what may happen tomorrow; reality is today. If you cannot play your part in the search for universal happiness, then at least be content with seeking your own.

God! It's nearly time for lights-out, and I haven't finished yet. There's so little time. I've neither the time nor the energy to work out a schedule for writing—I just write what I can in fits and starts, hoping they don't see me. Self-mutilation is not a simple subject, I must return to it later.

If[1] a man cuts a piece out of his own flesh, why not cut a piece out of his enemies too? He cannot or does not. It in no way exculpates the guards, but if you are bitten by a dog you have not the right to crouch on all fours and bite it back—there are more civilized ways; conditions which encourage the basest instincts; the Chinese way: to put some shit in your mouth and spit it in your enemy's face.

I remember a conversation, in 1969, with a young girl who worshipped the "Christian-Democrat Führer," Ogurtsov, with whom I had shared a cell in Vladimir:

"How did you get on with him?" she asked me.

"All right, I suppose; we nearly came to blows once or twice, but we parted on good terms, I suppose."

[1] Kuznetsov's thoughts here are disjointed.

"Surely your ideological differences weren't as keen as all that?"

"What ideological differences? Once we argued because of a bit of tobacco, and the other time because of the slop-bucket!"

Here, in a nutshell, is the principal unnaturalness of life: resentment at the unapproachability of those who occupy high positions of power. Briukhovetsky, who once set fire to himself, now works as a fireman in zone 3. Did something like this happen in Germany: didn't Hitler appoint someone who did something similar as fire chief?

In the camp you see things differently: the fact that consumer goods, which were once the prerogative of the Party elite, are now accessible to the masses, does not mean that inequality no longer exists. It means that the Soviet man-in-the-street is merely participating in a scheme whereby the prerogatives of the elite are subtly disguised by the stabilization of the regime.

27th June

A couple of days ago I was taken straight from work to the camp governor's office where I found before me the KGB vice-president, Mordovian ASSR, Lieutenant-Colonel Blinov —a thickset man with blue eyes—seated awkwardly and sternly behind a desk. There were three others with him all dressed in civilian clothes, but nowhere near as 'impressive' as Blinov himself.

When Blinov told me to speak about our case I refused. If you wish, you can find out about it through the official channels, I said. When he started telling me the usual about Russia being my homeland, I cut him off somewhat sharply. Israel, I said, was my homeland; the USSR was only a prison, so far as I was concerned. They tried to make me feel ashamed of not wanting to remain in Russia, and when this failed, asked me what nationality Yurka and Alik were: "You know very well what their nationality is, but you ordered your men—

174

convicts and police alike—to spread the rumour that they were Jews. Now they're 'yids' like me, with all the consequences that entails!" The KGB are so well-schooled these days. Even five years ago Blinov would have threatened me, "If only this were 1950 . . .!" Now you can only see it in his eyes. What will happen tomorrow, I wonder?

29th June

I am trying to collect information little by little about special regime prisoners. I thought of compiling a questionaire with 95 questions, but I realized how unrealistic this was. I couldn't even ask two consecutive questions here—they'd either threaten to expose me, or inform on me.

I'll keep to a dozen basic questions, which they could answer, I think, relatively safely (. . . I'll put this off for the time being, it's going to take too long).

Pity the authorities don't print their "mass" circulation "For Distinguished Toil" newspaper any more. They stopped bringing it out last year. A most curious thing, it was. From under that incredibly primitive, coarse and quite naive rubbish there were so many corners sticking out! Wasn't this what prompted some well-trained ideological checker from the capital to shut it down? When I was still at the "Mansion", I singled it out for special content analysis—the ridiculous views of the editors and correspondents about national, social and spiritual questions, what makes the good and bad convict etc.

1st July

I wrote Sylva a letter. But I've no means of knowing whether she will ever get it, as I don't know whether she's come to Mordovia or not.

I started working on the presses today, the hardest work you can do here. I tried to get out of it by saying I was short-sighted but might as well have saved my breath. I found out the authorities have been ordered to use me on the hardest jobs from now on.

The presses are antediluvian, the norms incredible; I'm not surprised a good dozen convicts have lost their hands over the last two years.

Special arrangments have been made for the three of us: every step we take is watched closely, and each of us has had 10 or so informers attached to us. It's no easy task to distinguish spitefulness from provocation. We will have to find ways of being careful which will not be construed as weakness, or we'll be in trouble: we're not exactly surrounded by well-wishers here.

5th July

When Berger describes his exploits in the underworld, he shouts enough to set the window-panes rattling. He rages most violently when he relates his trial in 1962: "Who were the witnesses? One of them was a wartime collaborator, another a homosexual, and a third a camp detective informer—and all of them bloody anti-semites! They'd had the Jews stuck in their throats for a hundred years! They call Mogila as a witness: Well, I think to myself, is it more than six months ago since I saved you from Hitler,[1] you bastard? (He'd been about to throw a brick at his head.) What have you been saying about me? I asked him. 'Let me never see freedom again, if I'm lying to you!' he says. The Procurator reads out his evidence: he'd been terrorizing, cutting ears off, inciting rebellion, etc., but Mogila denied it all, every last word of it. The judge had nearly broken him down when I spoke up. 'What do you want —another Beilis[2] trial? What are you trying to do—make a ritual murder out of it? I don't eat Christian ears! Do you understand? You'll never succeed. You can kill a hundred Nefedov's but you'll never get Berger!' 'Be quiet, Berger,'

[1] Underworld nickname.

[2] A reference to the notorious pre-revolutionary antisemitic trial.

the judge says, 'keep quiet', then he asked Mogila, 'Have you known him long?' He answers, 'Yes, I have'. "And what sort of person would you say Berger used to be?'. 'What can I say to you, esteemed citizen judge', says Mogila, 'you were never so afraid of Stalin as you were of Berger—at Dergachka, for example. There his word was law!' " . . .

15th July

I saw Lucia and Viktor[1] yesterday. All I had with Viktor was a 20-minute meeting. They tricked me as usual; they told me I could have four hours with Lucia, and then cut the time by half without warning me. Pure provocation! And they wouldn't even let me have a packet of cigarettes.

Today they took me straight from work to the governor's office. There were two men in civilian clothes there, one of whom was Major Lesnikov, the chief of the Leningrad investigators' group that had looked into our case. Same thing again: feeling their way, promises, threats, "Why did you steal two hours of my meeting yesterday," I asked them, "did you run out of tape?" "No, not at all, we've plenty of tape. You can count it as, shall we say, a little hint: behave yourself and you can have what you like." "What do you want me to do," I said, "collaborate with you or—perhaps you'd like me to reveal the full story in 'Izvestia'!" "Why not?" he smiled gently. I remembered my cell-mates would just be brewing some tea at this moment; if I weren't there, I wouldn't get any. "Well, I must be off now," I said, "My work won't wait for me." "Well, then?" the major wanted an answer. I had learned that if you give a direct "no" to a Chekist he'll lose patience and stop trying to win you over. Being delicate or ambiguous was of no use. "I don't know," I answered, "Whether it's true or not, what the Czechs used to say, "Even if they try and fuck us to death, we'll still never sign!" but for the next 15 years this is going to be my motto!" Then I left.

[1] Victor Khaustov, close friend of Kuznetsov.

When I left work this evening I went to see Kolgatin voluntarily. This was our conversation:

E.K.: Why did they give me four hours at first, and then . . .?

Kol.: I gave you two hours right from the start.

E.K.: The duty officer said four.

Kol.: I don't know anything about that.

E.K.: Why two and not four? I have no penalties as yet.

Kol.: Your behaviour has not been exactly outstanding, has it?

E.K.: You must give me some encouragement when I deserve it. A four-hour meeting is provided for by law and it can only be reduced as a punishment. What had I done then? Don't you like my face, or rather, "the colour of my skin"?

Kol.: I could give you two weeks in a punishment cell for daring to speak to me like that.

E.K.: (as clearly and assertively as possible) Just you remember, one more provocation like that, and you'll regret it, even if they kill me for it!

I expected him to press the button under his desk and to be dragged off to the punishment block, but he seemed taken aback. He rolled his eyes and said it wasn't him but orders from above.

The administration still cannot find the correct tone to take with us. They are prevented from doing so by the amount of fuss which has been raised by our case and the constant flitting to and fro of the boys in blue. It's very curious, but they (the administration) are sometimes misinformed intentionally. They have been told, for example, that we had links with the CIA and Shin Bet (Israeli Security Service), and that six people were shot when we tried our abortive hijack. And not long ago an article about us, published in the MVD magazine, "Towards A New Life", was read out over the local radio. Pure fiction—all of it!

20th July

According to a law passed in 1969, convicts who have served a third of their term, must be kept in normal (i.e. open) barracks, and not in cells. When Berger asked him, at work today why this law was being broken, Kolgatin said ours was a special regime camp, and we had our own laws. Rudenko[1] himself knew about it, he said, so everything was all right (!)

31st July

I'm finding it more and more difficult to write, I get so tired. Every day I have minor problems to solve. Even if I manage to solve them it doesn't make much difference and it tires me out just the same. If I fail, though, the results can be painful. Here's a typical example:

Someone told Repeikin (who, he won't say) that I was out to give him a beating (though why, he didn't know). In fact, I didn't even know who he was until I was asked why I wanted him. I went along to see my "victim" but my little bird had flown!

In the evening Vorobiov said he would put me in solitary if I should even dare to go anywhere near Repeikin again. Nobody will believe me when I tell them how ridiculous it is. The only time they listen to you is if you give them some information: anything else and they don't want to know!

6th August

Summoned by KGB Captain Kochetkov. Obviously in connection with yesterday's conversation of his with Alik. In an attempt to win Alik's confidence he had tried flattery: why should you, a Ukrainian, have anything to do with Jews, he asked. Then he promised him early release (in eight years time.) Yurka and I, he said, had long since offered to collaborate,

---

[1] USSR Procurator-General. Was chief Soviet prosecutor at Nuremburg trials.

but he had refused since we weren't dependable enough. Finally he had threatened to compromise him; but when even this didn't produce the desired effect, he said he would see to it that Alik got a further sentence. Alik had lost his temper completely: I've nothing to lose, he said, and if he had to drown he was quite capable of taking the KBG man down with him as well. I could see Kochetkov wanted to find out whether Alik had told us about this conversation:

Koch: What are all these protests of yours for?

E.K.: What are you talking about?

Koch: Your statement that your letters are being confiscated.

E.K.: Confiscation of letters, as you know very well, is quite illegal. This administration has a xenophobic complex: as soon as they see a foreign word, they think God knows what! . . .

Koch: You can tell Murzhenko I have forgotten all about his threats. We both got a bit excited, that's all . . .

E.K.: Why did you try and win him over like that?

Koch: What do you mean? Would you say I'd been trying to win *you* over?

E.K.: No, why should you? I never offered to help you either. Or did you forget to tell Murzhenko that?

Koch: What an imagination you have! What should I need you for? You've both got specific sentences to serve—I'd only be making difficulties for myself if I had anything to do with you.

E.K.: It's the other way round; I should have thought a long sentence was a guarantee of faithful service.

Koch: Not always. You'll soon be exposed and then you'll be an albatross round our neck: you'll start asking for privileges, clemency etc. and you won't be any good to us.

E.K.: That's not much of a threat.

Koch:	Don't be so clever! I could make things very hard for you.
E.K.:	How?
Koch:	I could have you brought to my office every day, and everybody would think you were an informer.
E.K.:	Is that all?
Koch:	I could put your name down on the list for strict regime. And since you've nowhere near done even half your sentence everybody would think you were collaborating with me.
E.K.:	My friends wouldn't believe it, and what the rest think doesn't interest me. It might even be for the better. In the camp even suspected collaboration can protect a man from many unpleasant things. So go ahead. Just as a matter of interest, how do you reconcile these methods of yours with the law?
Koch:	The law is the law and life is life. Dialectics! Sometimes you have to step back from the law to observe it all the better. You're on special here. This is not a corrective but a punitive institution. Our job is to bend you, till you're like putty in our hands. Do you understand?

11th August

We have decided to appeal to U Thant, using the draft I've prepared. It's quite possible U Thant will soon no longer be UN secretary general, and there'd be no point in addressing the secretary general personally. But this is unimportant. Here is the text of our "appeal", signed Fedorov, Murzhenko and myself:

To The General Secretary of the UN—U Thant   An Appeal

(Epigraph: "Whereas it is essential, if man is not to be compelled to have recourse, as a last resort, to rebellion against tyranny and oppression, that human rights should be protected by the rule of law ... Article 13–1—Everyone has the right to freedom of movement and residence within the borders of each state; Article 13–2—Everyone has the right to leave any country, including his own, and to return to his country; Article 14–1—Everyone has the right to see and to enjoy in other countries asylum from persecution. Article 15–2—None shall be arbitrarily deprived of his nationality nor denied the right to change his nationality; Article 19—Everyone has the right to freedom of opinion and expression; this right includes freedom to hold opinions without interference and to seek, receive and impart information and ideas through any media and regardless of frontiers."—"Universal Declaration of Human Rights.")

Dear Mr. U Thant,

We have taken the liberty of addressing several questions to you, the answers to which are to us a matter of life and death. We are, of course appealing to you not as a private person, but as a man who heads an organization, the aims and principles of which are very close to our hearts, and as a man who, in great measure, symbolizes for us the United Nations Organization. However, we ask you to examine our situation not only as the Head of the UN, not only as a man who has access to full and adequate information on those questions which concern us, but also as a human being. It is with the hope that you will understand the specific situation in which we find outselves, that we preferred to appeal not to any impersonal organization but to yourself.

Had we the slightest hope of an objective reaction on the part of the Soviet authorities in question or the slightest possibility of obtaining the information we seek from specialized literature, you may be sure, we would not have been so bold as to trouble you. Unfortunately, the Soviet authorities in question do not spare us their attention; at best, they entrust some semi-literate camp commander to carry out "educational-explanatory work" with us; whereas access to literature is strictly limited (Soviet, that is, for there can be no question—God forbid!—of access to Western literature, or to anything published in the so-called "popular democratic" countries).

We are; Edward Samuilovich Kuznetsov, a Jew, 32 years of age who, in 1968, finished serving a seven-year sentence of imprisonment for so-called "anti-Soviet activities" and was sentenced in 1970 to 15 years imprisonment by the Leningrad City Court for attempting to betray my homeland by crossing the frontier illegally; to 15 years imprisonment for organizational activities; to 15 years imprisonment for misappropriating government property of "particularly large dimensions" (i.e. an aeroplane); to 10 years for duplicating (in 2 copies), preserving and disemminating the "Memoirs" of Litvinov; to 10 years for duplicating (in 1 copy) preserving and disseminating, with the aim of weakening the Soviet régime, the book "Russian Political Leaders" by Shub; Aleksei Grigorevich Murzhenko, a Ukrainian, born 1942, freed in 1968 after serving a six-year term of imprisonment for anti-Soviet activities, and sentenced in 1970 to 14 years by the Leningrad City Court for attempted treason; Yuri Pavlovich Federov, a Russian, 28 years old, freed in 1965 after 3½ years imprisonment for anti-Soviet activities, sentenced in 1970 by the Leningrad City Court to 15 years for treason, 15 years for organizational activities and 15 years for attempting to expropriate an aeroplane. We are considered especially dangerous recidivists and are being held in a special regime camp.

During the trial we did not admit that we were guilty of the accusations made against us, although an article was printed in the Soviet press in which it was claimed that we had done so ("Izvestia" 1st January, 1971); and we now declare that we were tried for crimes which we not only did not commit, but did not even intend to commit. We are the victims of an intentionally broadened interpretation of the meaning of treason—an illegal politico-judicial device clearly condemned by the 1946 Nuremburg Trials—and of the illegal application of an article analogous to our case; due to the lack of any article referring to the hijacking of aeroplanes in the Soviet legal code, we were accused of intending to misappropriate the aeroplane.

While not denying the acts of which we are accused we consider they have been erroneously defined; we maintain that we are guilty of attempting to hijack an aeroplane, and not of attempting to misappropriate it, nor do we admit that we are guilty of betraying our country, but only of attempting illegally to escape abroad.

Mr. U Thant, the following questions worry us most profoundly; despite the fact that the text of the "Universal Declaration of Human Rights", or for that matter, of the Bible, or the Gospels, is regarded in a concentration camp as seditious material, we have dared to remember much of this text by heart. In the first instance Articles 13, 14 and 15. Magnificent words, great promises, a source of the brightest hopes! . . . Please tell us, does not ratification of the Declaration compel a government to fulfil its articles in practice? In what way does a government which has ratified the Declaration, guarantee that its provisions will be put into effect in reality? And how can that government be made to account for any constant infringements of any of the Articles of the Declaration, which have become an element of its policy? And most important of all, what is a man to do, when his rights are flouted continually over a period of many years, and when there is not the slightest hope of these rights being realized? Where can he turn to, and can he count on any active help from outside, if his interests as a man clash with those of the state to which he belongs?

Mr. U Thant, we have in mind an entirely concrete territorial-political context, and therefore advice to appeal to a court to solve the conflict between the state and a personality is unacceptable . . . It is unthinkable—particularly if at the basis of such a conflict there is at the very least the appearance of political undertones.

Imagine, Mr. U Thant, the situation of a man (or better

still, of a group of people) who, for whatever reason—not necessarily because he is fleeing from punishment for a crime, not even because he fears the opposition of the ruling party— wishes to leave for another country. He is no longer so naive as to take seriously newspaper prattle about freedom, but he sincerely expects he will be able to share in the benefits proclaimed by the Declaration, indeed, his very life would be a burden to him if he has not the opportunity of exercising these rights. So, imagine the position of such a man, if he has no recourse to legal emigration. He has no access either to military or to any other secrets, neither is he a scientist or politician of any description, who might wish to desert to the camp of the enemies of Socialism. What can he do, if life in the country in which he was born, (whether for real or imagined reasons) is like life in a hard-labour camp, if emigration is for him not the whim of one seeking the exoticism of foreign lands, and if the right to leave his country is more important to him than all other rights? Is he not likely to consider himself a slave, if he is deprived of this right? What can he do if he *knows* he will *never* be able to leave the confines of his country, which has for whatever reasons grown so hateful to him, that he will *never* become a citizen of a state freely chosen by him according to his personal taste or national sympathies, that he is condemned until the end of his life never to know of a life which is not full of concentration camps, and not to know what it's like to speak aloud his convictions?

Imagine, Mr. U Thant, the position of such a man and perhaps you will understand why he decided to commit such a completely reprehensible act as the hijacking of an aeroplane; reprehensible even in his view, but chosen by him only as an exceptional measure, and in no way a normal way out of a situation of conflict.

Having decided to hijack an aeroplane we were prepared to accept the whole burden of responsibility for our action. But *only* for our action, and not for what was attributed to us. . . . Escape abroad was for us the only means of achieving a worthwhile existence as we understood it. We are prepared to stand trial for hijacking, to stand trial in any country in which a man is not compelled to remain for ever in the place of his birth; however severely they might see fit to punish us, we would know that, after serving our term, we would never again have to bang our heads against the stone wall separating us from a world of free choice.

What are they to do whose whole world has been stolen from them, and who, having attempted to escape, are condemned to a long term of imprisonment knowing as they do, in all certainty that, even when they are released from prison, they will not be allowed the opportunity of leaving the country that has tortured them?

What *can* a man do, who does not wish to remain a citizen of this or any other state, that forcibly compels him to remain such, and is compelled to submit to a way of life which for him—who desires an ethical-political life, fashioned by the democratic thought of civilized humanity—is unacceptable?

In Article 29 of the Declaration it says that the implementation of the rights and liberties of a man "must in no way contradict the aims and principles of the UN". Into this category, of course, also falls the special resolution of the 25th November, 1970, adopted by the 25th Session of the General Assembly of the UN, concerning the hijacking of planes.

Unfortunately, we have the opportunity of acquainting ourselves with the resolution only according to the incomplete statement of it in the Soviet press. Is there not one word in the resolution about one of the most active means of combating hijacking? I refer, in fact, to compelling the UN member-states to put into effect Article 13 of the Declaration of Human Rights. Does this resolution not admit that people, organizations or governments which stand in the way of free emigration, are responsible for individual cases of hijacking?

Of course, however much circumstances may provoke a man to commit a crime, his guilt is not thereby removed.

However, a portion of it—and, in your case, a substantial one—rests on these very circumstances. An attempt to hijack an aircraft, indeed at the very time when the UN was appealing for the struggle against air piracy to be strengthened, is, evidently, to oppose the "aims and principles" of the UN Article 29 of the Declaration unambiguously condemns such actions. But there is another point of view in the same Declaration—paragraph 2 in the preamble—in which it is admitted that the possibility may exist where a man, whose rights are continually flouted, is "compelled as a last resort to rebel against tyranny and oppression". The flouting of our human rights was not a single action and was expressed not only in our lack of opportunity to emigrate, although we are here talking of this alone. We knew that phrases like "Rot here, but don't leave", were not only the personal wishes of Soviet officials, And if "tyranny and oppression" are too harsh an expression in our case, then our attempted hijacking of an aircraft was in no way a rebellion but rather a form of suicide, a cry for help—for *not one of us, on the evening before the decisive day believed that we would be successful* yet nevertheless not one of us refused to participate in this act of desperation. The investigation and the trial confirm that this was so. It is sufficient to relate the words of Sylva Zalmanson, spoken during the trial:

"We could clearly see that we were being followed, and we realized that we would be arrested. But like the others I decided that whatever was to happen—even prison—was preferable to my former way of life."

No, for us emigration was no sudden whim . . .

How can it be explained that, after our act of desperation, the number of Soviet emigrants increased more than tenfold, whereas the average age of the emigrants was sharply reduced, as was the percentage of the old and infirm? Is this not a tacit admission, euphemistically speaking, of a volte-face on the question of Jewish repatriation and emigration in general? If this is so, then why must we, the victims of this volte-face, bear the whole burden of its consequences?

Article 14 of the Declaration speaks of the right of a man to asylum in another country. But how were we to get to this other country? And can the very intention of asking for asylum, a right spoken of directly in the Declaration, be used as proof of any anti-Soviet objectives? On this basis alone are many of us accused of betraying our homeland. And this is in time of peace!

In the terms of the 25th November Resolution are we to be held equal before the face of world public opinion with criminals really fleeing from justice, with those who have stolen planes for mercenary or terrorist purposes, those who have the opportunity without obstacles of leaving their country and returning to it, yet who still hijack aircraft?

True, the threat to the lives of the passengers and the crew of an aircraft is a very important factor in the motives of those who undertake air piracy. But in our case there was neither any threat to the lives of the passengers of the aircraft, nor to the lives of its crew.

In excerpts of the text of the November Resolution of the 25th Session of the UN General Assembly, published in "Izvestia" on 28th November, it is said that the punishment for hijacking an aircraft must be equivalent to the crime. But what are the criteria for determining this? Surely the UN knows how easily such vaguely formulated appeals can be exploited by a demagogic government. Not for nothing was our trial, initially set for the 20th November postponed until the 15th December, with a total lack of legality: the planned severity of the sentences was to be justified by a reference to the UN resolution.

In no way do we see ourselves as politicians. Not only that, we feel no vocation for political activities, we have not even the slightest interest in politics. Although we were formerly tried for so-called anti-Soviet activities, all this really meant was that we did not conceal our convictions with enough care. At the present time one of us—Kuznetsov—has twice been sentenced to 10 years for reading, duplicating and keeping two books. If, in reply to your assertion, that Article 70, RSFSR Penal Code contradicts Article 17 of the Declaration, they should answer you that Article 70 provides for punishment for especially malicious activities, the object of which is the subversion of the Soviet state, do not believe them: the books of Shub and Litvinov are widely enough known, and each person can judge for himself whether they are worth ten years' imprisonment. Two of us—Murzhenko and Federov—were found guilty not of fleeing abroad, but of treason, only because we had, in the opinion of the court, anti-Soviet convictions. The presence of such convictions in the case of Murzhenko is proved only by the fact that, having served an earlier term, he refused to work; in the case of Federov, by a note to his mother, written in 1962 when he was 18 years old.

We appreciate that you are unable to intervene directly in the internal affairs of a country, but tell us to what extent we may count—if at all—on your co-operation in demanding a review of our case, a review, the essential precondition of which must be complete publicity?

The Soviet press labelled us thieves, bandits, political criminals and even agents of the Shin Bet and CIA but said not one word about the motives behind our attempted hijacking, let alone the fact that seven out of the 12 on trial had consistently, over a period of several years, appealed to the appropriate Soviet organs to be granted visas for Israel, and maintained, of course, strict silence about the fact that the remainder could not even permit themselves such a luxury as to admit publicly that they hoped to emigrate. We, having nothing to hide, desire the utmost publicity for our trial. You may well believe us: it was not *we* who wrote on the volumes of our case material; "Top Secret".

Availing ourselves of this opportunity we would like to ask you some questions which are not directly connected with the basic theme of this letter, for we have no other person of whom we may ask them, or rather, none from whom we may receive a reply.

Do we, as prisoners, have the right (according to Soviet law as well) to reject Soviet citizenship? If so, in what manner? That is, does Article 15-2 of the Declaration apply to political prisoners? Can we, while formally remaining Soviet citizens, seek the help of a lawyer of foreign nationality, and ask him to defend us? Is it true that the Soviet Union long ago was a signatory to a convention of rules governing the treatment of political prisoners? According to the regime of the camp in which we are prisoners, we are used only for physically hard labour, our right of correspondence is limited to one letter a month, only from 1978 onwards will we be permitted—provided we display the necessary degree of humility—a five-kilo food parcel once a year; foreign literature (including the publications of socialist countries) is categorically forbidden us, whereas it is extremely difficult to receive even Soviet literature. Without further mention of the other particulars of the regime of our camp, we would like to know whether the above limitations contradict any points of the above-mentioned convention? Do we have the right to ask for help from the Red Cross? If we have, under what pretext do the appropriate Soviet authorities reject those who try to help us?

Sir, it was not idle curiosity or an excess of energy seeking an outlet which compelled us to appeal to you . . . each of us needs answers to the questions worrying him, so as to somehow carry on living, so as to comprehend as fully as possible the situation in which he finds himself, so as to resist consciously those conditions which depersonalize a man and turn him into a half-insane creature, which many of those who inhabit camps have become.

We will, of course, have to pay in full measure for the very fact that we have appealed to you: the text of this letter will be called anti-Soviet, slanderous, libellous, in respect to the present political structure of the USSR, having the aim of subverting and weakening it. Probably, we will have to stand trial once again. But if you reply to us, and make certain that your reply reaches us, then we may have only the repression of the administration to deal with.

With great respect and in anticipation . . .

Yours, etc.

How can I get this letter over the wire? That's the problem. We're watched every second. When I was in Vladimir Central, I managed to write as much as I liked and get it past the censor; but here, there seems no way—at the moment. Even if you get sent to the hospital, you can't take a scrap of paper with you.

When they free you from the camp they take every single paper and book from you beforehand and search you thoroughly. Each time you have a meeting they examine every orifice in your body before they dress you in your "household" robe.

However much the guards speculate in tea and food, the very mention of the word "papers" is enough to make them turn pale . . .

13th August

Yesterday, after dinner, I'd just flopped down on some logs hoping for a little sleep before the hooter when "X"[1] came and sat himself down next to me. He proceeded to open his heart or half of it, rather, the objective being to illuminate the darker regions in the light most advantageous to himself. Whatever connections he has with the KGB are a secret between Pulcinella and himself. His idea was to make capital for himself by offering me his services; his plan was both to supply the Chekists with false information and to report on their intentions for us. I let him finish. As soon as Sinyavsky,[2] whom

[1] Name withheld.
[2] Andrei Sinyavsky, author and intellectual, tried with Y. Daniel in 1966, sentenced to 7 years, now living in Paris.

he'd met in the hospital, had told him we were in the camp, he'd sold himself to the Cheka to help us, he said . . . (I'll never again be a cynic!) It was he who'd arranged it for Yurka and me to share a cell—together with himself and the KGB office next door! I asked him what interested the KGB; "Everything, from the people you knew outside to your personal characteristics: your habits, your personality, temperament, degree of sociability, even your dreams." "How can you help us?" I asked. "Well, first: we could get one of your enemies jailed by giving them the impression he was playing a link-role between you and the West." (Hem!) "Secondly, we could give the Cheka some false, but genuine-sounding, information which would help my mother's efforts to get me clemency; my mother is an old Communist and she knows the right people . . . but she won't do anything for me till I reform and become a "Soviet man". She'd only have anything to do with it if she heard it directly from the authorities. Then I'd be free, marry a foreigner, gain access to some embassy and steal a child, a foreign child, of course. . . . Then I'd tell them, they'd never see that child again until they let Kuznetsov, Murzhenko, and Federov go."

"Kidnapping! But where would you hide the child? This isn't America, where everyone has a private house. . . ."

"I'd find somewhere. Perhaps we could just give him a sleeping-draught. And even if the child were to die for such a cause!. . ."

Just at that moment, the guard's voice brought me back to reality.

"Why aren't you working? I'll make a note of that!"

"But, commander, you don't know how to write!" This was quite true but it made him go wild;

"Kuznetsov," he shouted, "get to work! I'll report you, you lousy intellectual!"

Still no definite conclusions about Stovbunyenko's motives. I don't know whether it's stupidity or maliciousness or amorality or some sort of morbid need for a sentimental friendship. (Last year Dinmukhammedov slit his veins and asked Stovbunyenko to make sure the doctors didn't get to him. This incident took place in a cell they call the "palace" in the hospital zone; they'd been there together and apparently become friends. If they had really wanted to bandage Dinmukhammedov's arm, Stovbunyenko wouldn't have been able to stop them, but the doctors just stood by and let him bleed to death. Stovbunyenko wasn't working for the Cheka at that time; he was romantic and loyal to the promise he'd made . . . and he may have wanted to try and make things difficult for the administration by increasing the mortality rate!)

Before going to work I went to see him and told him I wasn't prepared to play his games, neither the one with the child, nor any other. The odds were incalculable; how could I compete with the KGB, particularly as Kochetkov now had a personal hatred for me (to persecute someone as an ordinary enemy is one thing, but to persecute them as someone they think is trying to outwit them, is another) and particularly when I shy away from any commitments?

Stovbunyenko said the Cheka were trying to find ways of making me talk as much as possible, whatever I talked about. He thinks they're going to "bug" me and trump up some evidence. Difficult to say how true this is.

22nd August

Simutis gave me a copy of the declaration he sent to the Supreme Soviet last year. He wanted to see if I could suggest any ideas for a new one. He had tried, he said, to avoid anything that might be construed as anti-Soviet, but he was not prepared to distort the real reasons for there being so many Lithuanians in prison.

I have decided to copy down his declaration without asking him, because I am sure that even if the Chekists should find my papers, the declaration, which will be on its way to the Praesidium, won't be among them.

To the President of the Supreme Soviet of the USSR
From Adomas Ludwikas Simutis—Declaration

I was five years old when I was shown the corpse of my father. Half his face was swollen, blue, while the other half was covered in blood. His eyes had been gouged out. On his arms and legs the skin was white, peeling, scalded. His tongue had been bound with a piece of string. His sexual organs were crushed (I found this out later). Round him lay many other distorted corpses. I remember the sobbing of my mother and many people I didn't know. They were cursing the Bolsheviks.

I had never before heard the word "Bolsheviks". This was the first evidence life had ever provided me of their existence: the only too visible evidence was disfigured corpses and the curses I could hear all around me. The Bolsheviks were cannibals, monsters, depraved freaks of nature, the scum of humanity . . . These curses came not from propagandists, but from mothers, wives and even men, who were literally fainting from horror and grief.

This was in June 1941, after the retreat of the Red Army. I was then five years old.

I was under the banner of the anti-Soviet organization "LLKS" ("Movement of the Struggle for the Freedom of Lithuania"), not because I didn't like the ideals of socialism— I was too young to understand theories—but because the Soviets, brought into Lithuania by the Red Army, had taken the law into their own hands with those who had refused to accept their incomprehensible new order.

The LLKS saw itself as a popular and inspiring force struggling against the occupation of Lithuania by the Soviet Army and against the enforcement of the Soviet order.

The struggle was uneven and therefore cruel. It was a struggle to the death—something not new in the history of peoples. If today the partisans in Vietnam get abundant help not only from the Soviet Union, but from the Communist Parties of many other countries, then nobody from the outside world ever helped those partisans that were defending their little homeland from its mighty aggressor. Almost all the honest people in the world (if after this they could be considered honest) watched in silence as the Soviet soldier tore the Lithuanians apart.

In the five years after the War, the shooting in Lithuania never ceased, and the people's blood was shed as they groaned both under Soviets and the LLKS. But I knew that the LLKS were Lithuanians, my own people, whereas the soldiers in the Soviet army spoke in an incomprehensible, foreign, tongue. I knew there had been no revolution in Lithuania, that the Red Army had come into our country and begun to build its order without any invitation and that this was called occupation. I knew—only too well—that it was not the LLKS which had made the fight so cruel, for the LLKS did not yet exist when the Chekists were boiling the skin off my father as he lay still alive and crushing his sexual organs.

I wanted to live and study and enjoy myself. But how can you live when your neighbour has been lying dead in the street for three days and no one is allowed to bury him? . . . How can you study when now one, now another, school friend stops coming to school—when, together with their families, they have been dragged off to Siberia in boarded-up cattle trucks? . . . How can you enjoy yourself when you hear adults weeping? . . .

Here are some figures which bear witness to the fact that I do not exaggerate, nor seek to slander anyone. From June, 1944 until December, 1945, 1,067 anti-Soviet underground organizations and groups were liquidated, 839 armed groups of bandits (our partisans are called bandits) and 11,870 counter-revolutionaries (Lithuanian Communist Party Central Committee Archives, op. 1771, collection 89, page 88). Compare: "During the years of the Great War of the Fatherland 9,187 people, of whom 1,422 perished, took part in the anti-fascist underground and partisan movement." (Shtaras "The Partisan Movement in Lithuania during the Years of the

195

Great War of the Fatherland"—Candidate's dissertation, 1965, page 243.)

There beat a living heart inside me, not a stone one. I could not remain on the side-lines, I could not!

My anti-Soviet activities were honourable and unselfish. I only did that which I sincerely believed necessary or useful for the cause of the struggle with a Soviet force alien to the Lithuanian people. I never did anything for personal gain or glory. I was convinced I was fighting against injustice, and fulfilling my duty as a citizen for the sake of my homeland, my people and all mankind.

I was not troubled—on the contrary, I was inspired—by the fact that the anti-Soviet movement in Lithuania, which, during the first post-war years, had united tens of thousands of people, had become, after ten years of fighting, very much reduced in number. I found it necessary to fight not only for myself, but also for those struck down by enemy bullets, and for those who fell into the hands of the Chekists, and, with numbers on their backs, died from starvation digging for coal in Vorkuta,[1] and for those who, afraid of torture in Siberia, and scared they might never see victory, either raised or lowered their arms.

I was arrested not in 1952 when the organs of Soviet state security received sufficient facts about my connections with the anti-Soviet underground, that I had ammunition and that I disseminated illegally-printed LLKS newspapers, booklets and leaflets. I was arrested after three years of involvement in anti-Soviet activities, in 1955, at a time when, immobilized by tuberculosis of the spinal column, I had gone into hospital for three years (according to the prognosis of my doctors) and was in a plaster cast and totally unable to walk.

This did not help to fill me with respect for the Chekists or to change my attitude to the Soviets. It was only public condemnation by the CPSU of the Stalinist cult of personality and the admission that many abnormal events, like repression

[1] Siberian town, centre of vast concentration camp area in Stalinist era.

196

against innocent citizens, cruelty, hypocrisy and cant, etc. had taken place in the country, and that this "must not be repeated" (Khrushchev), that made me ask: Will the Kremlin not change its policy so that any struggle against the Soviet regime will be rendered unnecessary?

At this time I had become fully aware that I was involved in political activity, not by vocation but by necessity; I could not become a politician for I had neither the necessary ability, nor the desire, nor sufficient education.

Therefore I began a peaceful, calm, working life. I began to raise the general level of my education and I acquired knowledge of a couple of trades. I began to work although due to the state of my health, I didn't need to do so. I exerted all my efforts in order to avoid infringing the established regime of the camp, although I cannot say it is just. Over the last eight years (until 1970) I have been consistently hungry. Things were very hard. But I kept silent although I cannot say that the attitude of the authorities in regard to the prisoners, particularly the political prisoners, was just. We more or less constantly receive bread of such a poor quality that even starving men have not the strength to eat the rations they give us. This same bread is provided also to those who live in the neighbouring settlements. But if citizens with full rights keep silent, then so must I, a prisoner, although I cannot regard this silence as normal. It does not correspond to the spirit of "the moral code of the builders of Communism". For we are no longer living in the post-war years; now, to judge by the newspapers, we have the ability to make bread as it should be made. I am often called a criminal or a bandit, by the representatives of the Soviet regime. I keep silent although I think that such a term is unjust; unjust not only because I am not a bandit, but because the official policy of the Soviet Government declares respect for those with different views.

And so on and so forth.

Until now I have not been full of trust in, nor of respect for, either the Soviet regime or the ideals of Communism. This is

197

probably because my imprisonment did not help me, but on the contrary hindered me. The representatives of the Soviet regime that are here, the fighters for communism (at least that's what they are supposed to be) often advise me: "Change your views. There is no other way to freedom." And these same people deprive me of the opportunity of addressing them and the representatives of their regime and Party with respect. For from whom, if not from them, can I get to know and understand the teachings of Marx—that the views of a man are formed as a result of many factors, and not because a man wishes to have such and such views?

Any educative work I do here, in the corrective labour special regime colony, where I am kept, leaves me with nothing more than revulsion, both towards the labour I perform and the administrators of this labour, who watch over me; I like to work for what I believe in, to toil creatively. The gratitude I have received in my own case for good work and exemplary behaviour testifies to this effect. But when they ask me to work here, and they give me neither the materials nor the necessary instruments, I am compelled to work badly; when in the first half of the month there is practically no work, and in the second half of the month I have to do work for two people; and when any attempt at manufacturing an instrument suitable for work, or its application, is accompanied by the suspicious glances of the guards or by a search, and is often considered an infringement of the regime—such work does not ennoble me!

I have spent 15 years of my life in prison. I realize that this term is too small to erase the pain in the hearts of the relatives of Osipov—who died by my hand. But in my very own heart the pain of the bestialities done by the Chekists on my tortured father, who was arrested on suspicion, and whose guilt was not even proved, has not yet gone. I cannot ever hope for his rehabilitation for he was tortured before any trial, and most probably never had a trial at all. Everybody who has ever known him has told me what a good man he was.

I am totally opposed to revenge. My behaviour in prison demonstrates that I am capable of leading a creative, peaceful way of life, of being loyal to the Soviets as long as they are seriously interested in redressing their mistakes.

I realize that this testimony is not necessarily bound to be accepted as proof. I know that there are many people who have been hypocrites all their life, not only for 15 years!

Nonetheless I am no longer 15 to 19 years old when I was capable of beating my head against the wall. I now want my score settled. I know that the organs of state security and the Soviet army long ago liquidated the LLKS. The newspapers and journals of Soviet Lithuania that I have had the opportunity of reading in prison confirm that the Lithuanian people realized that Communism was not only inevitable, but an excellent thing, that the alliance of Lithuania and Russia is not only enduring, but profitable and that there is no soil for anti-Soviet activities now in Lithuania. Consequently there are no grounds for supposing I would renew my anti-Soviet activities if I were freed.

Before I was arrested, as well as being anti-Soviet, I was able also to be a Young Communist, even an activist in this sphere. Now I have also learned to play the role of a repentant criminal, which here they want me to be. I could write a whole sheet full of praise for the detachment commander and the whole corrective-labour system of the Soviet Courts and the Soviet regime together. I could make a pile of beautiful promises. This would help the efforts of the administration to obtain clemency on my behalf. But I am not doing this, and will not. For it would not be from the heart. If I have no need to speak, I can keep silent about many things. But I have no wish to lie, and even less to lie for personal profit.

I believe in the triumph of justice. That does not mean that I see nothing good in the Soviet political structure. I am not speaking of that here. Here I am only emphasizing that I could not help fighting against the Soviet regime, that I was never a criminal and am not now, and my life in prison has not contributed to destroying my enmity to the Soviet state. There are no grounds for expecting the position to change in the near future, for the gap between the official line of the Soviet Government and the concrete situation is too wide. I do not have sufficient opportunity to observe the changes taking place on the other side of the fence, for I am strictly isolated from them. (Could anybody in this world believe that I have never seen a television set, or a transistor radio? But it is true.)

I appreciate that the Chekists had no choice but to arrest me and keep me a specific time in prison, once they found me fighting the Soviet regime with a gun in my hands. But I don't understand why, in prison, I was starved half to death, and humiliated in so many different ways. And now that the fight is over, that we have been defeated, my remaining in prison becomes meaningless. Worse—the state of my health has recently begun to deteriorate noticeably. If I am still able to work and earn a living, then in the future, under prison conditions, I may become unfit for work. Then freedom would indeed be bitter for me.

It follows therefore that to stay in prison any longer cannot nurture in me any respect for the authority of the Soviet state, but, on the contrary, can only show me, that despite all the promises, that which must not be repeated *is* nevertheless being repeated, and confirm the suspicion which has already begun to torment me, that in 1956, the President of the Supreme Soviet of the USSR commuted the death sentence of the Baltic Military Tribunal not only not to have me executed but also to torture me with the intolerable conditions of life in prison.

I beg you to free me.   A. L. Simutis

20.7.1970

Here is the text of another declaration by Simutis (10th December, 1971—the Day of the Defence of Human Rights).

To the Praesidium of the Supreme Soviet of the USSR
From Ludwikas Simutis, son of Adomas, born 1935.
Address : Udarny Post Office, MASSR 431140

I realize that to attempt to prove one's good qualities is a sign of stupidity and dishonesty. Therefore I find it exceedingly unpleasant and shameful to write this declaration. But I am in a "pit" where silence is a very expensive commodity, where modesty is valued as a sign of weakness and of good-for-nothingness, and where I am caused great pain not only in having to remind others that I exist, but having to shout to do it.

When I was 19 years old I was arrested for political activities directed against the Soviets in Lithuania.

I had always, since my very childhood, been a quiet, modest, obedient boy, who believed sincerely in God. I never had any intention of committing any crime, or of hurting anybody. On the contrary, the stories and tales my mother and grandmother used to tell me, and later the books I would read on the lives of the saints of the Catholic Church and others encouraged in me the desire to live a life as just and as courageous as these saints and fabulous, yet real, heroes had led.

It was not my fault that the norms of behaviour, morals and conscience instilled in me by life, by my environment, even my mother's milk, proved not to correspond with the demands of Soviet reality.

In prison I read a lot, educated myself, mixed with many different people of different nationalities and views, and I thought of the past, the present and the future. All this also had an effect on the formation, development and tempering of my attitudes. Today my views are very different from those I had when first imprisoned.

But again, I am not to blame if I never became a devotee of dialectical materialism, if I do not believe in the possibility of building Communism and if I have remained a Catholic.

My stay in prison, as a seriously disabled man, has been

extraordinarily hard, and since the state of my health is noticeably deteriorating, it has been becoming harder and harder. The severe daily timetables one has to follow, the insufficiency, lack of quality and monotony of the food, the dreadful conditions of life in the society of robbers, rogues, homosexuals and the mentally sick, and the 16½ years I have spent here have made me nervous, irritable, old before my time. But they haven't yet knocked out of me my honour or love of work, or my faith in the triumph of justice, my readiness to sacrifice myself for a cause in which I believe.

Life has taught me to be patient, restrained, to respect those views, causes and laws, which are unacceptable to me personally. This is proven beyond a shadow of a doubt by the fact that I have not once, during the whole of my term of imprisonment, broken the strict regime, nor have I ever received any penalties. Among the huge number of prisoners I know of only one other man who has been able to avoid penalties for 16 years. Not only that, but I have a series of grateful acknowledgements for my good work (I work, although as a seriously disabled man, I am not compelled to!) and my exemplary behaviour.

L. Simutis.

10.12.1971

I feel a desire to comment on the above declaration and give my impressions of Ludwikas himself. I will not, however, do this for the usual reasons: I give as little information as I can, so as not to harm anyone involuntarily. Maybe the time will come when I can make generalizations or draw my own conclusions, but even then I would still be very careful. Sometimes I feel like plucking up my courage and indulging in poetic licence, but this would hardly free me from my "criminal" responsibility for what I would have written.

Anyway, let me give some figures on the Lithuanians here: of the seven of them, only one, Bagdonas, works for the KGB. Captured in 1955, he helped the state security organs to arrest a group of partisans including Simutis, but was sentenced to be shot nonetheless. His sentence was then commuted to 25 years, 16 of which he has already served, in quiet co-operation with the KGB. When his request for clemency was rejected in spite of his collaboration, he was enormously discouraged.

One has the distinct impression that it was on Baltic and Western Ukrainian peoples most of all that the Soviets most forcefully demonstrated their existence, and that it was in these very lands where the rule of the most merciless vengeance held sway; he who does not bow the knee must rot his time away in prison, for the vengeance of those who possess absolute truth and who radically change the face of the world, is by its nature a bloody and implacable one.

In the camp at the moment there are 120 prisoners and 35 administrators, including the guards. The seven Lithuanians here comprise just under 6% of the camp population, whereas the proportion of Lithuanians in the population of 240 millions comprises about 1%. One of them, Shlimas, has had his sentence reduced to 15 years, while three others have had theirs increased for certain camp transgressions. Add all the seven convictions together and it comes to 182 years altogether, i.e. 26 years each on average; 125 years has been served, equalling on average, 18 years each. Their average age is 46. They are all Catholics. Not one of them has mutilated himself or inscribed any tattoos on his face (I suspect both of these are predominantly Russian forms of rebellion) and not one of them has become a drug addict or a homosexual. They have all retained a deep friendship and give the impression of being an association of countrymen. They are exceptionally decent, sober-minded people and keep their distance from non-Lithuanians (particularly the Russians). They show no signs of anti-semitism (or no evident signs at least), they are all extremely courageous men, and none of them has any time for physical "discussions". In the midst of all the criminals and wartime collaborators who set the tone here, they, the Lithuanians give the most gratifying impression. They have been promised release before the expiration of their terms provided they will condemn what they have done and sing the praises of their conquerors, but not one of them, except Bagdonas and Shlimas, has written a request for clemency; even so Bagdonas, in spite of all his collaboration with the Cheka, has been deceived, and Shlimas has had his sentence reduced to 15 years, apparently because he is thought to be insane (he has hardly spoken one word in 15 years).

Besides the Russians, Ukrainians, and a few Moldovians, Gypsies and Bashkirs, about whom I haven't yet collected any data, we have one Lett, one Estonian, one German, one Georgian, one Armenian, one Uzbek, one Cossack and four Jews.

There are four Jews, though if you were to believe the camp anti-semites, who imagine the Jews are everywhere (Brezhnev, Kosygin and the whole of the Kremlin host are Jews!), there must be at least twenty here. (And this is not to mention those suspected of belonging to the Chosen—or Accursed—Race, and who compete with one another in pathologically aggressive anti-semitism. Four Jews here, then,—3.3% of all convicts in the zone, whereas in the USSR Jews comprise less than 1% (not including Brezhnev and Kosygin!) In other zones (in Mordovia) the proportion of Jews is nearly 8%. Their average age is 35—and they've done 14 years each; if they should be released at the end of their terms (very possible) they will each have served 22 years on average, three are past criminals, three dream about Israel; two are criminals (in terms of their attitude to life) and one is an active homosexual; three have more than once resorted to hunger-strikes, and one has mutilated himself.

5th September

It is calculated that we each receive about one-fifth of our earnings (50% is immediately deducted for the necessities of the punitive apparatus; after this 14 roubles for food, five for clothes, etc.).

The intensity of the work on the presses is unbelievable,

	Letts.	Eston.	German	Georg.	Armen.	Uzbek	Cossacks
Age	32	43	55	75	35	36	32
Sentence	13	25	15	15	3	14	20
Executions		Yes	Yes	Yes			
Served	12	16	5	5	?	13	15
Stool-Pigeons	Yes	No	Yes	Yes	No	?	No
Drug-Addicts	Yes	No	No	No	No	Yes	No
Homosexual:							
Active	?	No	No	No	?	Yes	No
Passive	Yes	Yes[1]	No	No	No	No	No
Recidivists	Yes	No	No	No	Yes	Yes	Yes
Wartime Collaborators	No	No	Yes	Yes	No	No	No
Views[2]							
a Nationalist		Yes			Yes	Yes	
b Democratic							
c "Aggressive Philistine"	Yes			Yes			
d "Harmless Philistine"			Yes				Yes
Self-Mutilation	Yes		No	No		Yes	No
Hunger-Strike		Yes	No	No	Yes		No

[1] Imprisoned on account of participation in national-liberation movement. Certified as mentally ill: considers himself a woman.

[2] I have tried to keep this as general as possible.

a Nationalist: a man who takes a keen interest in the fate of his nation and is prepared to serve it unselfishly; might be monarchist or anything else—I have called him nationalist for want of further information.

b Democrat: he who has a tendency towards internationalism within the framework of a democratic society in the best Western tradition.

c "Aggressive Philistine": criminal variety; debauched, lacking spiritual feelings objective in life—to satisfy basest needs at whatever cost.

d "Harmless Philistine": creature without character, presently inoffensive but potentially aggressive (in above sense).

This page in the diary is in the form of a table. The footnotes are Kuznetsovs.

I work and work until my arms and my legs are shaky and stupefaction begins to set in. Maybe I will soon rebel.

19th September

From time to time information about our accomplices infiltrates through to us via the hospital. I hear they are all acting very courageously, which makes me happier than I can say. Once or twice they have managed to send us food, (sugar, powdered milk or tea). Tea is the main thing. Over where they are it's sold free in the shop, but we are forbidden it and it's three roubles a packet on the black market. This is quite profitable from the authorities' point of view, for they can fleece the zone, buy information on the cheap (everyone knows that the Cheka pays informers with tea), and exchange it for all kinds of trinkets, useless or otherwise, made by the convicts. Most of the tea channels are controlled by the camp detective. In our zone tea is still considered a drug, although not in other camps since 1969. One still hears the legend, perhaps apocryphal, about the harmful effects of what is known as "chifir".[1] (I've never seen anyone add more than 8–10 grammes of tea to 100 grammes of water.) Once this was only the incompetence of the camp authorities, now it is a covering veil for educative measures.

I think Sylva may be ill; it would appear so from some hints she makes in her letter: she can't forgive herself for the naivety with which she fell for the manoeuvres of her investigators. "The idea that I failed at the most critical juncture," she writes, "and that I conducted myself at the very least, unworthily, does not give me a moment's rest. I cannot forgive myself for accepting the 'proof' that was shown to me (i.e. that you and all the others had rejected me and were competing with one another to provide the necessary information.)." Ah, the KGB gives us all such bitter lessons in Soviet life (and not free lessons, by any means!).

Even the day before she was arrested Sylva was almost indifferent to anything which had no direct relationship to the problem of repatriation. For me the trial ended not so much with the judge's quickly reiterated, "death penalty, death penalty!" or with the handcuffs they put on us, but with Sylva's tears: "I hate everything here! I hate it!" And now I have her letter, each word full of anger and sarcasm all directed at its ill-concealed target! Her case is in no way exceptional. When once you enter (however inadvertently)

[1] A very strong brew of tea used as a stimulant.

the Cheka's labyrinth you will reach the exit with such a mighty store of hatred as would fill the whole of Vagankov Cemetery or Tel Aviv itself. From the moment the repressive apparatus of the state finds itself compelled to resort to more and more flexible forms of power and no longer able to kill off all its dissidents, it is faced with the problem of those crawling out of the labyrinth. The Russian repressive state inevitably lacks the flexibility necessary to integrate the dissidents into its system; it crushes them and turns them either into latent enemies or zombies who may one day rise again, albeit in certain defeat. Anyone who says to you, "The Czechs rose didn't they, and look what happened to them! You're wasting your time," can't see any further than his nose. To be victorious, in the long run, you need a tradition of fighting, you need myths and martyrs' haloes—otherwise national character will fall into decay. Anouilh's Joan of Arc says God wishes to give victory to the French only if they are heroes in battle and show themselves to be freedom-lovers. He does not squander his blessings like that, he offers them from above, and you rise to receive them.

24th September

This is the third day I've had stomach trouble, something I've never had before. I have never been ill, indeed, I used to boast that I would die of strain—either on a lavatory or on a woman! But now I get spasms of pain in the epistolatory region of my stomach, vomiting and the rest of it. Symptoms of an ulcer. Captain Tabakov, the head of the medical unit, a surgeon by profession and a Chekist by vocation, gave me the following diagnosis, word for word: "There's nothing wrong with you." "What do you mean?" I protested feebly (it's very difficult, after all, to be courageous and prove you're not putting it on when the pains are so indisputably real that the torture you're in must be evident to everyone). "And I've been vomiting . . ." "No vomiting whatsoever." Tabakov stared at me and prodded me a couple of times with his hand in the stomach obviously thinking I must have palpitations.

When I lie down on my plank-bed, it's not so bad, but if I pull on the press just a little too sharply I break out in a cold sweat, and double up from pain and nausea. Soda water relieves it for a while. But the tablets Tabakov gave me (he didn't say what they are) don't help.

27th September

The same but worse. I never expected to have to swallow any medicine. You can only get a diagnosis in the hospital (i.e. in camp 3) as there is no laboratory or x-ray machine or proper doctor here. People can cry out in pain for months before they're taken to the hospital, which isn't all that much help when you get to it. Tabakov said if the pains (at last he seems to believe I get them) don't stop, he'll (perhaps) send me to the hospital in February or March.

4th October

My patience is at an end. I've been sick all day, gritting my teeth from pain, and hardly able to wait for the working day to end, and for Tabakov to appear as though he were the magical liberator of all woes (such is the power of the white gown—when you're wracked with pain you forget who's in it!). He shoved three tablets into my extended palm, this time in a wrapping which read "enteroseptol". (No wonder we're forbidden to have medical or reference books.)

Had he not slammed shut the food-hatch in time, I would probably have slung some boiling water at him. I know enough about medicine to know that enteroseptol is prescribed for childrens' diarrhoea, dyspepsia and similar complaints. And he prescribed it as a sedative! As from tomorrow I'm going to declare a hunger-strike.

5th October

This morning I handed a statement to the duty officer: "For two weeks I have had dreadful pains and vomiting in spite of the fact that Captain Tabakov says I am quite well; they have not stopped. In my view, the prescription of enteroseptol as an antidote is humiliating. I demand qualified medical treatment. As from today I am on hunger-strike."

At last I am alone, everyone's gone to work. Until 5.15 I can drink in my solitude and the comparative silence (there is never absolute silence on special regime, even during the night: the guards are yelling, some idiot is beating against the door, begging for "something for my stomach, I'm dying!...").

Here is a happy thought! A hunger strike gives you the opportunity of reading and writing as much as you like! I have at my disposal a minimum of three days, then I'll be put in solitary, no books, of course, and no pen or anything to smoke. The latter is a good thing; fasting and smoking at the same time is not such a brilliant idea.

A few words about the history of the special zone. Until December, 1962, zone 10 comprised one barracks with a dozen small cells—one cell per five people. The OORs (especially dangerous recidivists) were kept in camp 4 about one third of a mile from camp 10. This is a normal camp, open, the convicts say, in the sense that you can move freely within its confines. Only those who broke the regime really badly were transferred for different terms—from two weeks to six months —to the cells in camp 10. However, in the summer of 1962 a new barracks was built. It was built by the convicts of the "foreign zone"; at that time the prisoner's tradition of not building prisons for their own use was still extant; how could you, after all, entrust the building of a prison to those who knew they themselves would have to live in it: they might build secret holes, tunnels for future escapes and such like. This new barracks is a low brick construction 100 yards long. On both sides of the corridor there are 30 multiple and 14 solitary cells. A multiple cell is 18 or 19 yards square, with two-tier wooden beds, a table, and all the rest. In 1963–64 I was in cell 21, where there were 15 of us. In the summer it's as stuffy as hell and the convicts walk about naked, except for a pair of shorts, with the sweat pouring off the sinews in their backs. Now at one end of the corridor, now at the other end, you hear someone howling pathetically, "Guard, let me have some water!" or the resounding clanging of a tin mug against the door, or someone whistling during the night, or the sound of breaking windows and "Doctor! Doctor!" meaning someone with heart trouble has "conked out". The winter's easier, but it's so cold—your fingers can't hold your pencil, your match fizzles out. . . . On Sundays we have an hour's "walk"— when people run as fast as they can to beat the queue and dive through the bathroom door! Sometimes freedom is using the toilet whenever you feel the need.

By morning the slop-bucket is always full to the brim, it's contents half-spilled on the floor . . . And then there are the scourges—the cold, the heat, the stuffiness, the overcrowding, the authorities, and, of course, the hunger. In six months only I've lost about 30–35 pounds weight, whereas some people have frequently been beaten to death (one just murdered) for stealing rations. No shop, no parcels, nothing. Thus it was until the Autumn of 1969, when the new "law on corrective labour institutions" alleviated the life of the OORs (OORs *only*, that is) to four-rouble purchases in the shop per month, two two-pound food parcels per year, one meeting per year and when half the prisoner's term is done, one ten-pound parcel per year for anyone who has "begun to reform".

On special then there were 450–470 men. Mostly ex-criminals. I can say nothing definite about how many were there on account of their religion; they were held separately, like the homosexuals.

In cell 21 there are three "politicals," one wartime-collaborator and 11 common criminals. Ripping open your stomach or pushing a wire into your penis is common practice. Prison in comparison is El Dorado (for there at least you get a parcel once every six months and you can buy things in the shop for two and a half roubles). New crimes have been invented just so as to get to prison.

I think I should say a few words about suicides, about those who have been murdered or those who have simply died, but at the moment I have insufficient data, and this is not a subject which lends itself to approximations. Perhaps I might just mention, in passing, the case of Susiei, a 22-year-old Lett, who, at the end of 1963, was in the punishment cell next door to me: that New Year's Eve he presented me with a pair of boots and foot-cloths, and the very next day hanged himself.

Enough for today. I must go and return a couple of books I promised ages ago to their owner.

6th October

I don't very much enjoy hearing my cell-mates chewing bread —it used to be dry, and sour, but now it tangs awfully.

In the camp now there are 120 people, and next week there will be 110: 10 are going to the general camp. This is an event in itself. According to the law, any convict who has done half his term, may be transferred to the strict zone if he behaves well,—but here, at least two out of three have done over half their time (and have served the authorities faithfully) but one infringement a year is enough to put an end to their hopes.

Now I have another person to add to my collection of information.[1] At the moment I have something on 90 of the men. The rest are difficult to get facts on: maybe they're invalids who are not forced to work, or rebels, spending most of their time in solitary, or minor offenders working in special cells. I never stop worrying about my papers, day and night. Shortly, I feel, there will be a time of more overt repression, which we shall try and resist. Anything may happen. Therefore I want to try and work over the material I've collected

[1] Name withheld.

and call a halt for the moment. I'll hide my papers as best I can and forget about the diary so all the stool pigeons in turn can forget what I look like with a pen in my hand—or they'll search me time and again.

I've got plenty of stuff to enrage the blue-boys. (They've been spreading the rumour that we've got plenty of money—seven or eight thousand roubles—so that the "rats" will keep their eyes on us the whole time hoping to make a quick profit. Their vigilance, spurred on by the thirst for profit, is so inexhaustible they might find something much more valuable. We *do* have money—23 roubles. This is an old Chekist trick. But, in this case, it's not only practical but has antisemitic overtones, which makes it all the more attractive. When we were arrested, rumours were spread throughout the country that we had tried to take gold with us in suitcases to Israel. Even though the judge said of ten of us "No confiscation of property, in absence of such!"

Ninety convicts, I suppose, are enough to make some generalizations. For example, the average age of our recidivist would have been higher if I had the opportunity of chatting with some still unburied old men in the invalid cells. Steal up to the food-hatch quietly and the guard bellows at you; ask quickly, "Grandad, how old are you?" and the mumbled reply comes back: "Very old, my son." "And how long do you have to stay here?" "Till the end of the Soviet regime, my son!" That's all the conversation you have time for.

Ninety people then; average age 45;—average of the Russians 45.5, Ukrainians, 44, Lithuanians, 45, Jews, 36, Moldovians 44; of these people, 41 are Russian, 29 Ukrainians, 7 Lithuanians, 4 Jews, 2 Moldovians, 1 German, 1 Georgian, 1 Buriat, 1 Estonian, 1 Lett, 1 Uzbek and 1 White Russian. Each on average has been here 16 years and if all of them should be released at the end of their terms (i.e. no amnesty, no review commission, no clemency only those who haven't been here five years yet believe in any of these!) then they will have done 24 years each.

The Russians have been here on average 18 years each, the Ukrainians, Lithuanians and Moldovians 16 years, the Jews 14 years. The Russians have yet to serve 26 years each, the Ukrainians and Jews 22 years and the Lithuanians 24 years and the Moldovians 21 years.

Of these ninety prisoners, 37 are collaborators, some secretly, some openly, and seven are suspected of collaboration. "Secretly" means that the collaborator tries to put a bold face on it, whereas there are some who don't make any bones about it, and make no attempt to hide the stigma of the informer and the spy. The Russians have 20 informers, and four suspected, the Ukrainians 11 and 2, the Lithuanians 1, the Jews 1 suspected, the German, Georgian, Lett, Uzbek and White Russian are all open stool-pigeons. Of the Russians' 20 stool-pigeons 8 are wartime collaborators and 12 common criminals; the four suspected are criminals. All without exception of the Ukrainian collaborators are informers. Eleven in all, whereas the 2 suspected are common criminals. Bagdonas I mentioned earlier. One of the "suspected Jews" is a criminal, the German and the Georgian are wartime collaborators, the Lett and the Uzbek are common criminals. The White Russian is neither one nor the other; he got the death sentence, later commuted to 25 years under Art. 58–8, for political terrorism, although in fact the murder he committed was non-political. I count as wartime collaborators those who worked with the Fascists to save their own skin. I count as criminals those who changed their criminal colours to political because, in the circumstances, it was more convenient to do so. In this way only 36 people are really political prisoners and the rest are wartime collaborators (21 informers) and common criminals (33).

7th October

The position on hunger strikes has changed; now they feed you according to "your daily condition" and not as before— after seven days and then every alternate day.

23rd October

Yesterday I came back from the hospital. On the 8th day of my strike Kochetkov summoned me from solitary and told me he would send me back to the hospital if I would break my hunger strike. From the 15th to the 22nd I was in hospital. They gave me no diagnosis (there was no x-ray machine), just one vitamin tablet per day, and watched me like eagles.

I still managed to exchange a word with one of "ours"! They have decided to declare a three-day hunger strike in protest on the anniversary of our trial, and 1-day strikes on the anniversaries of the Leningradites, Rigaites and Kishinevites.

17 November

Today we, (I, Yurka and Alik that is) sent off a declaration rejecting Soviet citizenship. Here is the text of mine:

To the Praesidium of the Supreme Soviet of the USSR
From Convict E. S. Kuznetsov—A Declaration

For many years I have not been a Soviet citizen, either in conscience or in political convictions. Having completed in 1968 a seven-year term of imprisonment for so-called anti-Soviet activities, I attempted to put into effect my inalienable right as a human being—my right to emigrate—by legal means. The obstacles in my path were unconquerable, and I was compelled to attempt to flee illegally across the border by means of seizing an aircraft. This action was falsely and premeditatedly called treason by the Leningrad City Court and I was three times sentenced to death. This was commuted by the Court of Appeal to 15 years imprisonment in a special regime camp. I consider myself—and I am such, not only by conscience, nationality and attitude, but factually,—a citizen of the State of Israel. I ask only that I be deprived formally of my Soviet citizenship, for I am de facto no longer a Soviet citizen.

214

My request is in complete accordance with Art. 15–2 of the Universal Declaration of Human Rights ("None Shall arbitrarily be deprived of his nationality nor denied the right to change his nationality").

Having been sentenced to 15 years deprivation of freedom, to 15 years of torture for an act which would only be a minor offence according to the laws of civilized states, I do not intend to back away from the insults with which I am daily rewarded for being a Jew, and a man who wishes to leave the confines of the USSR. Now and for ever: *I AM NOT A SOVIET CITIZEN AND I ASK NOT TO BE CONSIDERED AS SUCH.*

18th November

Alik has declared a hunger strike. We will join him on 1st December. His visit was cancelled for nothing. Our unit officer told us that the same would happen to Yurka and me. They have found our "Achilles heel". We will fast until this order is changed. We are being persecuted all the more. They are creating a "precriminal" situation, i.e. spreading all kinds of rumours, trying to set the common criminals at us. Three days ago, one convict swallowed some tablets, and came looking for Alik with a screw-driver in his hand. It's a good thing for Alik he stumbled on to me first and began telling me how wonderful I was, "I don't mind *you*, but I'll murder that Murzhenko." These recidivists are so intelligent!

We want to try and find a lawyer to protect ourselves as much as we can from pressure from above and below. The trouble is any lawyer needs a KGB pass—which they wouldn't give our man; alternatively, whoever they gave it to, wouldn't be our man.

Here is how they will answer my declaration: "The matter of your nationality can be considered only at the termination of your period of imprisonment."

23rd November

Received my third reprimand for not attending political study classes. The last class I went to, Lieutenant Bezzubov gave us the priceless information that, "In China the Zionists and the Red Guards are on the rampage. But the Chinese people are not stupid—they'll show them!" The academic level of these lectures is truly breath-taking!

28th November

In three days we shall be joining Alik. We must conquer or we are lost. Prepare yourself for battle Joseph Knecht![1]

In spite of the four volumes of the "Course of Soviet Criminal Law" (and what rubbish it is!), Tarasov and Tsvetkov will soon be condemned to death, under Art. 77–1. Tsvetkov tattooed Tarasov's face, which is construed as an act of terror against the administration of the camp. The reason: Tarasov was not given the medical treatment he needed.

[Sergei][2]

---

[1] Kuznetzov quotes this from Hermann Hesse's *The Glass Bead Game*.
[2] Person otherwise unidentified. Not in Kuznetsov's handwriting.

Proceedings of the Leningrad Hijacking Trial

The following account of the Leningrad hijack trial proceedings was recorded by a relative of one of the accused who was present in the courtroom. The question marks in brackets indicate uncertainty about whether the name was heard correctly in the courtroom.

Between the 15th and the 24th December 1970, in the City Court of Leningrad, the following were charged under the Articles of the Criminal Code of the RSFSR below: M. Y. Dymshitz, E. S. Kuznetsov, S. I. Zalmanson, J. M. Mendelevich, I. I. Zalmanson, Y. P. Fedorov, A. G. Murzhenko, A. A. Altman, L. G. Khnokh, B. S. Penson and M. A. Bodnya. (N. A. Yermakov, Chairman of the Leningrad City Court, presided; Prosecution—Leningrad Procurator S. E. Soloviov and N. Katunova; Social Accuser—USSR Civil Air Force pilot Metanogov).

Art. 64a : "Treason, i.e. an act knowlingly committed by a citizen of the USSR, prejudicial to the security, territorial inviolability and military might of the USSR . . ."

Art. 15 : "Responsibility for the preparation of a crime and for attempting to commit a crime."

Art. 70 : "Anti-Soviet agitation and propaganda, i.e. agitation or propaganda for the purpose of subverting or weakening the Soviet regime or for committing separate especially dangerous crimes against the State . . ."

Art. 93 : "Misappropriation of state or public property of especially large dimensions."

The trial took place in a hall with a seating capacity of 300, of which only 20 or 30 seats were occupied by defendants' relatives who appeared on the lists. The remainder were allowed to enter upon presentation of special passes. There was in the building a large number of policemen whose function was to send away any others who might wish to enter the courtroom. The public who sat in the Court were hostile to the defendants. When the court rose for recess the opinion was frequently voiced that "they should all be hanged!" On the day after the commencement of the trial the newspaper *Leningradskaya Pravda* referred to the defendants as criminals.

According to the bill of indictment the defendants' intention had been to use the AN-2 12-seater passenger aircraft to take off along the Leningrad-Priozersk route and fly to Sweden. M. Y. Dymshitz, S. I. Zalmanson, I. I. Zalmanson, B. S. Penson and M. A. Bodnya pleaded guilty. I, M. Mendelevich, E. S. Kuznetsov, A. A. Altman, A. G. Murzhenko and L. G. Khnokh pleaded guilty in part only. Asked "Do you plead guilty?" Y. P. Fedorov replied, "Not under these articles."

Of the eleven defendants, nine (excluding Murzhenko and Fedorov) testified that the single aim of their planned seizure of the aircraft had been to reach Israel. S. I. Zalmanson, her husband E. S. Kuznetsov, I. M. Mendelevich, A. A. Altman, B. S. Penson and M. A. Bodnya had, on more than one occasion, attempted to leave for Israel by official means, but either they had met with refusal at the OVIR[1] office or they had not been given the necessary employment reference, without which the OVIR would not accept their application.

The first of the defendants to be cross-examined was Dymshitz.

Cross-Examination of Mark Dymshitz

MARK DYMSHITZ, born 1927. Was a member of the

[1] Soviet government agency responsible for exit procedures.

CPSU (Communist Party of the Soviet Union) even up to the time of his arrest, but then expelled. Studied at flying school, and joined up as military pilot. In 1960 demobilized. Unable to find specialized work in Leningrad, where he worked two years as a civil pilot. Returning to Leningrad he entered the agricultural institute. He then became an engineer.

Mark Dymshitz stated that he was unable in the Soviet Union to give his children a Hebrew education. He spoke of three factors motivating him to leave for Israel:

1 Antisemitism in the USSR.
2 Soviet foreign policy in the Middle East.
3 USSR domestic policy over the nationalities question, towards the Jews.

In 1948 the Soviet Union had voted for the establishment of the State of Israel and, when the war started, it was the Arabs that had been the aggressors. The same war still continued and the aggressor could not have changed. The only question was: who broke the truce first?

He himself had hit upon the idea of leaving the USSR. He had never applied to the OVIR. He had wanted to construct an air balloon, then build an aeroplane himself, and then hijack one. Having thought of this last idea he had realized he could not cope alone and had begun to seek others. At the same time he had begun studying Hebrew—though without much success. All these plans had matured in his mind during the years 1967–8.

In the autumn of 1969 he first met Butman, who took him along to an "ulpan"[1]. Butman knew of his plans and they began to search for people together. At first Dymshitz's wife did not agree, but then, "having created within his family an atmosphere of despotism and oppression" (prosecutor's words), he won her and the children over. Their daughters

---

[1] Israeli-style school for learning Hebrew.

were told of the plan of escape. There were three basic alternative plans:

1 The seizure of a TU 124 (48–52 passengers) on the Leningrad-Murmansk route. This plan was called "Operation Wedding". They rejected the last days of April and fixed their escape for 1st-2nd May. But then the Leningrad "centre" decided to ask Israel for its opinion, and Dymshitz was forbidden to try anything before an answer was received.

According to this plan Dymshitz received 50 roubles from Butman to fly to Moscow but, since the pilot of the aircraft was an old friend of his from Bukhara, he travelled in the pilot's cabin for nothing. Having acquainted himself with the structure of this type of aircraft, he gave 35 roubles back to Butman and squandered the other 15 in drink. Butman did not know that he had flown free of charge.

Asked by the prosecution what he had been intending to do when he got to Israel, Dymshitz said he would have been a civil pilot or a chauffeur or a tractor-driver.

2 Plan 2 was conceived by Dymshitz at the end of May and he asked Kuznetsov to come over to Leningrad to discuss it. The idea was to seize an aircraft (a 12-seater AN 2) from an airfield during the middle of the night. Dymshitz and Kuznetsov (together with Kuznetsov's wife, Sylva Zalmanson) visited Smolny airport towards the end of May and realized this would not work (because of the searchlights, dogs, etc.). Kuznetsov left for Riga thinking the whole thing was over and done with. But on 5th June he received a telephone call from Dymshitz asking him to come and talk over yet another plan. This was on 5th June. Kuznetsov came, summoned Fedorov to Leningrad, and on 8th June the three of them flew to Priozersk and agreed on Plan 3 for the 15th June.

3 Plan 3 was to seize an AN 2 at Priozersk airport. The problem was, everything had to begin at Priozersk. Twelve people

(Dymshitz, Kuznetsov, Mendelevich, I. Zalmanson, W. Zalmanson, Dymshitz's wife and daughters Lisa and Julia, Fedorov, Murzhenko, Altman, Bodnya) had to fly there as normal passengers. When the aircraft stopped they were to tie up the first and second pilots—making sure they did not receive a single scratch—put them in a tent in sleeping-bags—and then take aboard the four who were waiting at Priozersk (A. Khnokh, M. Khnokh, S. Zalmanson, B. Penson), then they would fly to Sweden.

Thus, *the hijacking bid had not yet even begun* when the twelve were arrested at 8.30 at Smolny airport, and the four near Priozersk at 3 o'clock in the morning.

The only gun found among the group (with Fedorov) belonged to Dymshitz. He had made it himself when he was still in Bukhara.

Cross-examination of the defendant S. Zalmanson

SYLVA ZALMANSON, born 1943. Lived in Riga where she worked as an engineer. Married E. S. Kuznetsov in January 1970. Confirmed she had reprinted the first number of the literary journal *Iton* [Hebrew word for newspaper].

She was a Zionist, she said. When asked by the procurator if she was aware that Zionism was inimical to Marxist-Leninist ideology, she said she was not aware of this, but thought that Zionism had in it aspects which were not inimical to our ideology, the most important of these being the ingathering of the Jews within one state. She had first applied to the OVIR for an exit visa in 1968 but had been refused. In 1970 she had once again received the necessary invitation[1], both for herself and for her husband Kuznetsov, but she had been unable to obtain the reference the OVIR demanded. From about 1968 she had been printing Zionist literature on behalf of Shpilberg.

[1] i.e. from Israel.

She had brought to Dreisner (?) in Leningrad a suitcase of literature with which she was unacquainted. When Butman and Dymshitz came to Riga with their plan of escape she had introduced them to Kuznetsov. The latter, who was new to Riga and knew no one there, she had also introduced to a number of intended participants. Although she was on very good terms with her younger brother she thought Kuznetsov would be more authoritative than she and therefore entrusted him to talk to Izrail. When Kuznetsov talked things over with him he agreed readily. In May her second brother[1] came home from the army and he too, after a short discussion with his sister, agreed. Asked by the prosecution whether she had been aware how inimical Zionist ideology was to us, Sylva Zalmanson replied she still did not think this was so and remained a Zionist nevertheless. (Generally she had little to say and answered questions put by the procurator, defendants and their lawyers, for the most part indistinctly.) When asked what she had intended to do in Israel, S. Zalmanson said she was prepared to do anything.

Cross-Examination of Iosif Mendelevich

IOSIF MENDELEVICH, born 1947. He said he had been brought up in a family which cherished Jewish traditions, he had always taken a keen interest in the history and fate of the Jewish people, and he and his family had long been convinced that Israel was their spiritual and historic homeland. They had several invitations to go to Israel and had received permission to enter the country from the Israeli Ministry of Foreign Affairs. They had applied three times to the OVIR, and three times they had been refused. When told of the impending flight his family had been in the midst of applying to the OVIR, and he had said that if they met with a refusal he would participate. The refusal came several days later. He left his studies at the Polytechnic Institute feeling, in

[1] i.e. Wulf

spite of his great desire for education, that it was somewhat immoral to study at Soviet expense. He did not think this was so great a sacrifice, for he was sure he would be expelled for his desire to emigrate to Israel in any case. In Riga he edited the journal *Iton* and wrote articles. He kept an index-card questionnaire. He wrote a letter which they wanted to leave behind in case of failure. This letter was considered by the prosecutor a slanderous anti-Soviet document. Asked whether he considered himself "as being of Jewish nationality or a Zionist" he replied, "I am a JEW." Furthermore, he said as far as the USSR was concerned he had no pretensions, and the country really had little interest for him. The only thing he wanted was to go to his Homeland. The procurator then remarked that the Russian people had made Birobidjan available for this purpose, and why did he not go there? To which he answered: "Please be so kind as to allow *me* to decide which state—not region—is my Homeland!" In addition to his own speech he replied in full to the peremptory and extremely ignorant questions of the prosecution, and to those of the lawyers. He conducted himself in a highly honourable manner, neither shielding himself nor placing the guilt on others.

He had bought some lead for the knuckle-duster, he said, after someone had told him (who, he couldn't remember) that lead couldn't be got anywhere. He had been walking past a shop, he had seen some and bought it. He took it back to the Zalmansons and put it on the table. He had no idea who had done it, but he saw the knuckle-duster was wrapped round with rubber and then covered in a plaster cast to soften the blow. This was not, he said, noted in the experts' findings.

Asked why he had attempted to flee the country, he replied, "to get to Israel". Why had the others taken part?—he did not know. When asked what he would have done in Israel he said that the material aspect did not concern him, but that he was very sure he would be able just to live there. It transpired that during the investigation he had been sent to Riga for a month's psychiatric treatment.

16th December, 9 a.m.: proceedings began with the cross-examination of the defendant E. Kuznetsov.

EDWARD SAMUILOVICH KUZNETSOV

Born 1939. Passed examinations for Moscow University. Faculty of Philosophy, 1960, with distinction. Arrested in second year of his studies, and in 1961 convicted under Articles 70 and 72 and sentenced to seven years imprisonment. In a camp in Mordovia he was subjected to the judicial process of the administration of the camp and spent half his term in a cell in Vladimir prison together with Igor Ogurtsov. Freed in 1968, he was held under police surveillance in Strunino, Vladimir district. After marrying Sylva Zalmanson he moved to Riga where he worked in a hospital.

When asked about his nationality Kuznetsov answered that he was a Jew. When the prosecutor remarked that his passport said he was a Russian he replied "You asked me about my nationality, not about what it says on my passport".

Kuznetsov attempted to outline the circumstances which had brought him to the defendants' bench. The aim of our group, he said, was to cross the Soviet-Finnish border and head for Sweden. He described the plan for crossing the frontier. "Tell us the facts", interrupted the procurator "It's not a question of facts but of the circumstances that led up to them, and which have universal characteristics. I should like to make several observations with regard to the charges against me. I have been charged with many things, including the dissemination of anti-Soviet literature. As far as the memoirs of Litvinov are concerned I should like to point out that their dubious authenticity has not been proved. Nevertheless I do not consider this document to be anti-Soviet, for its subject is Stalin's entourage and Stalin himself. It is a document no more revealing than those of the 20th CPSU Congress."[1]

[1] Kuznetsov refers to the 1956 Congress in which Khrushchev made his now famous "secret" speech denouncing the Stalinist "cult of personality".

224

Question : Where, and in what circumstances, and for what purpose, did you make a photocopy of Shub's *Russian Political Leaders?*

Answer : After receiving a microfilm from a friend. But I made the copy myself so I could read it through. I do not find it particularly interesting.

Question : But anti-Soviet?

Answer : Yes.

Question : Whom in Leningrad did you give it to?

Answer : To Abram Shifrin, who is now in Israel.

Question : What have you to say about your statement?

Answer : The statement was only to be released in the case of our dying. As far as Art. 64-15 is concerned, I found out about the escape plan from Korenblit and later from Butman in Riga, who before this had talked it over with my wife, Sylva Zalmanson. I did not consider Butman a representative of an organization but a private individual. He did not make a very serious impression on me. However, I agreed to go to Leningrad to discuss the plan. Butman, Korenblit and myself discussed Plan 1 (the Leningrad-Murmansk one—the seizure of an aircraft in the air). Also, Sylva, Altman and Izai knew of it then. Plan 1 was forgotten: to seize an aircraft in the air was deemed impossible. But not the idea. We started to consider Plan 2—seizing an aircraft on an airfield during the middle of the night. But we rejected this also. We had asked Israel and they asked us not to go ahead with it. Then we decided, without Butman and Korenblit, to try Plan 3. Dymshitz rang me on 5th June and I went to Leningrad. The three of us—Dymshitz, Fedorov and I—flew off to Priozersk. We decided on 15th June. Towards the end of April I persuaded Fedorov to join us and suggested bringing Murzhenko.

What was it that motivated me to do all this?—I considered myself a Jew. My father died in 1941. When I was sixteen my mother persuaded me to register as a Russian. I wasn't particularly bothered at that time. Only when I was in the camp did it first begin to be of any significance.

When I came out I asked to be registered as a Jew, but I was refused.

Question : Do you consider yourself a citizen of the USSR?

Answer : Formally.

Question : But during the investigation you said you did not acknowledge, nor wish to live by, the laws of this country. Is that correct?

Answer : In substance—yes, it is.

Question : But you have lived and worked in this country.

Answer : Yes, lived, worked *and* served time!

After leaving the camp I found living under the constant surveillance of the Strunino police very hard indeed. They wouldn't allow me to live with my sick mother. I came to Moscow for the day and was forced to stay the night with friends. In January 1970 I married Sylva Zalmanson and moved to Riga. Then I decided to take advantage of the right our Soviet Constitution provides to leave the confines of the USSR. But I was unable to get my papers accepted by the OVIR, since neither I nor my wife had been given the necessary reference. This right, therefore, existed only on paper. I was not the only one to become such an unfortunate victim of the general attitude towards Jews who desire to go to Israel. Unlike many traitors it was not my intention to give any foreign powers any information about Soviet military potential. Therefore I could not (nor was I intending to) indulge in any actions prejudicial to the security of the Soviet Union. Thus, I do not understand this part of the charges against me. The issue here is evidently one of prestige, in case our attempt might have proved successful. Only in countries inside the communist bloc are people tried for attempting to escape.

Judge : Please do not speak here of other countries. We know ourselves. Keep to the point.

Kuznetsov : As far as Art. 93-1 is concerned, this defines the

226

act we were intending to commit. If a crime has not been committed how is it possible to talk of misappropriation. There's an old Jewish law: no crime—no punishment!

I should like to refer to the article which says I was involved in anti-Soviet agitation and propaganda; there just happened to be some interested people whose views I shared.

Procurator : Were you in the army?

Answer : Yes.

Question : Do you know what your reference said?

Answer : Yes.

Procurator quotes : "Did not attend political lectures . . ." Do you think this is typical of a Soviet citizen?

Answer : I never strove to be a typical citizen and I did not like the regimentation in the army. I avoided political lectures because they were given by illiterates.

Question : What did you intend to do when you got to Israel?

Answer : It was a matter of indifference to me.

Question : Have you anything to say about the parcels you received from abroad?

Answer : They must have been from my relatives in Israel whom I heard from occasionally (?). I was surprised and didn't know what to do with them.

Public Prosecutor : If the weather had been bad in Sweden what would you have done?

Answer : I left this to Dymshitz.

Lawyer : You committed this crime for political motives?

Answer : No, I was guided by considerations of a spiritual and moral character.

Lawyer : Were you intending to cause damage to the Soviet Union?

Answer : Not at all.

Lawyer : Were you not worried as to how this might be received by the enemies of the USSR?

Answer : It's not my fault that it has enemies.

Lawyer : Were you intending to call a press-conference when you got to Sweden?

Kuznetsov : Butman mentioned this, but I think this was just playing around and we never discussed it in concrete terms.

Procurator : To whom did you mention your intention of bringing Fedorov in?

Kuznetsov : To Dymshitz and Butman.

Procurator : What sort of reference did you give Fedorov?

Kuznetsov : More or less, that I'd known him for a long time.

Procurator : Whom did you personally bring in to this treasonable act of yours?

Kuznetsov : Fedorov, Mendelevich, Izia, Sylva and practically all the others.

Procurator : Explain the meaning of the word "Zionism".

Kuznetsov : I do not agree with the common Marxist-Leninist definition, that "Zionism is a tool of imperialism".

Procurator : Do you not think that antisemitism is caused by Zionism?

Kuznetsov : Zionism has existed only in the twentieth century, but there has always been antisemitism. Surely you know that.

Procurator : Where and what legal literature have you read and from whom did you receive instructions?

Kuznetsov : Soviet literature. Permit me to quote . . . (Takes out a note).

Procurator : There's no need to quote.

Kuznetsov : I was going to quote from *The Nuremburg Trial*, Moscow, 1970, edited by Rudenko.

Procurator : There you are, bearing a grudge against the Soviet regime; yet, when all's said and done, you were convicted of a crime and you still didn't reform! Your camp reference says you shirked work and were transferred to prison—why is this?

Kuznetsov : I like to educate myself—there are people who like to—and in prison there is a good library and time for studying.

Question : Did you make the knuckle-duster?

Kuznetsov : Yes.

Question : Sylva Zalmanson says she made it.

Kuznetsov : She takes too much upon herself.

Question : Whose idea was it that Fedorov and Murzhenko should be brought into your plan so as to conceal the national character of your action?

Kuznetsov : Butman's. But I had already brought in Fedorov and Murzhenko—before this conversation of 1st–2nd May. I had spoken to Fedorov about the end of April.

Question : You told Fedorov the group contained only Jews?

Kuznetsov : Yes.

Question : What was his reaction?

Kuznetsov : Nothing particular . . . [i.e. Fedorov's no antisemite]

Cross-examination of Izrail Zalmanson

IZRAIL ZALMANSON 21 years old, brother of Sylva Zalmanson, born 1949, youngest of the defendants. Student at Riga Polytechnic; in June 1970 had passed all his fourth year examinations. Says he wants to go to Israel, he's a Jew. His family received an invitation in 1965 but his father decided not to go. It was only later that he had the idea of flying—all the more so when his sister, Sylva, her husband, Kuznetsov, and then his brother Wulf, agreed to go also. He does not think he has caused any damage to the interests of the USSR—he could see no other way. He thought he would not be causing any material harm to the USSR since the aircraft would be returned, and, by and large, he didn't think about this too much anyway. He had signed the statement not only for himself but for others, since he had not attached much significance to it, and, anyhow, hadn't read it carefully.

He answered questions put to him in such a way as to try and shield his sister Sylva (accused of printing literature) and Kuznetsov (accused of preparing the bludgeons). Said he had done these things himself.

On the second day of the trial, although the statement was much discussed, its text was not read to the court.

ALEKSEI MURZHENKO, born 1942. Lived and worked in Lozovaya, studied by correspondence course. He began with the reasons he had participated: due to my unsettled state of mind I hadn't been able to get into an institute, and things had been difficult at home. The charge against me is based on my first conviction, but I do not agree with this since, after I was freed, I did not disseminate any anti-Soviet literature, nor express any anti-Soviet views, nor read Samizdat.

I do not agree with the charges: 1) that I acted in accordance with any anti-Soviet views—my reasons were purely personal; 2) that I was involved in the preparation of the action—I did no such thing; 3) that I intended to steal the aircraft—I was sure it would be returned.

Learned everything through Fedorov but not in detail: the results of my unsuccessful attempt to build a life for myself leaving the camp were decisive factors in my desire to leave the USSR. I received no orders: when Kuznetsov gave me the bludgeon that morning I asked him why he was giving it to me. He said, "In case . . ." When I asked him what I should do, Kuznetsov said, "Use your own discretion."
Judge : Things do not happen like that!
Murzhenko : But that's how it was.

17th December, 1970
Cross-examination of defendant Leib Khnokh

LEIB KHNOKH, aged 25, born 1944. Worker. Was brought up in a family in which Hebrew was spoken and the traditions and festivals observed. He thinks the Jews can only have a future as a nation in Israel. He applied to the OVIR but was refused a visa. An official there told him he was too young and he wouldn't be allowed to go. In his view refusing the Jews a visa for Israel is a violation of the Universal Declaration of Human Rights. He was the co-author of letters to Kosygin,

CP secretaries and U Thant, but is convinced there was nothing slanderous or anti-Soviet in any of these letters. He was arrested together with three others—Mary Khnokh, Penson, Sylva Zalmanson—at 3 a.m. on 15th June in a wood near Priozersk.

I consider myself a Jew, I have always wanted, and still want, to live in my Homeland. As far as I am concerned, the USSR is my homeland in a formal sense only. I came to hear of the flight from Mendelevich and agreed immediately to participate. I did not previously apply to the OVIR for personal reasons (I had married Mary Mendelevich on 23rd May).

I do not plead guilty under Art. 64, since Israel is my Homeland. I am sure the others, like myself, did not intend to steal the aircraft and thus I do not plead guilty under Art. 93. I would like to say something about the group waiting at Priozersk. We left the Finland station, Leningrad, for Priozersk on 14th June. As we journeyed we felt we were being followed and we therefore got off the train twice in order to get on the following one. We thought of turning back, but we were unsure and so continued our journey. We removed from our rucksacks anything that might have been compromising— the map which Dymshitz had given us, and the two bludgeons which Penson showed us were in his bag. We got to Priozersk considerably later than we had expected through having changed trains twice. We left the city, entered the wood, and lost our way; we didn't know where either the airport or the station were. We lit a fire and went to sleep. One of us (at first Penson, then Khnokh) kept watch, but at 3 a.m. we were arrested. This Priozersk group came about because there were too many people and they couldn't all get in the twelve-seater "Smolny" aircraft. We decided it was safer in Priozersk and the women should be there. [It's still not clear what happened to Dymshitz's wife and children—Khnokh probably didn't know about them.]

Khnokh went on to answer questions appertaining to Arts. 70 and 72, under which he also refused to plead guilty. The articles, "Nehama has returned" and about the "native language" (title imprecise), he said, were not anti-Soviet. In one sentence in one of his articles he *had* exaggerated (namely, that in the 30s the entire flower of the Jewish nation in the USSR had been destroyed)—"entire" was too strong— but there was nothing slanderous or anti-Soviet in anything else.

The procurator asked Khnokh many questions which Khnokh answered thus: this is not in the charges against me so I refuse to answer. There were some names in these questions but they don't spring to mind. After five or six similar answers the judge cut him short. "Why have you decided to answer the court in this manner?" Khnokh replied he had the right to do so, but could not remember which article said so. The lawyer Sarri asked him if he meant Art. 254, Code of Criminal Procedure, and read it out loud. (This was probably to the defendant's benefit.) Khnokh answered some of the procurator's questions by saying they differed somewhat from the investigation protocol. He then protested about how the investigation had been conducted: though he had not been threatened and the investigation had been conducted in a proper manner, he had not at times been able to get the investigator to note down his answers correctly. Unfortunately he didn't manage to write them himself.

Cross-examination of the defendant Boris Penson

BORIS PENSON, 23 years old. Born 1947. Has close relatives in Israel. Artist. Previous conviction (was present at multiple rape).

I will explain my motives. My father is 72 years of age, a pensioner and sick man, his closest relatives are in Israel and he dreams of joining them before he dies. My mother was born in a small Jewish town, speaks very poor Russian, and finds it impossible to assimilate within the USSR. We applied to the OVIR several times but were rejected. Because of me,

I think, for I am young and healthy; were it just the old people they would have let them go. Therefore, when I heard about the plan I agreed to participate without any hesitation: if I got to Israel, my parents would quickly be given permission to leave. I heard about it at the end of May or the beginning of June, but I was scared—I suppose it's a feature of my character—so I asked them to let me join the Priozersk group, thinking that if I changed my mind I could get out again without any trouble. I asked someone, Izrail Zalmanson perhaps, to sign the statement for me, since I was in a hurry going somewhere at the time.

When asked by the procurator where he had put the two bludgeons, he replied, "I threw them through the window when I realized we were being followed; but I must tell the court that Kuznetsov did not give them to me. I must have put them into my rucksack myself by mistake instead of my sausage, which was also wrapped up in a newspaper. The whole of the time we were in the forest in Priozersk I was scared and wanted to go, but I couldn't leave the fire as I was keeping watch."

He pleaded guilty in part under Art. 64. As for Art. 93, he said, "This is obviously a lot of nonsense. Who could possibly believe we were intending to steal an aeroplane?"

Cross-examination of the defendant Mikhail Bodnya

MIKHAIL BODNYA, 32 years old. In 1944 our family disappeared; we didn't know what had become of my mother and brother. I stayed with my father, who soon married again. My step-mother is a Russian, and while I am very grateful to her for the care and kindness she has shown me, I have always wanted to find my mother and my brother. In the 50s we found out that, after having gone through a great ordeal, they had finally managed to get to Israel. Since then I have on several occasions applied for a visa for Israel and each time been refused. The last refusal was not so long ago. It was for this reason that, when I heard of the plan, I immediately agreed to participate.

In answer to the questions of the procurator and his lawyer he said he was a metal-worker, a labourer, although disabled (a splinter had completely blinded him in one eye while the other was going blind). He received a disability allowance of 35 roubles, and had obtained many certificates and testimonials during the years he had worked at his plant. He had been the chairman of his local commitee and sports association.

I never intended to betray my homeland, but wished, and still wish, to join my mother.

Cross-examination of Witnesses, 17th December, 2 p.m.

GILIA BUTMAN, 38, engineer, married with one child, member of Leningrad "centre". Introduced, in the autumn of 1969, to Dymshitz by someone by the name of Vania [identity not clarified by the court], who had lived not far away. Dymshitz soon began to tell him about an organized plan of escape. Butman took Dymshitz along to the ulpan, where L. L. Korenblit taught Hebrew. He confirmed everything that had been brought to light by previous cross-examination.

He had accepted Plan 1 ("The Wedding"), but the Leningrad "centre" had rejected it. Dymshitz still wanted to try and decided to ask Israel. The question was passed to the relevant quarter by means of a foreign tourist, but the reply was a decisive *no* [it is uncertain whether there really was any enquiry or not]. Dymshitz promised Butman he wouldn't take his enquiries any further, but he was still not pacified. He suggested to Kuznetsov that they try Plan 2, and then, on the 5th–6th June, Plan 3. In order to determine whether Dymshitz would give up his plans, Butman asked him to put his signature to a letter—a telegram—of condolence to the mothers of the children who had perished in the school bus attack.[1] Dymshitz refused, but asked him to get the documents for the

[1] i.e. the Arab terrorist attack on an Israeli school bus, in which eight children were killed and twenty wounded (23rd May, 1970).

OVIR—he would attempt to leave by legal means. Butman promised to find some fictitious relatives.

L. L. KORENBLIT, about 50 years old, brought from prison where he had been since 15th August, senior scientific worker, physicist, member of Leningrad "centre", principal editor of *Iton*, and Hebrew teacher in one of the ulpans. Grown a lot thinner, looks ill. Nonetheless, answered questions in his characteristically intellectual, educated manner, and managed to get the procurator not to yell at him so much. Knew of Plan 1, was against it and press-conference if flight was successful: such a press-conference, he thought, would not help those Jews in the Soviet Union who wished to leave, since it would draw the world's attention not only to them but also to their "criminality".

Last time he saw Dymshitz was 24th or 25th May; in heated conversation tried to persuade him to give up all plans, but without success. The following day Butman told him Dymshitz had dropped plans and he (Korenblit) was pacified. Saw Dymshitz once again—studying at his ulpan—but did not speak. Dymshitz was his pupil.

In answer to the procurator's questions Korenblit spoke of his editing work and meetings connected with it, to which Mendelevich had come from Riga. Said Mendelevich was author of two articles in *Iton* (No. 1) and of a leading article in No. 2. He had thought no attempt would be made to seize an aircraft, and that Dymshitz had agreed to this. Asked why, out of all those from Riga, it was Mendelevich who was the author of *Iton*, Korenblit (or Maftser, or Shpilberg?) replied it was because he had journalistic ability and knew two Jewish languages. The prosecutor several times enquired about this and gave the impression he did not know what was meant by "two Jewish languages".

ARON SHPILBERG, 36 (?), engineer, inhabitant of Riga, in prison since 4th August 1970. Stated he had never been involved in any anti-Soviet, slanderous or Zionist activities.

Intent upon trying, the whole time, to reach agreement with the court, and particularly with procurator Soloviov, as to the precise meaning of the word "Zionism", but not given the opportunity. Said he had gone to some station near the coast, where he had left a suitcase with literature. He had taken Sylva Zalmanson with him only because it was pleasant to be in the company of an agreeable lady. He considered the contents of the suitcase neither Zionist, nor slanderous, nor anti-Soviet. He was allowed to name only three of the books in the suitcase, 1) a collection of poems by the Jewish writers Marshak, Bialik and a third whose name I don't remember, 2) a separate edition of Bialik's poems, 3) Exodus. There was another title he was unable to give. (Defendants' relatives from Riga said this was a Hebrew textbook.)

He said he had entrusted Sylva with taking the suitcase to Leningrad and giving it to one of their mutual acquaintances. But Sylva said she had given it to Dresler (?). He tried to prove Sylva had never received from him twenty copies of a pamphlet on their "native language", and consequently could never have distributed them. In spite of what Shpilberg said, Sylva confirmed the evidence she had given at the preliminary investigation—that she had received from Shpilberg, and distributed, the above-mentioned pamphlet. Shpilberg conducted himself well, even eloquently, and very courageously, giving the impression of great mental and physical steadfastness. He was asked one more question—how had he got to know about the suitcase with literature? From a friend, he replied, who had long since been in Israel. (Did he name him?)

BORIS MAFTSER, witness, 26 (?), engineer, in prison since August 1970, native of Riga. Said *Iton* had been printed at his home in Hebrew. Altman, Mendelevich, Izrail Zalmanson (?) had taken part also.

MISHA KORENBLIT, witness, stomatologist, arrested August (September) 1970. Introduced to Dymshitz by Butman.

The three of them had become good friends and accepted Plan 1. But towards the end of April they had dropped it and he had not known about Dymshitz's other plans. The evidence he gave was very complicated. They kept on interrupting him, the prosecutor particularly abruptly and coarsely. You sensed he wanted to talk about Dymshitz and his wife, but he wasn't given the chance. One sentence only got through: "I used to think Dymshitz was an honest fellow suffering for the Jewish people, but. . . ." Here the procurator cut him short. He had told Dymshitz after cancellation of plan "Wedding" not to give up his job. But one day he heard from Dymshitz that he had already done so, and that they might as well go through with it, since he was out of work now. He even asked "What am I going to do now?" To which Korenblit answered, "Find yourself a job, and fast!" Then he heard from Butman that he (Dymshitz) had given his plans up. When, on 13th June, the Leningrad Jews were signing their letter to U Thant, Mogilever (apparently because Dymshitz had dropped his plans) suggested to Korenblit that they go and see him and get him to sign the letter. He had always been treated as one of the family in Dymshitz's house and so he was amazed when, at first, they wouldn't let him in, but then shut the doors to all the rooms and let them come into the kitchen only,—"and I saw . . .!" (possibly in the sense of "understood")[1]. Here he was interrupted and, while literally being thrown out, just managed to shout, "I ran and telephoned Kaminsky at the "centre" as well and said: "You must ring Edik[2] in Riga, they all know about it. . . !" He was removed with neither the defendants nor the lawyers being given the opportunity to question him.

WULF ZALMANSON, witness, 28 years old, mechanical engineer, but of late in the army—an officer. Arrested 15th June at Smolny airport as a participant, but appearing here as a witness since he was to be tried separately by a military

---

[1] Did Korenblit see a KGB man or informer on this occasion?
[2] i.e. Kuznetsov.

tribunal at the end of this case.[1] Conducts himself very well indeed, replies clearly, briefly and firmly. He had heard of the plan from his sister and agreed to participate. He had never taken any part in the preparation of the plan. Came to Leningrad on 14th June with his brother Izrail and Iosif Mendelevich. Said his task at the airport at Priozersk was, together with Bodnya, to tie up the second pilot.

Procurator : Who was to tie up the first pilot?

Zalmanson : I don't know, all I know is what my task was. The others, I suppose.

Procurator Katukova : If all the others were to, there might have been a lot of confusion and the whole thing have fallen apart for lack of organization?

Zalmanson : That's what *did* happen! (Stir in the hall).

Question : Did you ask for leave?

Answer : No, I deserted.

Question : What would you have done in Israel?

Answer : I would have got a job as a mechanical engineer.

Question : Perhaps you would have served in the army?

Answer : No, I was not sufficiently trained to do that.

Question : What do you mean—that the Soviet army doesn't train her soldiers to fight well enough?

No answer

Question : You do not agree with the policies of the Soviet Union?

Answer : That is so.

Question : In which sphere?

Answer : National policy.

Question by the defendant Mendelevich : In national policy with regard to the Jewish question?

Answer : No, national policy in general.

18th December—Fourth Day of Trial
Cross-examination of witnesses not in custody
PELAGEYA SERGEYEVNA FEDOROVA, mother of

[1] He was sentenced to ten years in a corrective labour camp on strict regime.

Yuri Fedorov, lives in Moscow. After Yuri's first term of imprisonment, she said, he was ill, didn't leave the house, couldn't sleep, occasionally went away for no reason (south to the sea), and complained he was being followed. In part she thought this fear of his was an illness, yet at the same time there were grounds for it. She herself had been to check and had seen him being followed along the street. The psychiatrist in the hospital where Yuri had been for more than a month, and from which he had been discharged with a diagnosis of psychosthenia, (this is apparently quite normal after leaving a camp), said all he needed was peace and quiet. It was because of this that she had gone to the Lubianka and asked them to leave her son alone. He was a good boy at heart and inclined towards studious pursuits. For example: he had once watched her beating a carp on the head with a hammer before cleaning it. Yuri had said that preparing carp was a disgusting business and he wasn't going to eat any more fish or meat, although he didn't consider himself a vegetarian.

Fedorova was called as a witness by the lawyer Toropova, who asked the court to prescribe a further course of psychiatric treatment. The court agreed to her request, and permitted the following questions to be put to experts:

1 Was he in need of hospital care?
2 Was he mentally distressed?
3 Was he of sound mind?

ALEVTINA IVANOVNA DYMSHITZ, lives in Leningrad, where she works as a laboratory assistant. She spoke much, and for a long time, about how her husband had kept on trying to persuade her to leave, but how she wouldn't agree, because she was a Russian and this was her homeland. This was why they had separated. But she had always been extremely happy with her husband (although he had lived in Bukhara and she in Leningrad). Her husband loved his flying very much, but it scared her, and she wanted him to live on the ground, and not in the air. On 19th April—her birthday—he had come to see her (uncertain whether of his own accord or whether she had invited him), and she had agreed to go with him if only to keep the family together. It was she who had told their daughters that they would be leaving. She had read Shub's book and Litvinov's memoirs which Kuznetsov had given her, and what Lenin had said on the national question. Asked by Kuznetsov whether he had, in fact, given her these memoirs, she said he hadn't really given them to her, but had just taken them out of his briefcase and put them on the table before going out to the shops, and she herself had looked to see what sort of books they were.

It became clear from the cross-examination that her divorce from her husband was official and that she was no longer called Dymshitz, but some other name (new name uncertain).

ELIZAVETA DYMSHITZ, 19 years old, seamstress. Added nothing new. Said she had known about the flight.

JULIA DYMSHITZ, 15 years old, grade 9 in school. Said she knew of flight. She had flown to Priozersk because her father had asked her to—to book a trip and have a look at the situation there.

OLIA KOZLOVA. Grade 9 in school. Had become good friends with Julia and flown with her to Priozersk. (She wasn't asked if Julia had told her why they were flying; nor was it made clear why she'd been called as witness, as she was asked no questions by the prosecution.)

MIDDLE-AGED MAN, technion teacher and high-school acquaintance of Dymshitz; had since met on occasion. In the spring Dymshitz had brough him two or three full suitcases and asked him if he would look after them for him because, he said, he was going with his family to the south and he was afraid to leave them at home—they lived on the first floor. Dymshitz borrowed 500 roubles from him at an interest rate of 3%, saying he needed the money to get to Tbilisi to buy a visa for Israel (again vague).

MIDDLE-AGED WOMAN (can't remember her name). Friend of Bodnya's. He had stayed at her apartment on the night of 13th–14th June. He told her he had come to Leningrad on a business trip. On the 13th they had gone for a walk in the city and dined out together. He hadn't mentioned the flight to her. (Why was she called?)

THE FLIGHT COMMANDER who had been on the AN-2 and was its pilot. Spoke of aircraft's technical details. The procurator asked him to speak about the case: "What case?" he asked, "I taxied towards the landing point, the passengers were accompanied out and they were arrested near the plane. That was all. (Laughter in the hall—Procurator angry.)
Question : Would you have been pleased if they'd gagged you?
Answer : Would *you*?
Question by the defendant Kuznetsov : I am going to ask you some rather more concrete questions. When the second pilot goes out to meet or lead out the passengers, does the cabin door remain open?
Answer : It all depends.
Question : Should it be open?
Answer : It should. (Stir in the courtroom.)

The general impression given by the pilot was that he had nothing against the defendants, whereas the procurator irritated him with his pointless questions. It would have been, he said, very possible indeed for them to have bound him without any bloodshed whatsoever, had they taken him by surprise. (Earlier, when the defendants were interrogated, it had been said that if the door had been closed the operation would be cancelled.)

THE PILOT with whom Dymshitz had flown to Moscow. Revealed nothing new. But his opinion, after serving with him in Bukhara, was that Dymshitz was a very good pilot. When a pilot had been needed in some Leningrad squadron, he said, he himself had gone along with Dymshitz, and he couldn't understand why they wouldn't take him—there were *other* Jewish pilots, after all!

A TEENAGE GIRL who had become acquainted with Dymshitz a couple of weeks before 15th June. Dymshitz had told her of the flight and even asked her to come. She had refused. Said she liked Dymshitz because of his passion for flying.

BORIS, stomatologist, 26–27 years old. Asked by the procurator if he was a member of any anti-Soviet organization, he replied that he was a member of an educational organization, whose task was to study the language, history and culture of the Jewish people. He had met Dymshitz towards the end of 1969, had known about the plan, but had not been prepared to participate. Dymshitz had asked him to buy a starting pistol.
Procurator : A firearm?
Answer : A starting pistol is used for sports and is no more of a weapon than a stick.

MURZHENKO'S WIFE LIUBA. Has a one-year-old daughter. Didn't know of the flight. Had received letter of farewell from Moscow after 15th June.

On the day of the trial material evidence was presented: several bits of white linen cord and two gags—stockings stuffed with cotton wool. The pistol and other arms were not presented.

In his speech the prosecutor made much of the "intrigues of international Zionism". In the Soviet Union, he said, there was not, and could not be, a Jewish question.
"Some people say this is a trial against the Jews, but this is

untrue. This trial is not about Jews. This is a criminal trial, in which the majority of the criminals are Jews. Though I do not consider Kuznetsov a Jew: I think he is a Russian. This is, as far as I am concerned, a group case, and this court must decide not on the guilt of any one individual, but on the guilt of all."

Procurator Soloviov pointed out that the defendant Bodnya had shown genuine repentance. In his view, Bodnya, unlike the rest, had no anti-Soviet convictions. The prosecutor concluded, "In my view, the motives of all the accused, with the exception of Bodnya, were anti-Soviet. I ask you to find all the accused, except Bodnya, guilty under Articles 64/15, $93^1/15$, 70 and 72. As far as Bodnya is concerned, taking into account his genuine repentance, his sincerity and frankness, as well as his personal motives for committing this crime, I ask you to find him guilty under Art. 83 (crossing the border illegally) and Art. 93^1. I ask the court to apply in the case of Bodnya Art. 43 of the Criminal Code of the RSFSR," (i.e. a lighter punishment than that prescribed by law).

Procurator Soloviov demanded that Kuznetsov, Fedorov and Murzhenko be acknowledged as especially dangerous recidivists; that Kuznetsov and Dymshitz be sentenced to the supreme penalty of execution, that Fedorov be given 15 years special regime, Murzhenko 14 years special regime, Mendelevich 15 years strict regime, Khnokh 13 years strict regime, I. Zalmanson, Altman and Penson, 12 years strict regime, S. Zalmanson 10 years strict regime, and Bodnya 5 years hard regime.

All defence counsels stated that Art. 93^1 was totally unsuitable, as the defendants had obviously not been intending to steal the aircraft. Drozdov, S. Zalmanson's counsel, demanded that Art. 93 be removed from the bill of indictment, and each of the other counsels demanded that Art. 93^1 be changed to Art. 91 (robbery with intent to take possession of state or public property).

Defence counsels for Mendelevich, I. Zalmanson, Altman,

Fedorov, Murzhenko, Khnokh and Bodnya (Arya, Ilina, Lesko, Toropova, Sarri, Suistunov) pointed out that it had not been their clients' intention to subvert the might of the Soviet Union or to prejudice in any way its external security, and without any such intention there could be no mention of Art. 64. Aria, counsel for Mendelevich, said, "Ever since 1968 my client has had a great yearning to go to Israel, which he mistakenly thought his own homeland . . . And if Mendelevich had fled to Israel to worship his own God and maybe even to censure the USSR, this could not have harmed our external security in any way."

Defence counsels for S. Zalmanson, Mendelevich, I. Zalmanson, Altman and Khnokh felt that the actions of their clients, of which they were accused under Art. 70, had been much overrated. Khnokh's lawyer, Sarri, said, "It is absurd to imagine that the structure of the Soviet State could possibly be weakened by the dissemination of such material as "Nehama has come", or "Your Native Language", and even less so by keeping them in one's possession. Altman's motives for participating in the editing of the journal *Iton* (a journal about the life and history of Israel) were not, his counsel Lesko said, anti-Soviet.

For all these reasons the above-mentioned defence counsels asked that their clients be charged not under Art. 70 but under Art. 190[1].

Ilina, Murzhenko's counsel, asked the court to consider that, excepting his former conviction, the charges against her client indicated that there was no proof as to his having any anti-Soviet views. This, in turn, was repeated by Fedorov's counsel, Toropova.

The counsels asked the court to take into account all the mitigating circumstances.

Lury, Kuznetsov's counsel, asked the court to consider what his client had said to Bodnya: "We must try and manage without any violence—the pilots must not even receive one scratch." With regard to the supreme penalty demanded by prosecution, Lury said, "Is it necessary to use this measure if the crime is uncompleted? Thanks to the organs of state security[1] the aircraft was not removed nor the pilots harmed. I do not think that such an extreme measure should be used here."

Defendants' Final Pleas

M. Y. DYMSHITZ

Obviously every criminal considers his punishment too severe. Nevertheless, I should like to express my opinion with regard to the proposed punishment. In my view what the procurator has demanded is extremely cruel. The procurator frequently used the word "if". He has, I think, exhausted the whole of his stock of the most terrifying suppositions. *If* we had landed in Finland, and *if* we had been extradited, what then? . . . What *if* there had been passengers? I am no liberal and I understand perfectly well what a struggle is. You need such a harsh punishment to prevent this happening again. I myself proposed the first plan, but we ourselves dismissed it. The prosecutor spoke on behalf of the pilots. It is a pity that those in the squadron from whom I sought employment were not sitting at his side. *They* could have stopped me—before the autumn of 1969; but after that only the organs of the KGB could have stopped me. We defendants are of varying characters. Many of us have but recently come to know one another. I find it comforting that we have not lost—even here—our human qualities; that we have not begun to bite one another like spiders trapped in a jar. I thank the security organs for the humanity they have shown to my wife and my daughter. I ask the court to treat me with justice and humanity.

SYLVA ZALMANSON

I am completely overwhelmed . . . I am stunned by the

[1] i.e. the KGB.

sentences the prosecution has demanded for us. The procurator has just demanded the death penalty for something that has not been done. If the court agrees to this then such outstanding men as Dymshitz and Kuznetsov will perish. I do not think that Soviet law can possibly regard someone's intention to live in another country as treason, and I am convinced that those who unlawfully violate our right to live where we wish ought themselves to stand trial. Let the court at least note that, had we been permitted to leave, this "criminal conspiracy", which has caused us—not to mention our relatives—so much pain, would never have happened. Israel is a country to which we, as Jews, are tied both spiritually and historically. It is my hope that the Soviet Government will decide this question positively in the near future. The dream of returning to our ancient homeland will never desert us. Several of us did not believe that our undertaking would be successful, or had little confidence in it. Even when we were at the Finland Station we noticed we were being followed. But it was too late to turn back—to return to the past, to continue to wait and to live in our suitcases. Our dream of living in Israel was not to be compared with the fear of the pain it might cause us. By leaving this country we would have harmed no one. I wanted to live there as part of a family and work. I would not have been involved in politics. My entire interest in political matters was exhausted by my simple desire to leave. Not even now do I doubt for one moment that I will one day live in Israel whatever happens. This dream of mine, consecrated by 2000 years of waiting and hoping, will never desert me. Next year in Jerusalem!! And I repeat:

"If I forget thee, O Jerusalem,
May my right hand lose its cunning!"

(She repeats these words in Hebrew. The procurator stops her.)
I have finished.

246

IOSIF MENDELEVICH

I should like to say that I acknowledge the guilt of my actions—my attempt to seize an aircraft and to cross the border illegally. But my fault lies in the fact that I allowed myself to be undiscriminating in the methods I used in order to achieve my dream. These last six months have taught me that emotions must be subordinated to reason. I realize that I must be punished and I urge the court to be merciful to my comrades.

EDWARD KUZNETSOV

The state prosecutor proceeds on the assumption that, once abroad, I would have engaged in activities prejudicial to the interests of the Soviet Union. He makes this assumption on the basis of my so-called anti-Soviet views, which, however, I have never expressed to anyone. I had no intention of harming the interests of the USSR. All I wanted to do was to live in Israel. I did not see a possible request for political asylum as a hostile political act. This is incorrectly stated in the bill of indictment. I have never expressed any wish to speak at any press conference, nor have I ever discussed this with anyone. Without going further into the reasons why I had no such intention, I will say only that my characteristic sense of irony reliably insures me against the making of political speeches. I sincerely regret having given my agreement to participate in this affair, and I plead only guilty in part under Art. 64—a/15 and Art. 72, Criminal Code of the RSFSR. I beg the court to show mercy to my wife Sylva Zalmanson, and I ask for justice for myself. We have only one life, after all.

IZRAIL ZALMANSON

The only thing which inspired me was my desire to live and work in the state of Israel, my spiritual homeland. This desire became the principal aim of my life. Consequently, I have come to realize how mistaken my actions were. I wish to assure you that, in the future, no circumstances will ever compel me to break the law.

ALEKSEI MURZHENKO

Before I speak of my own case, I beg the court to show mercy towards Kuznetsov and Dymshitz.

I am in complete agreement with my lawyer. The procurator has asserted that I am anti-Soviet and that it was for this reason that I participated in this action. But this is not true. My first conviction totally unsettled my life. The fact that I took part in this undertaking is the consequence of my inexperience of life. My life has been up to now—eight years in Suvorov Military College, six years in camps for political prisoners, and only two years of freedom. Living my life in the backwoods I have never had the opportunity of applying my knowledge and I have had to bury it. You are deciding my fate, my life. If, as the prosecution has demanded, I receive fourteen years' imprisonment, then this means you consider me incorrigible and have decided to abandon me to my fate. I have never pursued criminal objectives. I beg the court to determine such a term of imprisonment as will allow me to hope for happiness, for the future both of myself and my family.

YURI FEDOROV

When I reflect upon what we did I am convinced that our sole purpose was to leave the USSR. Not one of us intended to cause harm to the Soviet Union. I think we took all the measures we could to secure the lives of the pilots. I plead guilty only to attempting to cross the border illegally, and I am prepared to bear the responsibility for this, but I cannot, in all conscience, consider myself guilty—I did not *do* anything. The prosecutor did not stint his demands for punishment, but has he any conception of what even three years in a camp can mean? The public prosecutor spoke against the seizure of an aircraft

248

and one can agree with this. As far as the revolver is concerned it was taken in case we used the Finland plan. As for my anti-Soviet views, I abandoned them even when I was in the camp. When we were going to hijack the plane we never thought that some were more guilty and others less guilty. Each person did what he could. Then, all of a sudden, it seems that Dymshitz and Kuznetsov are guiltier than the rest of us. Dymshitz at least was to fly the aircraft, but I cannot understand why Kuznetsov suddenly proved to be any guiltier. With regard to the possible consequences I may say that, since the action did not take place, it is fruitless to speculate on what might have happened. I beg the court to show mercy to Kuznetsov and Dymshitz. I would like to emphasize that I myself insisted that I participate, whereas Murzhenko was brought in by me, even in spite of Kuznetsov's wishes.

ANATOLY ALTMAN

I appeal to the court to save the lives of Kuznetsov and Dymshitz and to prescribe the minimum punishment for the only woman amongst us—Sylva Zalmanson. I wish to express my deepest regret that I and my comrades should be sitting on these benches. I hope the court will find it possible not to punish us very severely. I do not say that I should not be punished for my participation in this crime, but there is one thing which bewilders me. In 1969 I appled for a visa for Israel, that is, I wished to change my homeland. Whereas in that instance my wishes evoked the contempt of others towards me, in this instance I am standing trial. This bewilderment I feel is not for nothing: I refer to the isolation, deprivation of freedom and pain caused to our families. I was born in the Soviet period and I have spent all my life in a Soviet country. I have never had the opportunity of learning the class nature of Zionism, but I do know that peoples and countries experience, at different times, diverse political conditions, and become as a result of this neither better nor worse.

On this day, when my fate is being decided, I am elated and sad. It is my hope that Israel will live in peace. I send you today, my country, my wishes that you may do so. Shalom Aleichem! May you see peace, my country Israel!

LEIB KHNOKH

I ask the court to show mercy to our two comrades and leniency towards the only woman among us. I can only repeat yet again that my actions were not directed against the security of the Soviet Union. My single aim was to live in the State of Israel, which I have long regarded as my own country, a country where my people first arose as a nation, where there once developed, and now develops, a Jewish state, where my own language is spoken, and where my relatives and friends live. I have no anti-Soviet views. Two witnesses have misinterpreted them. Obviously they live in those parts of the USSR where Jews do not apply to the OVIR. Both told the court that I had not touched upon the essential nature of the socialist system. My only aim is to live in Israel, the true homeland of the Jews.

BORIS PENSON

During the course of the entire investigation I testified as to my intentions, and it is in vain for the procurator to assert that I have changed them. This is not so. It is simply that for the first few days I gave no evidence. I did not change it. I had consistently doubted whether we would be successful and whether there was any point in doing it at all. But my desire to make my family happy was great, and I did not see the degree of risk involved; thus I went ahead. However, once I reached the forest, I decided to leave. But I did not succeed, for we were arrested. I ask the court to take into account the fact that I repent of my deeds; I should have sought to leave by legal means, although the organization which deals with this gives no hope whatever that it will ever grant a visa for

Israel. I am prepared to bear the responsibility for what I did not carry through. I beg the court to consider that I have aged parents.

MENDEL BODNYA

I beg the court for mercy and leniency. All I wished was to see my mother. I beg the court to take into consideration that I have promised henceforth never to violate the law.

On 25th December, 1970, the Leningrad
City Court, Chairman Ermakov, sentenced:

Dymshitz, M. Y.	to the supreme penalty, the death penalty with confiscation of property.
Kuznetsov, E. S.	to the supreme penalty, the death penalty, without the confiscation of property, in the absence of such.
Mendelevich, I. M.	to 12 years strict regime, without confiscation of property, in the absence of such.
Fedorov, Y. P.	to 15 years special regime, without confiscation of property, in the absence of such. To be recognized as an especially dangerous recidivist.
Murzhenko, A. G.	to 14 years special regime, without confiscation of property, in the absence of such. To be recognized as an especially dangerous recidivist.
Khnokh, L. G.	to 13 years strict regime, without confiscation of property, in the absence of such.
Altman, A. A.	to 12 years strict regime, without

	confiscation of property, in the absence of such.
Zalmanson, S. I.	to 10 years strict regime, without confiscation of property, in the absence of such.
Penson, B. S.	to 10 years strict regime, with confiscation of property. (At beginning of preliminary investigation all pictures, studies and sketches impounded, as personal property subject to confiscation.)
Zalmanson, I. I.	to 8 years strict regime, without confiscation of property, in the absence of such.
Bodnya, M. A.	to 4 years hard regime, without confiscation of property, in the absence of such.

The announcement of these sentences was greeted with applause by the "public", whereas from the relatives came cries of "Fascists, how dare you applaud the death penalty!" "Good lads!" "Don't give up!" "We're with you!" "We'll wait for you!" "We'll be in Israel together!"

Whereupon the applause ceased.

Public Protests after the Trial

December 27th: A letter, signed by V. N. Chalidze, A. C. Volpin, A. N. Tviordokhlebov, B. I. Tsukerman and L. G. Rigerman, was sent to N. V. Podgorny, Chairman of the Praesidium of the Supreme Soviet. In it they requested that the murder of Kuznetsov and Dymshitz should not be allowed; that all who wish to leave the Soviet Union should be allowed to do so; that the right of the Jews to repatriation should be acknowledged.

December 28th: Academician Andrei Sakharov sent a letter to the President of the USA, R. Nixon, and to the Chairman of the Praesidium of the Supreme Soviet of the USSR, N. V. Podgorny, in support of Angela Davis; and M. Y. Dymshitz and E. S. Kuznetsov, sentenced in Leningrad.

December 30th: A declaration was addressed to General Franco and the Chairman of the Praesidium of the Supreme Soviet of the USSR, Podgorny, by a group of Soviet citizens "profoundly disturbed and shaken by the present wave of cruelty which is manifested in the death sentences passed in Burgos[1] and in Leningrad." They appealed for the lives of those condemned.

Suddenly in contravention of Art. 328, a review of the appeals of the condemned and their lawyers was fixed for 30th December. As copies of the sentence had been given to the condemned on 26th December, the court of appeal should have begun to sit, according to Arts. 328 and 103, Code of Criminal Procedure, no earlier than 5th January.

About 20 of the "public", including several relatives of the accused who had been able to come to Moscow, gathered in the small hall. The session on 30th December continued until 2.30 in the afternoon, when it was unexpectedly adjourned for one and a half hours.

After the adjournment the session continued for another twenty minutes. Then a further adjournment was made until the following day. (It may be recalled that on this day, 30th December, General Franco commuted the death sentence passed on the Basques.)

During the 30th December session the case was put before the court and the defence lawyers spoke.

On 31st December the session lasted thirty minutes only. Procurator Pokhlebin (USSR procuracy) spoke in favour of commuting the sentences of death, whereupon the appeals court retired for an hour-long consultation. At about 11 a.m.

---

[1] i.e. the sentencing to death of six Basque patriots by the Franco regime, 29th December, 1970.

the judicial board on criminal affairs of the Supreme Court of the RSFSR (chairman L. N. Smirnov, members—M. A. Gavrilin, V. M. Timofeyev) announced the following decision:

Taking into consideration that the criminal actions of Dymshitz and Kuznetsov were halted before they could come to fruition, and that the death penalty is the supreme measure of punishment, the board of the Supreme Court has found possible not to apply the above sentence in the case of Dymshitz and Kuznetsov.

The judicial board of the Supreme Court has decided upon the following sentences:

1	Dymshitz, M. Y.	15 years strict regime, with confiscation of property.
2	Kuznetsov, E. S.	15 years special regime, without confiscation of property in the absence of such. To be recognized as an especially dangerous recidivist.

In addition the board passes the following sentences:

3	Mendelevich, I. M.	12 years strict regime, without confiscation of property in the absence of such.
4	Khnokh, L. G.	10 years strict regime, without confiscation of property in the absence of such.
5	Altman, A. A.	10 years strict regime, without confiscation of property in the absence of such.

For the rest of the accused the original sentences were maintained. However, a telegram from the Supreme Court of the RSFSR to the Leningrad City Court indicated a change in the sentence of I. I. Zalmanson from 8 years to 7 years strict regime.